A Dictionary of Bible Knowledge

Also available in this series:
A Dictionary of Bible Symbols
A Dictionary of Theological Terms

A Dictionary of Bible Knowledge

I. Stringer B.A.

General Editor H. J. Appleby

Grace Publications

GRACE PUBLICATIONS TRUST
139 Grosvenor Avenue
London N5 2NH
England

Joint Managing Editors:
    H. J. Appleby
    J. P. Arthur M.A.

© Grace Publications Trust 1992
First printed 1992
Second impression 1996

ISBN 0 946462 27 5

Distributed by
EVANGELICAL PRESS
12 Wooler Street
Darlington
Co. Durham DL1 1RQ
England

Printed in Great Britain at the Bath Press, Avon.

Cover design by Insight Ltd, Ipswich, Suffolk, IP1 5NP.

Aaron

Aaron was the elder brother of Moses, who led the Israelites out of Egypt to the borders of the promised land. Aaron was Moses' spokesman (Exod.4:14-16). God also chose Aaron as Israel's first high priest, and he and his sons represented the Israelites before God (Num.3:10; 1 Chr.6:49). All priests in the Old Testament had to be men from Aaron's family, without any physical deformity (Lev. 21:16-23).

An Israelite who wanted to offer a sacrifice had to ask a priest to do it for him at the tabernacle or, later on, in the temple. On the Day of Atonement, Aaron and those who became high priests after him went into the Most Holy Place to represent the whole nation of Israel before God (Lev.16).

Aaron and his duties were a picture of Jesus Christ and the atonement he made for his church. Christ is both the priest who represents his people before the holy God (Heb.9:11) and the sacrificed lamb (John 1:29; Heb. 9:28). Now that Christ has fulfilled Aaron's priesthood, no more high priests or sacrifices are needed to cover sins (Heb.10:18).

See Priest.

Abba

Jesus spoke in Aramaic, which was the language used by the Jews who lived in Palestine during New Testament days. Abba was Aramaic for 'father'. Small children called their father 'abba'.

The Jews did not pray to God as 'abba'. They felt that the word was too familiar to use of God. Jesus, however, did use it. The word shows something of the closeness between Jesus and God, especially at a time of deep distress in Gethsemane (Mark 14:36).

Our Lord's use of 'abba' was copied by the early disciples (Romans 8:15; Galatians 4:6). In all these cases, it was followed by the Greek word for 'father', probably to help those who did not speak Aramaic.

Abomination of desolation

Daniel prophesied this (Dan. 11:31) and our Lord reminded his disciples of Daniel's prophecy (Mark 13:14). The abomination of desolation was something particularly detestable to God and his people. It would be set up in the temple, taking the place of the daily sacrifices (Dan.11:31).

On December 25, 167BC, the Greek king Antiochus IV walked into the Holy of Holies. He set up a pagan altar over the altar of burnt offering as part of a campaign to impose Greek culture on the Jews. This led to the Maccabaean rebellion.

Christ used the prophecy to warn his disciples. In AD66, more than thirty years after Christ's resurrection, the Jews revolted against the Romans. In AD70 the Roman army entered Jerusalem, killed thousands of Jews without mercy and destroyed the temple. The abomination of desolation was the Roman standard, or army banner, on which the image of the emperor was fixed.

The Christians escaped this slaughter as they remembered Christ's words and fled from Jerusalem at the beginning of the revolt.

Abraham

Abraham's life is told in Gen. 11:27-25:11. God made a covenant with him, promising that he would be the father of a great nation; that they would have the land of Canaan (Gen. 15); and that through Abraham, all nations on earth would be blessed (Gen. 12:3). The great fulfilment of this promise is Jesus Christ, whose humanity was descended from Abraham (see Gal. 3:16).

God changed the name 'Abram', which means 'exalted father', to 'Abraham', which means 'father of many' (Gen. 17:5).

Abraham was particularly noted for his faith (Gen. 15:6; Heb. 11:8-19). His faith led to obedience (James 2:21-24). The Jews were proud of having Abraham as their father. Christ, however, said the true children of Abraham were those who copied his life, not all those who were born into the Jewish nation.

Paul says a similar thing in Rom. 4 and Gal. 3: the true children of Abraham are those who share his faith. This means that even

Gentiles are Abraham's children if they are true Christians. All Christians inherit God's blessings and heaven, as did Abraham (Gal. 3:26-4:7; Heb. 11:16).

Abraham's bosom

This phrase is found in Jesus' parable of the rich man and Lazarus in Luke 16:22-23. At Jewish feasts, people reclined at table. This meant that one person's head was next to the bosom of the person who reclined above him. The most favoured guest would have his head next to the host's bosom (see John 13:23).

As Lazarus was beside Abraham, he had a highly favoured place in the feast in paradise. This was in great contrast to his position on earth and also a great contrast from the eternal state of the rich man (Luke 16:26).

Abyss

The Greek word means 'bottomless'. In the New Testament it describes a very deep place. In Rom. 10:7 it is the word used of the abode of the dead. In Luke 8:31 and Rev. (e.g. 9:1; 20:1) it is used to describe the prison of demons and the place of torment.

Adam

Adam was the first man and appears in Gen. 1-4. He was created sinless, but sinned after the temptation (Gen. 3). Because Adam sinned, all mankind is sinful and dies (Rom. 5:12,19). The Hebrew word 'adam' also means 'mankind'.

In 1 Cor. 15:45, Christ is called the last Adam. This means he is the head of the new, redeemed, humanity just as Adam is the head of the old, sinful, humanity. Physical birth into the first Adam gives human beings sinful minds and death. New birth into Christ, who purifies from sin, brings them into the family of God.

Adoption

The word only appears in Paul's letters, but the idea is found throughout the Bible (e.g. Exod. 4:22; 1 John 3:1) describing the change that Christians experience, from being slaves of sin to children of God (Gal. 4:3-5). This adoption was planned by God through Jesus Christ in eternity (Eph. 1:5); it gives his children the right to call God 'Father' (Rom. 8:15); and gives them an inheritance in heaven (Rom. 8:17). Rom. 8:23 teaches that the full glory of this adoption will be made public when believers receive their new spiritual bodies at the resurrection.

Advocate

AV only. NIV: 'The one who speaks in our defence'.

The Greek word for advocate is 'paraclete'. The basic meaning is 'called to the side of'. An advocate is someone who comes to another's side in order to help.

Christ is called our Advocate in 1 John 2:1. In New Testament times, advocates were often friends of accused people who spoke in law courts in their defence. Christ speaks in the defence of his friends before God the Father. His argument is that his death has dealt with their sin.

The same Greek word is translated 'Counsellor' in John 14-16. Here the Counsellor is the Holy Spirit who is the helper at the side of Christians. He teaches them (14:26). He speaks all the time about Christ and strengthens those who witness about Christ (15:26,27). He also convicts the world in regard to sin, righteousness and judgment (16:8-11).

Almighty

Only God can be called almighty. All power in the universe is completely in his control and is used by God for his own purposes. Human beings and evil spirits use the powers of nature only as God graciously grants them the ability to do so.

Alms

Godly living according to the Bible includes having pity on the poor and giving them what they need (Deut. 15:11; James 2:15). Giving alms became the most important religious duty for Jews after they stopped offering animal sacrifices. Every city had officers who collected and distributed money and food.

Jesus taught that his disciples should have a right motive when they give alms (Matt. 6:2-4). The early church made sure that their poor were cared for (Acts 4:34). All those who truly have God's love in them will have pity on the needy (1 John 3:17).

Alpha and Omega

The names of the first and last letters in the Greek alphabet. God the Father (Rev. 1:8) and God the Son (Rev. 21:6; 22:13) call themselves the Alpha and Omega. This means that God is the beginning and end of all things, as alpha and omega are the first and last letters.

Although these words do not occur very often in the Bible, they teach an important fact about God. It is the same as saying that God is the first and the last (Isa. 44:6; Rev. 2:8).

Altar

Burnt offerings were a central part of Old Testament worship. Altars were built by the patriarchs (Gen. 8:20; 12:7,8; 26:25; 33:20), Moses (Exod. 17:15), Gideon (Judg. 6:24), David (2 Sam. 24:18) and Elijah (1 Kings 18:31,32) among others. These were usually made from earth or stone (Exod. 20:24,25).

The tabernacle had an altar for burnt offerings (Exod. 27:1-8) and another for incense (Exod. 30:1-10). They were both made of wood, the first overlaid with bronze and the second with gold. Similar altars were built for the temple (2 Chr. 4:1,19).

Moses told the Israelites to destroy the Canaanite altars (Deut. 12:3). They were to worship God only in the way he told them, and they were to do so only in the place he chose (Deut. 12:4-7). When the tribes who lived on the east side of the Jordan made another altar, there was a threat of war until they explained they only built it to show they all worshipped the same God and they would not use it for sacrifices (Josh. 22 - especially v. 26).

When King Ahaz met Tiglath-Pileser in Damascus, he saw an Assyrian altar. He had a similar one made for the temple which is an example of his failure to do right in God's eyes, for he was honouring the Assyrian gods (2 Kings 16:10-16).

Amalek

Amalek was a grandson of Esau, Jacob's brother (Gen. 36:12). His descendants were nomads who lived in Sinai and the Negeb. During the time of the judges, they pressed further north to the country of Ephraim, which is towards the centre of Palestine (Judg. 12:15).

When the Israelites came out of Egypt, the Amalekites fought them at Rephidim. God told the Israelites to punish them by destroying them completely (Exod. 17:8-16; Deut. 25:17-19). This is why Samuel told Saul to attack them.

The Amalekites were a warlike people (Num. 14:45; Judges 3:13; 6:3; 1 Sam. 30:1). They declined in numbers later and by King Hezekiah's day were quite few. A group of Simeonites killed the last of the Amalekites then (1 Chr. 4:43).

Amen

A Hebrew word meaning 'true', or 'truly', or 'surely'. Listeners say 'Amen' in the Bible to show they agree with what someone has said (1 Kings 1:36). In prayer, it can mean that the congregation identifies with the prayers someone has spoken aloud (1 Chr. 16:36), or it can underline the importance or truth of a prayer (Rom. 1:25). Jesus used the word at the beginning of some of his great sayings. It is translated 'verily', or 'verily, verily' in the AV (Matt. 5:18; 6:2,5 etc.).

Ammon

Abraham's nephew, Lot, had two sons by his daughters. The younger was Ben-Ammi, the father of the Ammonites (Gen. 19:38). God told Israel to treat them kindly (Deut. 2:19). But they were not allowed in the congregation of Israel up to ten generations, because they had joined the Moabites in trying to corrupt Israel (Deut. 23:3-6).

The Ammonite territory was east of the River Jordan. Ammonites often appear in Old Testament history, with various wars (e.g. Judg. 10; 1 Sam. 11; 2 Sam. 10) and intermarriages (1 Kings 14:21; Ezra 9:1,2).

Their religion helped to corrupt Israelite faith. It included child sacrifice to their god Molech.

Amorites

The table of nations shows the Amorites were descendants of Canaan (Gen. 10:15). They were originally desert people with little evidence of civilisation. Shortly before Abraham's time, they entered Mesopotamia and soon ruled in that area. They absorbed the culture and much of the religion of the civilisation they conquered. Their religion was evil (Gen. 15:16) and was later used to show how wicked Ahab's (1 Kings 21:26) and Manasseh's (2 Kings 21:11) religion was.

Abraham had Amorite allies in his battle against the four kings who were led by the king of Sodom (Gen. 14:13,24). At the time of the Israelite invasion of Canaan, the Amorites were in control of much of the hill country on both sides of the Jordan. Sihon and Og ruled on the east side (Num. 21:21-35) and Joshua had to face more Amorites across the Jordan (Josh. 3:10). From about that time, the Amorites' power declined, and by David's time they were quite weak. Solomon used them as forced labour (1 Kings 9:20).

Anak

A people descended from Arba (Josh. 15:13) and the Nephilim (Num. 13:33). They lived in Canaan before the conquest by Israel, particularly around Hebron in the south (Num. 13:22). They were a warlike and tall race (Deut. 9:2) but Joshua (Josh. 11:21) and Caleb (Josh. 15:14) destroyed all those living in the Judaean hills; only in Philistine country did they survive (Josh. 11:22).

Angel - 'Angel of the Lord'

The word means 'messenger'. The same word is used for human and heavenly messengers (e.g. Genesis 32:3; Hag. 1:13; Matt. 11:10).

God created the angels (Ps. 148:2,5). Some sinned and followed Satan (2 Peter 2:4) but a great number remain true to God (Rev. 5:11). They are constantly in God's presence (Matt. 18:10) and have a special brilliance and beauty (Matt. 28:3, cf. Acts 6:15). Angels praise God (Ps. 148:2) and rejoice in his works (Job 38:7; Luke 15:10).

They carry out God's will by bringing messages to people (Matt. 1:20), interpret them (Zech. 1:9), intercede for God's people (Zech. 1:12), protect individuals (Ps. 91:11) and nations (Dan. 12:1), guide (Gen. 24:40), execute judgment (2 Sam. 24:16), and help believers (Heb. 1:14). They are an order of creatures higher than human beings (Ps. 8:5) and yet in glory, Christians will judge angels (1 Cor. 6:3). Angels have various ranks, such as archangels (1 Thess. 4:16) and the list of spiritual authorities in Col. 1:16.

In the Old Testament, the 'angel of the Lord' is the appearance of God, or Christ in a pre-existent form. One example of this is Judges 13:21,22. These appearances of the divine Person prior to the birth of Christ are called 'theophanies'. See a Theological Dictionary.

The New Testament warns against regarding angels too highly, mainly because some people started to worship them. Paul tells the Galatians that the truth of the gospel is more important even than messages from angels (Gal. 1:8). Heb. 1 points out that Christ is far above the angels and is worshipped by them. Paul says something similar in Col. 1:16.

Anger - See Wrath.

Anoint, Anointing

Objects (Gen. 28:18) as well as people (Zech. 4:14) were anointed with oil. This act showed that they were set apart to God for a special purpose. Kings (2 Kings 9:6), priests (Exod. 28:41) and sometimes prophets (1 Kings 19:16) were anointed. God told Moses to make a special blend of oil to anoint the tabernacle, its furniture and the priests. This oil could not be used for anything else (Exod. 30:22-33).

Oil was a sign of joy (Ps. 23:5; Isa. 61:3) and also brought healing (Isa. 1:6; Luke 10:34; James 5:14). Its link with joy and strength makes oil a fitting symbol of the Holy Spirit. A man set apart for the work of prophet, priest or king needs the power of the Holy Spirit to carry out his tasks (1 Sam. 16:13; Isa. 61:1).

In the New Testament, oil is not used for setting apart men for a ministry, but God still anoints with the Holy Spirit (Acts 10:38; 1 John 2:20,27). Even in the Old Testament, God did the anointing through his servants (1 Sam. 10:1).

The words 'Messiah' and 'Christ' both mean 'the anointed one'. Jesus Christ, above anyone else, was God's special person for God's special task. See Christ, and Messiah.

Men and women also anointed themselves with olive oil after washing (Ruth 3:3; 2 Sam. 12:20; Matt. 6:17). This was a normal practice and had no special meaning behind it. In the same way, people would anoint the bodies of the dead (Mark 16:1).

Anti-Christ

This name only appears in 1 and 2 John. Paul calls him the 'man of lawlessness' (2 Thess. 2:3). Similar teaching is found in Daniel and Revelation.

'Anti' can mean either someone who opposes or someone who takes the place of Christ. Probably we should take both meanings. The anti-Christ opposes Christ by seeking to take his place. 2 Thess. 2:4 supports this view.

Although John talks of the anti-Christ who is to come (1 John 2:18), he focuses completely on the spirit of anti-Christ which was seen even as he wrote his letters. There were many anti-Christs (v. 18). They were once members of the churches (v. 19) but they teach things that are damaging to the very centre of the gospel message (v. 22; 2 John 7). They therefore deny Christ, and by denying Christ deny the Father (1 John 2:23).

In Revelation we read of the dragon (Rev. 12:7), which is a symbol for Satan. We also read of beasts who are associated with Satan and do his work (11:7; 13:1,11). The dragon and the beast from the sea were worshipped (13:4). The beast from the earth did a great miracle (13:15). These show teaching very similar to Paul's man of lawlessness and John's anti-Christ. There are many different interpretations as to when all these events in Revelation will take place and what the different symbols such as the beasts stand for. However, these all support the fact that Satan works through people and people's organisations to oppose Christ and set up alternative religions and other world views.

Apostle

The word apostle comes from a Greek word meaning 'someone who is sent on a mission'. He is a messenger with authority given to him by the one who sent him. God sent Christ into this world on a mission, and he is therefore called an apostle in Heb. 3:1. In some places in the New Testament, the word apostle is used in the Greek where it simply means messengers sent by the churches (e.g. 2 Cor. 8:23; Phil. 2:25). They were not apostles in the way that Peter was, but the same word is used in the Greek.

Usually, the word apostle refers to a small group of men who had a special task in the early church. Mark 3:14-15 tells us (1) Christ gave them the name 'apostle', (2) They spent time with Jesus, (3) They were to preach, and (4) They had a special authority over demons. Acts 1:21,22 adds that their special task was to be witnesses to the resurrection.

Paul's apostleship was on the same basis as that of the other twelve. He received a special calling (Rom. 1:1), learnt his gospel direct from Christ (Gal. 1:12), witnessed the resurrection (1 Cor. 9:1; 15:8), was sent to preach (Rom. 1:5) and did miraculous signs (2 Cor. 12:12).

The New Testament occasionally calls 'apostles' men other than the twelve and Paul (e.g. Acts 14:14). Some at least of these may have been no more than messengers from their churches, others such as Barnabas were leading missionaries. It is safest to restrict the full meaning of the apostleship to the twelve and Paul. We also know of false apostles (2 Cor. 11:13; Rev. 2:2).

The apostles' authority was in their teaching (Acts 2:42). However, one apostle who was doing something wrong could be corrected by another apostle (Gal. 2:12-14). Their authority was firm, but not harsh. They investigated Philip's work in Samaria and placed their hands on the Christians so that they might receive the Holy Spirit (Acts 8:14-17). In Acts 15 they consulted the elders in an important doctrinal matter (v. 2,22,23).

The apostles were a direct link between Christ and the church. As such they had to be chosen directly by Christ, be taught directly by Christ and witness his resurrection. It is obvious, therefore, that there could be no more apostles after the first ones died. They were there to provide the foundation of the church (Eph. 2:20). Their teaching and authority continues today in the writings of the New Testament.

Areopagus

Areopagus is the name of a hill in Athens. The name means 'the hill of Ares'. Ares was the Greek god of war.

Long before New Testament times, the important Council of the Areopagus met on this hill. It had lost some of its original power by Paul's day, but was still very highly respected. Its main concern was morality and religion.

When Paul preached in Athens about Jesus and the resurrection (Acts 17:18), the Council asked him to explain his teaching to them (v.19). They wanted to give their verdict on this new religion.

Ark

God sent a flood to destroy the evil world during the time of Noah. He told Noah to build a floating home for himself and his family, and for representatives of every kind of animal. A description is found in Gen. 6:14-16.

Ark of the Covenant

While the Israelites were camped at Sinai after the exodus from Egypt, God gave Moses the law and details of the tabernacle and its worship. The ark of the covenant was a box about 1100 millimetres long, 700 millimetres wide, and 700 millimetres high, made from acacia wood covered with gold. It was placed in the most holy place in the tabernacle. The proper way of carrying it from place to place was by Levites holding poles which threaded through rings at the side of the ark. On top of the ark was the mercy seat and two cherubim with outspread wings facing each other (Exod. 25:10-22; 26:33,34).

The ark held two stone tablets with the ten commandments inscribed on them (Exod. 25:16), a pot of manna, and Aaron's rod (Exod. 16:34; Num. 17:10; Heb. 9:4,5). It also was the place where God met with his servants (Exod. 25:22).

Asherah (Grove, AV)

Asherah was a Canaanite mother-goddess. She is often linked with the fertility god Baal in the Old Testament. The name was also given to wooden images made for that goddess. God told the Israelites to cut down (Deut. 7:5) or burn (Deut. 12:3) these images. The Israelites were constantly ensnared by this goddess.

Ashtoreth

Astarte was a Semite (tribes descended from Shem — Gen. 10:21,22 - see also Hebrew) goddess worshipped by the Canaanites.

She was goddess of fertility, love and war. Ashtoreth is the plural form of Astarte, with vowels changed by the Hebrews probably to imitate the vowels of the Hebrew word for shame.

Soon after Joshua died, the Israelites started worshipping the Ashtoreth (Judg. 2:13). After Saul's death, his armour was put in her temple at Beth-Shan by the Philistines. Despite the Israelites' rejection of Ashtoreth in Samuel's day (1 Sam. 7:3,4; 12:10), King Solomon brought back her worship in Israel (1 Kings 11:5).

Assistant

In the Old Testament, the Hebrew word can mean 'one who gives personal service' to an important person (Gen. 39:4; 2 Chr. 22:8), or it can mean 'someone who is involved in work done in worship' and who therefore is in a special relationship to God, such as a priest (Deut. 17:12), or an angel (Ps. 103:21). A high rank may be intended. God told Moses every detail of the work that was to be done in the tabernacle and later the temple. The priests and Levites had various duties which covered the whole of the worship of the Old Testament. The work of the temple, therefore, was carried out by certain people, but not by the whole nation of Israel (Num. 8:26). Another example is Joshua, Moses' minister (Exod. 24:13) who succeeded Moses as leader of Israel (Josh. 1:1-5). It is a different word from slave or servant (Exod. 4:10; Isa. 42:1; Jer. 33:21,22).

In Rom. 13:6 the Greek word originally meant someone who worked in a public office, such as a magistrate, at his own expense. Then it came to mean any public servant. The same word is used in Romans 15:16; Phil. 2:25; Heb. 1:7; 8:2. This word is close in meaning to the Old Testament word described above.

See Deacon.

Assurance

Sometimes refers to the reason for being sure about something (Acts 17:31). Paul told the men of Athens in this verse that God has given proof, or a reason for being sure, by raising Jesus from the dead. The Greek word here is translated 'faith' in most other places.

Assurance more often means the feeling of being sure — in other words, a conviction. Here the Greek word gives the idea of being full. The assurance of faith (Heb. 10:22) means to be fully convinced. When Paul preached to the Thessalonians, they became certain that his preaching was true (1 Thess. 1:5).

Christian belief is God convincing us about his truth, followed by our knowing that it is true. It is not a feeling that we could be right in what we believe, but being fully persuaded (Rom. 8:38,39; 2 Tim. 1:12). With this faith, we can be assured that we are God's children because the Spirit tells us so (Rom. 8:16). There is, of course, the possibility that we may be wrong in feeling that we belong to God. Some people have a false assurance. But we can test our feeling of assurance that we belong to God by testing our lives (Titus 1:16; 1 John 2:3).

Atonement

The Hebrew word for atonement is closely related to its word for a ransom. A ransom is a price paid in order to gain someone's freedom. In the Old Testament, the price of an atonement was sometimes money (Exod. 30:16) but the main atonement price was the life of an animal (Lev. 1:4). Sinners deserve God's anger and death but in their place an innocent animal was killed. The animal died that the sinner might live.

In the New Testament, we find that Christ is the atonement for sin. We deserve God's anger for our sin, but Christ's life was given instead. His life was innocent. Christ died that we might live.

See a Theological Dictionary for other theories of the atonement.

Atonement, Day Of

The Day of Atonement was the most solemn of all the holy days in the Old Testament. It was held on 10th Tishri, the seventh month (about September/October). No work was to be done and a fast had to be held, the only annual fast in the Mosaic law. Also, the high priest went into the Holy of Holies only on that day. The ceremonies are described in Lev. 16.

Lev. 16:34 says that atonement was made that day for all the sins of the Israelites committed during the year. This means that the Day of Atonement showed the Israelites that the many regular sacrifices made during the year were not enough to atone for sin.

Even this special day only made them clean in an outward, ceremonial way, as Heb. 9:13 points out. Heb. 9 and 10 show that the Old Testament Day of Atonement was a picture of the real atonement for sin made by Christ on the cross. Just as the high priest went into God's presence in the Holy of Holies once each year with blood, so Jesus went into God's presence in the real Holy of Holies, heaven itself, with his own blood. He had to go only once for all time, not once each year.

Heb. 13:11,12 also refers to the Day of Atonement. The bull and goat used for the sin offerings had to be burned outside the camp (Lev. 16:27). Jesus Christ died outside the city of Jerusalem.

Authority

Authority is the rightful power a person has in order to do something. Jesus' enemies asked him by what authority he was allowed to teach in the temple (Luke 20:1,2). This power may be over others. Jesus, for example, showed authority over the evil spirits. There are exceptions to the power being rightfully held. Satan, for example, usurped authority.

The Bible teaches that all authority belongs to God. He is King and Ruler over all (Ps. 93), including the most powerful of men (Dan. 4:34). Christ has been given all authority (Mark 1:22; 2:10; Matt. 28:18).

God delegates authority to people. This authority is found in the church (Heb. 13:17), the home (Eph. 5:22; 6:1-3) and in government (Rom. 13:1-5). As God has entrusted authorities with their respective powers, those powers should be used carefully and in the way that God has indicated. To resist proper authority is to resist God. The only time to refuse to obey any God-given authority is when we are asked to disobey God's Word.

Baal

In Hebrew, Baal means 'lord', 'owner', 'husband'. The Canaanites had many baals. In fact, each piece of ground had its baal, or divine owner. The chief god of the Canaanites was also called Baal. Baal worship was a particularly vile fertility cult.

As Yahweh was Lord and husband of the Israelites, the name Baal seems also to have been given to him by the northern kingdom of Israel. Hosea attacks this practice (Hosea 2:16, where the Hebrew word for master is baal).

Babylon

This city was on the River Euphrates in what today is Iraq. Its origins go back to before Abraham's time (Gen. 10:10) and at a very early stage it rebelled against God (Gen. 11:1-9). Under Amorite rule, it flourished as the Old Babylonian Empire until it was defeated by the Hittites (1894-1595BC, i.e. during the Israelites' stay in Egypt).

For several centuries, Babylon was weak and became dominated by Assyria. Nabopolassar became king of Babylon in 626BC and during the next few years gradually drove the Assyrians back until he finally defeated them in 612BC. Nebuchadrezzar was the next king (605-562BC). He invaded Judah, taking its leading citizens into exile to Babylonia and sacking Jerusalem in 587BC.

The New Babylonian Empire did not last long. It fell to the Medes and Persians in 539BC. Cyrus ruled in Babylon and allowed the Jews to return home.

The Old Testament prophets warned the people of Judah that God would punish them by the Babylonian exile. They also saw Babylon as under God's judgment because of its pride, wealth, tyranny, idolatry and vice. Babylon became a symbol of human pride in opposition to God and under judgment by God. John's description of Babylon in Rev. 17-19 fits Rome, especially as Rome had seven hills (Rev. 17:9). This does not mean that Babylon in Revelation is exclusively Rome, because the description fits any human authority setting itself up against God.

The Babylon in 1 Peter 5:13 could mean the ancient city or a town with the same name in Egypt. It is more likely, however, to be a symbolic reference to Rome.

Baptism

John the Baptist baptized Jews in the River Jordan (Matt. 3:6). There were other Jewish sects at the time which practised similar baptisms and it may be that official Judaism baptized Gentile converts as early as this. Certainly they did later.

In John's and Christ's baptism, the command is first to repent, then to be baptized (Matt. 3:11; Acts 2:38). Baptism symbolizes sin being washed away (Acts 22:16) through an appeal to God to forgive (1 Peter 3:21). It took place without delay after a person professed faith in Christ (Acts 16:33).

The word baptism comes from the Greek word meaning 'to dip in or under water'. Baptism was a total dipping (immersion) under water. This showed that Christians are united with Christ in his death, burial and resurrection (Rom. 6:3,4). Through this union with Christ, their sins are forgiven and washed away.

A baptism in the Spirit is mentioned in the New Testament. This is used to contrast the baptism of John with the ministry of Christ (Matt. 3:11). Pentecost was a fulfilment of this, together with other comings of the Spirit to people at regeneration, as Peter remarks in Acts 11:15-17.

Barbarian

The Greeks called all non-Greek speaking peoples barbarian. It often meant 'foreigner' (e.g. Acts 28:2,4), but sometimes also meant someone who lacked culture (Col. 3:11).

Bath

A liquid measure of uncertain size, the same size as an ephah. It held probably about 22 litres (Isa. 5:10; Ezek. 45:10).

Belial

Belial means someone who is worthless, or very wicked. The name is given to Satan (2 Cor. 6:15).

Binding and Loosing

The Jewish rabbis used the terms 'binding' and 'loosing' to show
their followers what was forbidden and what was allowed. When
Christ gave this authority to the apostles, therefore, it was in order
that they might teach and discipline church members.

This does not mean that anyone, even Peter, could decide for
himself what was forbidden or allowed. They must be true to
Christ's own teaching, or what the Bible teaches. Christ condemned
making rules which were out of harmony with God's Word (Matt.
15:1-20).

Christ gave this authority to Peter as representative of the twelve
apostles (Matt. 16:19) but also to the whole church (Matt. 18:18).
This exercise of authority must be directed by the Holy Spirit
working in a Spirit-filled community (John 20:22,23).

Blasphemy

God's name should be honoured. When instead it is cursed or
reviled, God is blasphemed. In the Old Testament law, the penalty
for this most serious sin was death by stoning (Lev. 24:10-23).
When the people of God turned to idols, that too was blasphemy, as
it was an insult to God's honour (Ezek. 20:27,28).

Jesus said blasphemy can be forgiven, unless it is against the
Holy Spirit. As the glory of God was hidden in the person of Christ,
insults against him can be forgiven because it was done in ignorance.
Those who blaspheme against the Holy Spirit, however, see the
clearest evidence of God at work and yet harden their hearts and
refuse to repent of their insults against God's honour. In fact, they
even say that what is so clearly done by God was done by Satan
(Matt. 12:24-32).

As this unforgivable blasphemy is a stubborn refusal to repent in
the face of the clearest evidence of God's works, no people who are
troubled as to whether they have committed this sin need to worry.
Their tender consciences and willingness to repent show they
cannot have done so. Paul's blasphemies before his conversion were
forgiven because he did them in ignorance and unbelief (1 Tim.
1:13).

Blessed, Blessing

When a person is said to be blessed, it means that person is happy in the highest and purest way. This happiness is given by God. Godly people may at times seem to be pitied, but in fact they have an enviable happiness (Matt. 5:3-11).

A blessing can be a material good (Prov. 10:22) or the greater blessing of a right relationship with God through the gospel (Rom. 15:29). A blessing can be invoked through words (Gen. 27:27-29).

Blood

In the Bible, the word blood often indicates a violent death, for example, by murder (Gen. 4:10). Blood was also central to the Old Testament sacrificial system. It is important to remember this when the Bible talks of 'the blood of Christ'; the meaning of this is that his violent death on the cross was a voluntary sacrifice for sin.

Body of Christ

The New Testament makes it clear that Christ's physical body was a real one (1 John 4:2). Christ had to be a complete human being in order to save human beings (Heb. 2:5-18; 4:15).

At the Last Supper, Jesus broke bread and said: 'This is my body' (Luke 22:19). Some people, such as Roman Catholics, teach that at the communion service, the bread is changed from bread to the actual body of Christ. Others say the bread stays as bread, but at the same time carries with it the actual body of Christ. These both misunderstand Jesus' words.

Jesus cannot have meant that the bread was his real body because he had not yet died and his body was standing there as he said these words. The disciples would have understood him to mean that the bread represented, or symbolized, his body. Jesus often used symbols.

A third use of the phrase 'the body of Christ' is found in Paul's letters where he used it to mean 'the church'. In Rom. 12 and 1 Cor. 12 he talked about the body of Christ to show how members of each local church are related to each other. Church members differ from

invite or summon someone. When God is the one who calls, or who is being called, the word has a special significance.

People call on God's name (Gen. 4:26; Isa. 55:6). This has no effect when the caller persists in sin (Hosea 11:7) but when it is a call of faith, the call brings God's presence to the caller (Ps. 145:18). God's presence in turn brings salvation (Isa. 55:6; Joel 2:32) or other help (Ps. 17:6; 34:6). Calling on God's name could be by prayer for God to act (1 Kings 18:24,36-38), in thankfulness (Ps. 105:1) or in worship (Ps. 80:18).

God calls people. He invites them to trust him for salvation (Isa. 43:1; Rom. 1:6). In Matt. 22:14 Jesus means a general gospel call because many refuse it: the called are those who hear preaching. In other places, especially in the New Testament letters, the called are not just those who hear gospel preaching, but those who also respond to it in faith: the called are those whom God predestined to salvation (Rom. 8:30). There are no people who are called but who are not believers.

God also calls people for special tasks or service (Isa. 49:1; Rom. 1:1). In the New Testament only the apostles received a direct commission from God for their ministry. Others such as the elders were appointed on the basis of the gifts God had given them (Acts 14:23; Titus 1:5-9). On that understanding, we can say that all whom God calls for salvation are also called to serve God (1 Cor. 7:15; 1 Peter 2:20-21).

The 'calling' (AV) of 1 Cor. 7:20 that Christians were in when God called them to salvation is their situation when they were converted. When God saves, he saves the whole person, which includes outward circumstances. Paul is saying that they should not try to change things just because they are now Christians. They should remain married and not leave their partner. They should remain circumcised, or uncircumcised (v. 19), or slaves (v. 21). If there are other reasons for changing, however, they are free to do so (v. 21).

Calvary

See Golgotha.

Canaan, Canaanites

Canaan was a son of Ham, and the father of peoples who occupied all of Palestine (Gen. 10:6,15-19). This occupation took place before Abraham's time (Gen. 12:6).

The Canaanites lived in the plains by the sea and west of the Jordan, whereas other tribes lived in the Negev and the hills (Num. 13:29). Canaanite can refer to almost all the peoples living in Palestine before the Israelite conquest, or to one racial group in parts of Palestine. This double meaning of the word Canaanite is also found in ancient writings outside the Bible. This shows how Canaanite culture and religion had spread to at least some of these groups, especially the Amorites.

The Canaanites lived in small city-states ruled by kings. This means they were not united politically. Their greatest achievement was in writing and their scribes could write in various languages. They are credited with the invention of the linear alphabet, which is the ancestor of the alphabets used in many parts of the world today. Trading was another important part of their culture, especially exporting timber and textiles. This brought great wealth, especially in the early days of their history.

Their religion is of particular importance in understanding the Bible. This was a vile form of paganism, emphasising debased sexual practices and cruelty. An important part of this religion was the myth of the death and resurrection of Baal, which corresponded with the annual death and resurrection of nature in winter and spring.

Censer

A metal vessel for carrying live coals (Lev. 16:12) or for burning incense (Ezek. 8:11; Rev. 8:3).

Census

The Romans regularly imposed a census on their territories in order to find out what taxes should be paid to the imperial exchequer. Two are mentioned in the New Testament. The first is in Luke 2:1, which brought Joseph and Mary to Bethlehem when Jesus was born. The second took place in AD6 when Judaea was made a Roman province. This census sparked off a rebellion led by Judas of Galilee, the founder of the Zealots. Judas considered that giving tribute to a pagan overlord was treason against God. This rebellion was mentioned by the Jewish teacher Gamaliel in Acts 5:37.

Centurion

The smallest division of the Roman army was called a century, which officially comprised 100 men. In practice they were a little smaller than this. The commander of a century was a centurion. Unlike higher officers in the Roman army, he was a professional soldier promoted from the ranks. For an example, see Luke 7:2; Acts 10:22.

Chaldaea, Chaldeans

Chaldaea was in south Babylonia, on what is now the north coast of the Persian Gulf. Abraham came from this area (Gen. 11:28).

With the rest of Babylonia, Chaldaea was for many years under Assyrian rule. When Sargon came to the Assyrian throne in 721BC, Merodach-Baladan, who was the ruler of a Chaldean district, seized the Babylonian throne. He rebelled against the Assyrians, but Sargon eventually defeated him in 710BC. When Sargon died in 705BC, Merodach-Baladan tried again to gain independence from Assyria with the help of some states to the west. These events are the background of Isa. 23:13, and chapter 39.

Nabopolassar was a Chaldean governor who came to the Babylonian throne in 626BC. He gradually defeated the Assyrians and set up the new Babylonian empire. The whole of Babylonia became known as Chaldaea during this time (Dan. 5:30). Astrologers, who were much respected by the Babylonians, were also called Chaldeans (Dan. 2:10).

See Babylon.

Chariot

Heavy two or four wheeled vehicles drawn by asses were used for war and ceremonies before Abraham's time. Not until the light, two-wheeled vehicles drawn by horses were introduced into Asia did they have any military importance. The Hittites and Egyptians used them to great effect and the Canaanites in the plains had them by the time of the conquest. They were only of use in the plains, however, and could not be used in the hill country.

In Samuel's day they were already a symbol of kingly splendour (1 Sam. 8:11). In the reign of Solomon they became an important part of the Israelite army. Like the Hittites, the Israelite chariots had a crew of three: a driver, a warrior and a shield bearer.

Cherubim

These heavenly beings guarded the tree of life (Gen. 3:24). God also told Moses to make two gold cherubim to cover the ark, where they formed a throne for the invisible God (Exod. 25:18-22; 1 Sam. 4:4). The picture of God riding a cherub is found in 2 Sam. 22:11.

Cherubim were depicted in Solomon's temple (1 Kings 6:23-29). Ezekiel described them in his visions of the glory of God where they are seen as God's throne (Ezek. 10:18). We cannot be sure what these representations of the cherubim looked like, but they seem to have been a mixture of human beings and certain animals. These animals etc. are of course only symbols which stand for the spiritual beings who attend on God in his glory.

The - im ending is the Hebrew form of the masculine plural.

Christ

This word comes from the Greek word meaning 'anointed', which is the Greek equivalent of the Hebrew word for Messiah. Jesus of Nazareth is the Messiah (or Christ) foretold in the Old Testament - the man anointed by God as the Leader and Saviour of his people.

In the Gospels, Peter recognized Jesus as the Christ (Mark 8:29). Jesus told his disciples not to tell anyone, probably because the Jews thought of the Messiah as a military leader who would defeat the

Romans, whereas his kingship is not of this world (John 18:36).

Jesus' triumphal entry into Jerusalem on Palm Sunday was a demonstration that he was the Christ, or King, of Israel (Matt. 21:5). He rode on a donkey, the animal of peace, to show that he is the king of peace. Later, the high priest asked Jesus if he claimed to be the Christ. When Jesus said he did, the high priest and the Sanhedrin condemned him for blasphemy (Mark 14:61-64). The Roman court accused Jesus of the political crime of claiming to be a king (Mark 15:2,26). After pentecost, the apostles preached to the Jews that the man who was crucified was the Christ (Acts 2:36).

See Anointed.

See also Messiah.

Christian

The word only appears three times in the Bible (Acts 11:26; 26:28; 1 Peter 4:16). It was probably a well-known name in New Testament days for Christ's followers, but there were other names such as 'disciples', 'the Way', 'believers', that they preferred to use.

Christian means 'Christ's one', a follower of Christ, a 'disciple' (Acts 11:26).

Church

The Greek word for church means 'an assembly' or 'meeting' called for some purpose. A church is therefore a local congregation of Christians. The Jews also used the word for the Old Testament congregation of Israel (Acts 7:38).

The New Testament does not use the word church to describe a building, nor groups of congregations. Paul wrote to the churches in Galatia, not to the church in Galatia (Gal. 1:2). Acts 9:31 may be an exception, although some texts have 'churches' (see KJV). Alternatively, the word could be used loosely.

It is unclear if the church in Aquilla and Priscilla's home (1 Cor 16:19) was the entire Ephesian (see v.8) church.

In addition to individual congregations, the New Testament has only one other meaning for church, and that is the heavenly reality of the whole number of the redeemed (Eph. 5:25; cf. Rev. 21:2).

Circumcision

Genesis 17 says how circumcision among the Jews began. God gave it as the sign of his covenant with Abraham and his descendants (v. 11) and all boys had to be circumcised when eight days old (v. 12). Uncircumcised males could not be included in God's people (v. 14), which is why they could not eat the passover, the meal which celebrated God's redemption of his people from slavery in Egypt (Exod. 12:43-49). The cutting of the flesh, and the bleeding which followed, may be designed to indicate that a covenant had been made. See Covenant.

Circumcision was the sign of the covenant, pointing to God's grace in choosing and saving his people. Unless, therefore, it was accompanied by devoted obedience to God, it was of no use. Their hearts had to be 'circumcised' (Deut. 10:16; Jer. 9:25).

In the New Testament, some Jewish Christians said Gentiles could not be saved unless they were circumcised (Acts 15:1). Paul and others strongly opposed this teaching and the Council of Jerusalem agreed with Paul (Acts 15:1-29).

Paul developed the Old Testament teaching that circumcision is a matter of the heart. Indeed, Christians are the new circumcision because of their relationship with Christ through the Spirit (Phil. 3:3). Christians have been 'circumcised by Christ' (Col. 2:11); in other words, Christ has purified their hearts through the new covenant in his blood.

So the New Testament equivalent of circumcision is the saving work of Christ applied to the Christian by the Holy Spirit. It is an inward reality, not an outward sign. Baptism points to the fact that Christ has cleansed us from sin through his death, burial and resurrection, but it is not the New Testament successor of circumcision.

Paul said that it made no difference whether a man was physically circumcised. What was important was a new life in Christ

(Gal. 5:6; 6:15). Abraham's circumcision was the mark which proved that he was right with God through faith (Rom. 4:11).

Paul opposed circumcising the Gentiles as necessary for salvation because that would completely change the gospel (Gal. 1:6-9). If Gentiles became Jews through circumcision, Christ's death was not enough: they would also have to be saved by keeping the law of Moses. This was no longer a gospel of God's grace received through faith (Gal. 5:3-6).

Claudius

Mentioned in Acts 11:28; 17:7; 18:2.

See Caesar.

Clean and Unclean

People in Old Testament times in Bible lands thought bodily cleanness was very important. No one could approach God unless clean.

Cleanness in the Old Testament was not simply a washed body. Someone could be unclean because he touched a dead body (Num. 19:11), had an infectious skin disease (Lev.13:45) or because of many other reasons. A woman was unclean if she had given birth to a child (Lev.12:2). Certain meats were unclean and therefore forbidden to the Israelites (Lev.11). This distinction between unclean and clean animals goes back at least as far as Noah (Gen. 7:2).

Unclean people had to keep away from holy things, including other Israelites (2 Chr. 23:19; 1 Sam. 20:26). They were, however, still allowed to eat the passover (Num. 9:10). After their time of ceremonial uncleanness, the Israelites had to be ceremonially purified.

By New Testament times, the Jewish teachers had added to the biblical rules. Jesus pointed out the real meaning of the Old Testament ceremonies when he said that cleanness was a moral, not a ritual, matter (Mark 7:1-23). Mark comments that Christ declared all foods clean. Christians are therefore not bound by these Old Testament ceremonies, but their real meaning remains true: no one can approach God unless clean inside — that is, clean from sin.

Comforter

See Advocate.

Communion

The word 'communion' (fellowship) means sharing. The root Greek word is used for partner, where the men shared a fishing business (Luke 5:10) and for communion, where Christians share in the Holy Spirit (2 Cor. 13:14).

People who share together in something are bound together. The good king Jehoshaphat was condemned because he joined with the wicked Ahaziah in a business venture (2 Chr. 20:35-37). Likewise, Christians are told to separate themselves from evil associations or they would share in their sins (Rev. 18:4). There is such a thing as fellowship with demons (1 Cor. 10:20).

Christians have fellowship first with God and his Son, Jesus Christ (1 John 1:3). In fellowship there is a giving and a receiving. Christians receive Christ and have the right to become God's children (John 1:12). They share the blessings gained by Christ on the cross. They give themselves to God in repentance and faith (Rom. 6:13). This submission to Christ includes submission to his teaching and the Word of God (Matt. 11:29; 1 John 2:20-23).

Christians have fellowship secondly with other Christians, especially with members of the same local church. Christians are bonded together in Christ Jesus (Gal. 3:28). They share together in worshipping Christ (1 Cor. 10:16-18), witnessing for Christ (Phil. 1:27), suffering for Christ (2 Cor. 1:7), persecution (Heb. 10:33), in meeting other Christians' needs (Acts 4:32), and will share the coming glory of Christ (2 Thess. 2:14). Fellowship also leads to respecting one another, helping one another, teaching one another, confessing sins to one another (Phil. 2:1-4; Col. 3:12-17; James 5:16) and sharing in the Love Feast and the Lord's Supper.

Compassion

Compassion is part of the character of God (Exod. 22:27). This is why he forgives sin, although this compassion is not shown to those who continue in their sin (Exod. 34:6-7). God is therefore not compassionate to everyone; he selects those to whom he shows compassion (Exod. 33:19). Because God is compassionate, godly people are also compassionate (Deut. 10:18,19; 24:19).

Compassion was a mark of Christ's ministry (Matt. 9:36; Mark 1:41). He taught others to show pity to everyone in need (Luke 10:29-37). Christians therefore should show compassion to all in their church (Col. 3:12,13) as well as to other people. Those who are not compassionate clearly do not have God's love in them (1 John 3:17).

Confess, Confession

The word 'confess' translates a Greek word meaning 'to say the same thing'. So if we are confessing sins, we are 'saying the same' that God says about our sins. If we are confessing the faith we are 'saying the same' that other believers say about what we believe.

Confession is also used in a further way. Confessing one's faith is to declare in public that one has a personal relationship with God. Believers confess a person, Jesus Christ, not a religious system. This confession may be costly (John 12:42) but will lead to Christ confessing us before his Father in the judgment (Matt. 10:32). The Holy Spirit enables believers to confess Christ (1 Cor. 12:3). In fact, Jesus confessed before Pilate that he was the Christ (1 Tim. 6:12,13).

Believers may confess their sins before other believers (Acts 19:18; James 5:16), but some sins may be too shameful to speak about (Eph. 5:12). Confession to God, however, must hide nothing. Nowhere does the Bible tell believers to confess their sins to a special officer of the church who in turn will absolve them from those sins.

See a Theological Dictionary for Confessions of Faith.

Congregation

In the Old Testament, congregation means an assembly of Israelites who met together for a particular purpose. Often this assembly was by appointment, and to worship or otherwise serve God (e.g. Num. 10:7).

See Church.

Conscience

The idea of conscience is found in the Old Testament (e.g. Job 27:6; 1 Sam. 24:5), but is more fully developed in the New Testament. It is the inner voice which judges the morality of what we think, say or do, causing us to feel guilt when we do wrong, or guiding us to do what is right.

In Rom. 2:12-16 Paul tells us that God gave the Old Testament law to the Jews, but he also gave Gentiles an instinctive knowledge of his law. Conscience is not the same as this instinctive law written on our hearts, but it does use this inner law to condemn our faults or defend our right actions (Rom. 2:15).

Our consciences are not infallible. They can be weak, condemning what is not necessarily wrong (1 Cor. 8:7), or they can be corrupt, failing to condemn what is wrong (Titus 1:15) or even seared, that is, not bothered about right and wrong at all (1 Tim. 4:2). Our consciences need the Holy Spirit to apply biblical teaching to our minds.

Conversion

The word 'conversion' comes from Latin 'convertere' — 'to turn, change'. Conversion is the act of turning; a convert is a person who converts or is converted; not just an outward change of behaviour, but a humble and sincere seeking after God (Deut. 4:29,30). The Hebrew word 'sub' and the Greek 'epistrepho' (both translated convert, verb) have this meaning of turn; i.e. to turn from sin to God.

In the Old Testament, an individual (Ps. 51:13) or a whole nation (2 Chr. 30:6) could turn to God; indeed, there is a looking forward to a worldwide turning to God (Ps. 22:27). New Testament conversions are mainly by individuals, but sometimes whole families turned to God (Acts 16:31-34).

The New Testament reserves the word conversion for a once in a lifetime event. Peter's repentance in Luke 22:32 is the one exception to this. Conversion is a turning from sin, from idols and the rule of Satan to the worship of God (1 Thess. 1:9). Backsliders are urged to repent rather than convert (Rev. 2:5).

Conversion includes turning from sin in repentance (Acts 3:19) and turning to God in faith (Acts 11:21). It is a deliberate act. The Bible clearly teaches that turning to God is the result of God's work first in people's lives (Lam. 5:21; Acts 16:14).

See Repentance.

Cor

A dry or liquid measure the same size as a homer (probably about 220 litres, Ezek. 45:14).

Cornerstone

The cornerstone carried the weight of a building and also bound walls together. The Old Testament uses this as a picture of the foundation of the created world (Job 38:6) and of the coming King, or Messiah (e.g. Zech. 10:4).

The New Testament teaches that this cornerstone is a symbol of Jesus Christ. Is. 8:14 and 28:16 are quoted together to show that Christ can be a stumbling block to unbelievers or the one who unites believers (Rom. 9:33; 1 Peter 2:6,8). Ps. 118:22 is quoted to show that the one who was rejected became the most important person (e.g. Matt. 21:42; 1 Peter 2:7).

Ps. 118:22 may refer to the keystone which completed an arch or other structure at the top of the building, rather than a foundation stone as in Isa. 28:16. Christ is both the foundation on which the church is built and its crowning glory.

Counsellor

See Advocate

Covenant

The Hebrew verb for making a covenant is 'to cut a covenant' and this is seen in Gen. 15:9-18.

The Greek noun 'diatheke' comes from a verb meaning 'to dispose of one's own property'. In secular Greek, it meant a will, and the word means this in Heb. 9:15-17).

In the cultures of nations of Bible times, covenants were agreements entered into by two or more parties (Gen. 31:44). These are confirmed either by erecting a stone (Gen. 31:45) or by a sacrifice where animals were cut in two and the people making the covenant walked between the pieces (Gen. 15).

Covenants made by God in Old Testment history were not agreements made by two parties. Instead, God sovereignly and graciously bound himself to fulfil certain promises. God entered into covenants with Noah (Gen. 6:18; 9:8-17), Abraham (Gen. 15; 17:1-14), Phinehas (Num. 25:12) and David (Ps. 89:49, cf. 2 Sam. 7:12-17). In Gen. 15, for example, God walks alone between the sacrificed pieces, whereas if Abraham were also a party to the covenant, he too would have walked there. All these covenants include the descendants of those with whom God made the agreement.

These divine covenants often included obligations on the part of people to keep the covenant. This could be by entering the ark with the animals (Gen. 6:18-21), circumcision as the sign of the covenant (Gen. 17), obeying God's commands, as in the case of the nation of Israel at the Sinai covenant (Exod. 19:5).

Finally there is the new covenant promised in the Old Testament (Jer. 31:31-34) and fulfilled in Christ (Heb. 8:8-13; Luke 22:20).

These covenants should not be thought of as entirely separate from each other. They are all covenants of God's grace. Deut. 29:13 shows that the Mosaic covenant is an extension of the one with Abraham, and indeed, the new covenant in Christ is a fulfilment of the covenant with Abraham (Gal. 3:15-29).

Creation

We cannot begin to understand the Bible's teaching about God unless we see him as the creator of all things (Gen. 1:1). This theme of creation is found throughout the Bible (e.g. Job 38; Ps. 8:3; Isa. 40:26-28; Acts 17:24 and the other texts quoted in this section).

A biblical understanding of creation comes through faith in God (Heb. 11:3). God has revealed it. On the other hand, God's character shines through what he has made, giving sinners no excuse (Rom. 1:20).

Heb. 11:3 with Gen. 1:1 show that God created the universe out of nothing. Physical matter is not eternal. Only God is eternal. It follows therefore that God is not part of creation, but is separate from it and exalted far above it.

Not all creation was made out of nothing, however. The animals (Gen. 2:19) and man (Gen. 2:7) were made from the ground; woman was made from man (Gen. 2:21).
The whole triune God - Father (Gen. 1:1), Son (John 1:1) and Holy Spirit (Gen. 1:2) - was involved in creation. And God alone created everything (John 1:3), as no creature has that supreme power.

God created all things for his own glory and purpose (Rev. 4:11). He continues to keep the universe going (Col. 1:17) and will bring the present creation to an end, replacing it with a new heaven and a new earth (Rev. 21:1).

Cross

Before the Romans, the Phoenicians and Carthaginians practised crucifixion. The Romans used wooden crosses of four different shapes to execute slaves, provincials and the lowest form of criminal. Very seldom was a Roman citizen crucified.

After being condemned, the criminal carried the cross beam (not the whole cross) to the place of execution, which was always outside the city. In front of him walked a herald who carried the title (written accusation). On arrival, the condemned man was stripped naked, laid down and nailed or tied to the cross before it was raised upright.

The victim was left to die of hunger, exhaustion and suffocation. It was a very painful death which could take several hours. Death was sometimes made quicker by breaking the victim's legs, which made it impossible for him to pull himself up in order to breathe. This was not necessary in the case of Jesus.

Crucifixion was brutal, shameful and humiliating and yet the cross of Christ was God's power and wisdom as shown in the gospel.

Cubit

The distance between a man's elbow and the tip of his finger. The standard cubit was 17.5 inches (six handbreadths). The long, or royal, cubit was 20.4 inches (seven handbreadths).

Cupbearer

Rulers such as Pharaoh of Egypt (Gen. 40:1) and Solomon (1 Kings 10:5) had cupbearers to bring in their wine and taste it before they drank it, to make sure it was not poisoned. Foreigners were sometimes used, but often they became trusted men who had political influence with the king. Nehemiah was one such man (Neh. 1:11).

Curse

A curse spoken by God brings misery and death to sinners. God's main intention is to bless his creatures, but those who reject his blessing receive his curse instead (Deut. 11:26). Human curses call for God's judgment on others (Num. 23:8; 2 Kings 2:24) or on the speakers to test the truth of what they are saying (Mark 14:71).

The person who curses God is guilty of the worst sin and deserves to die (Job 2:9). Cursing one's parents, or the king of Israel, was equal to cursing God, because they represented God in the family or nation (Exod. 21:17; 1 Kings 21:13). The Bible does not treat curses as empty words, but a real threat. A curse was as much a danger for a deaf man as a rock in the path of a blind man (Lev. 19:14). However, the power of a curse is related to the one who utters it. The blessing of God will more than compensate for the curse of any human person (Ps. 109:28). God's curse is God's judgment on sin (Jer. 29:18) and is against those who break God's law (Deut.

27:26; Zech. 5:1-4). Christ became a curse to release sinners from the curse of breaking God's law and to open the way again to God's blessing (Galatians 3:13,14).

Christians must not curse anyone, because a curse seeks to bring God's judgment on that person, to be shut out from God's grace. Instead, Christians should bless those who curse them (Rom. 12:14).

Curtain (veil, AV)

See entry under Temple.

Dagon

In the Old Testament, Dagon is a main Philistine god. Samson died destroying Dagon's temple in Gaza (Judg. 16:23-30). In Ashdod a few years later, the image of Dagon fell down in front of the captured ark of God and broke (1 Sam. 5:2-7). After King Saul was killed, his head and armour were put in the temple of Dagon by the Philistines (1 Chr. 10:10).

People in Mesopotamia were worshipping Dagon about 1000 years before Samson. Later, some north Canaanite stories call Dagon the father of Baal. The Philistines took over this Semitic religion.

For a long time, scholars thought that Dagon was a fish-god. This was mainly because of an image of a fish-tailed god found on coins in sites of towns not far from Gaza and Ashdod. But this god was called Atargitis. It is more likely that Dagon was a corn-god. The Hebrew word for corn 'dagan' seems to be related to the name of the god, Dagon.

David

David was the youngest of the eight sons of Jesse. Jesse was from the tribe of Judah and lived in Bethlehem. When God rejected Saul, the first king of Israel, he told Samuel to anoint David instead (1 Sam. 16).

David was a shepherd, but became a soldier after killing Goliath (1Sam. 17). Saul became jealous of David's successes and eventually forced him to flee from the court. He then became the leader of a private army of malcontents. David became king of Judah (and seven years later, king of all Israel) after Saul and his sons died in the battle of Mount Gilboa.

David's reign was marked by military success (2 Sam. 8,10). In his personal life, however, he committed adultery with Bathsheba and had her husband Uriah killed (2 Sam. 11). David's family life was painful at times, especially when one of his sons led a rebellion which was later defeated (2 Sam. 13-18).

Despite his faults, David was a godly man. He captured Jerusalem and brought the ark there after many years of neglect (1 Samuel 7:1,2; 2 Sam. 6). A skilled harpist (1 Sam. 16:18), he wrote many psalms. He also wanted to build a temple but God told him that because he was a soldier, he must leave this task to his peaceful son Solomon (1 Chr. 17). David undertook preparation work for the temple (1 Chr. 28-29).

God promised David that the throne would always be occupied by one of his descendants (1 Chr. 17:7-14). When the kings of Judah ceased after the defeat by Nebuchadrezzar, the Jews continued to look for the son of David, the Messiah, who would restore the glory of Israel. Jesus of Nazareth, a direct descendant of David, is this Messiah.

Day of the LORD

In Amos' day, the Israelites were expecting that God would make their nation the head of all the nations in the 'day of the LORD'. But Amos and other prophets told them that the day of the LORD would bring judgment on them for disobeying God (Amos 5:18-20). Other nations too would receive God's judgment for their brutality and sinfulness (Isa. 13:6,9; Obadiah 15).

In the New Testament, 'the day of the Lord' is the second coming of Christ, when God will punish the wicked and reward the faithful (1 Cor. 1:8).

Devils, Demons

Devils are spiritual beings hostile to God. They were created by God as angels, but sinned against him. (See Job 1:6 where Satan appears with the 'sons of God' [angels] as one of their number).

Devils can enter into people, and we mainly find this happening in the Bible in the Gospels. Probably demonic forces were especially active at that time in order to fight against the Son of God.

Devils are powerful creatures. No one should think they are of little importance. Even angels take great care in dealing with them, even though they are stronger than devils (2 Peter 2:10,11; Jude 9). Demons are present in idol worship (1 Cor. 10.19f).

God will punish all devils in hell, which was prepared for them (Matt. 25:41).

See Satan.

Deacon

Jesus called himself a deacon (Luke 22:27). The word translated 'servant' is the same word as is translated 'deacon' in other parts of the New Testament. Sometimes it is translated 'minister'. Deacon means servant, often table servant, or waiter.

All Christians are to follow Christ, serving each others' needs (1 Peter 4:10). The apostles described themselves as deacons of the Word (Acts 6:4; Col. 1:23).

But there is also a special group of people in churches called deacons. The seven men in Acts 6:1-6 are nowhere called deacons, but they did wait at table. Probably the diaconate of 1 Tim. 3:8-13 grew from the seven in Jerusalem.

We are not told what the deacons of 1 Timothy 3 did. No doubt they attended to the social needs of the church, as did the seven, releasing the elders for prayer and the ministry of the Word (cf. Acts 6:4). Soon after New Testament days, we read of deacons visiting the sick and doing other tasks.

Although deacons were entrusted with social work in the churches, they still had to be spiritual people (Acts 6:3) who lived upright lives and had a good knowledge of the faith (1 Tim. 3:9).

It seems that women could act as deacons. 1 Tim. 3:11 is more likely to mean women deacons than deacons' wives. Phoebe is called a deacon of the church in Cenchrea (Rom. 16:1).

Death

We normally think of a person as being dead when the physical body no longer has any life in it. This is sometimes what is meant when the Bible uses this word (Josh. 1:1). There is much more meaning to the Bible's teaching on death, however.

Death is the punishment for sin (Rom. 6:23). God told Adam that if he disobeyed, he would immediately die (Gen. 2:17). Adam's body did not die until much later, but his perfection before God, his fellowship with God, and his ability to please God, did die straightaway. This is what death really is. Bodily death is a picture of real, i.e. spiritual, death in God's sight.

This means that people who are physically alive can be dead spiritually (Eph. 2:1-2). Everyone needs to be born again (made alive) in their relationship to God (John 1:12,13; 3:3). We should not be afraid of physical death because to Christians that is little more than sleep (1 Thess. 4:14). There is also a second death for the ungodly which Christians need not fear (Rev. 2:11; 20:14).

The Christian good news is that Christ has conquered sin and death. Death no longer holds any terror for the Christian (1 Cor. 15:54-57) because Christ is life and the giver of eternal life (John 11:25,26).

Devoted thing

Something which must be surrendered to God without reserve and cannot be reclaimed. This can be something used exclusively in the service of God (Lev. 27:28; Josh. 6:19), or something which must be destroyed because of grave sin (Lev. 27:29; Josh. 6:21). The rule was misused by the Pharisees (Mark 7:11).

Disciple

Jewish and Greek teachers in the ancient world often gathered groups of pupils (disciples) around them. The word disciple is also used of people who accept the teachings of another person (cf. John 9:28, disciples of Moses). The word means 'a learner'.

In the Gospels, the twelve are called disciples (Matt. 10:1) but so are other followers of Christ (John 6:66). Acts also describes all Christians as disciples (6:1).

Divorce

Jesus made it clear that God intended marriage to be permanent (Matt. 19:4-6). Because men and women are now sinners, Moses gave permission to men to divorce their wives (Deut. 24:1-4). Moses did not command men to divorce their wives, but sought to prevent abuse of the wife when divorces were carried out. A legal document was handed to the wife and she was free to remarry. The man could not remarry his ex-wife.

The Old Testament law gives two cases when divorce was not allowed. These are when a husband falsely accused his wife of unfaithfulness before their marriage (Deut. 22:13-19) and when the wife's father made the couple marry after the man raped the girl (Deut. 22:28,29).

The exiles who returned to Judah married pagan wives. Their leaders commanded them to divorce these wives (Ezra. 9,10; Neh. 13:23-27). These were exceptional events in order to maintain religious purity and are not applicable today.

Jesus taught that divorce is not for those who wish to obey God unless the marriage is broken through adultery or similar sexual unfaithfulness. Divorce on any other grounds makes remarriage adultery (Matt. 19:9).

Paul repeated Christ's teaching that marriage is permanent. If a couple do separate, they should remain unmarried, or become reconciled (1 Cor. 7:10,11). When two unbelievers marry and one later becomes a Christian, the Christian partner should not leave the other. If, however, the non-Christian leaves, then the Christian is not bound to keep an impossible union.

Eden, the garden of

We cannot be sure exactly where the Garden of Eden was (Gen. 2:8). Four rivers are mentioned in Gen. 2:11-14. We do not know what Pison and Gihon are today but the other two are the Tigris and the Euphrates. This leads us to think that the most likely place is somewhere at the north of the Persian Gulf.

The name Eden seems to come from an ancient word for a plain, or flat country. The Hebrew language has a similar word which means delight, and the meaning of Eden in the Garden of Eden has taken on this meaning as well. The garden was a place of delight. This leads to the Bible linking the garden with paradise (Rev. 2:7, cf. Gen. 2:9). The garden is also called the garden of the Lord (Isa. 51:3) and the garden of God (Ezek. 28:13). The Bible does not tell us what happened to the garden.

Edom, Edomites

Edom means red and is another name for Jacob's brother Esau (Gen. 25:30). It became the name of his descendants and their land - Mount Seir at the south of the Dead Sea. Esau settled in this land (Gen. 32:3).

The Edomites refused to let the Israelites pass through their land on the way to Canaan (Num. 20:14-21) but despite this, the Israelites were told not to hate their brothers (Deut. 23:7). David conquered the Edomites (2 Sam 8:14). They tried to rebel (1 Kings 11:14; 2 Chr. 20:1,10) but were subject to the kings of Judah until Jehoram's reign (2 Kings 8:22).

When Jerusalem fell to the Babylonians, the Edomites rejoiced (Ps. 137:7) but the prophets foretold judgment on Edom for their hatred towards God's people (Obadiah). Some Edomites moved into southern Judah which became Idumaea. Various groups of Arabs raided and defeated Edom proper in the fifth to third centuries BC. Malachi, written about 450BC, refers to these earlier raids (Mal. 1:3).

Between the Old and New Testaments, the Jews under the Maccabaeans defeated the Edomites, forced them to be circumcised and incorporated them into the Jewish nation. The Herods of the New Testament were Edomites, sons of the spiritually insensitive Esau.

Egypt

The history of the Egyptian nation starts before Abraham, who lived there for a while (Gen. 12:10-20). Egypt was one of the more powerful nations of the ancient world, especially from shortly before Abraham to the time of the book of Judges. Its power declined during the thousand years before Christ, although there were times of revival under more vigorous leaders. It was ruled for a time by the Assyrians and later by the Persians. Alexander the Great conquered Egypt and after his death it was ruled by Greeks until it became part of the Roman empire in 30BC.

The great act of redemption in the Old Testament is the exodus from Egypt. This theme is recounted many times in the Old Testament.

Elder

In Old Testament days, cities and nations were ruled by elders (Gen. 50:7; Num. 22:7). The elders of Israel first appear in Egypt and were most likely the heads of the families (Exod. 3:16). They continued to be important during the monarchy (1 Kings 8:1; 20:7) and afterwards (Ezek. 8:1). Their duties were mainly civil rather than religious and included sitting in the city gates as judges (Deut. 19:12; 21:2; Ruth 4:1-12).

By New Testament times, the Jewish elders were more concerned with religious than civil affairs. They are often mentioned in the Gospels and Acts (Mark 8:31; Acts 4:5). Elders also ruled the synagogues.

Christian churches are also ruled by elders (Acts 14:23; 15:2; Titus 1:5). The same men are also called pastors or bishops. (See Pastor). They must be gentle and upright men with a mature faith and able to teach that faith to others (1 Tim. 3:1-7). They are not necessarily old men.

Although they rule the churches by the Word of God, they should not do so harshly (1 Peter 5:2,3). They are to correct the erring (1 Thess. 5:12), visit the sick (James 5:14) and set apart others for gospel work (1 Tim. 4:14). Some but not all elders work in preaching and teaching (1 Tim. 5:17).

The twenty-four elders in Revelation (e.g. 4:4) seem to stand for the redeemed of all time. The number is made up from the twelve tribes, representing the godly in Old Testament times, plus the twelve apostles representing the New Testament era.

Elements

The Greek word had several meanings. The important meanings for understanding the New Testament are:

1. Basic principles of knowledge. This meaning developed from the use of the word to describe the letters of the alphabet as the elements of speech.

2. Basic material parts which make up physical things. (Some Greek philosophers thought they were earth, water, fire and air).

3. Angels or demons.

In Heb. 5:12 the meaning is obviously the basic principles of knowledge (1).
    2 Peter 3:10,12 clearly demands the basic parts which make up the universe (2).
    Some people argue that meaning (3) occurs in Gal. 4:3,9 and Col. 2:8,20. One problem with this theory is that this meaning does not seem to have been used until two or three hundred years after these letters were written. The meaning angels or demons probably did not exist in Paul's day. It is better, therefore, to assume meaning (1) in these verses. The basic principles of knowledge could be Jewish religious rules or pagan belief and philosophy.

Ephah

The name of a container big enough to hold a woman (Zech. 5:6-10). It was used to measure cereals and was probably about 22 litres. The equivalent measure for liquids was a bath.

Epicureans

Epicurus (341-270BC) founded this Greek school of philosophy. He believed the greatest good is to avoid fear and pain, and to seek the quieter pleasures of life, especially friendship. This led him to advise people to avoid public life and marriage.

Epicurus hated religion because it made people afraid of the gods and of death. His teaching sought to defeat this fear. According to him, the gods were only interested in their own pleasures and not at all concerned about people. As everything was made from atoms including the soul, all that happened at death was that the atoms dispersed. So there was no life after death.

Part of Paul's audience at the Areopagus were Epicureans (Acts 17:18). His message was opposed to their philosophy because he preached about God's concern for mankind, and about judgment after death.

Ephod

Linen ephods were worn by priests (1 Sam. 2:28; 22:18), although David wore one on at least one sacred occasion (2 Sam. 6:14). These were probably simple linen garments like modern day skirts.

The high priest's ephod was an ornate dress reaching from the breast to the hips, attached by shoulder straps (Exod. 39:1-26).

There was also an ephod which was hung in the temple and used for oracles (1 Sam. 21:9; 23:9).

Eternal, Eternity

The Hebrew and Greek words translated 'eternity' and 'forever' do not always mean endless time. The same word is translated 'old' (Deut. 32:7) and means 'a long time'. It also appears in 1 Sam. 1:22: 'he will live there always', and means the length of Samuel's life. When it is intended to express the idea of endlessness, the word is often repeated: 'for ever and ever' (e.g. Rev. 4:9).

The Jews spoke of two ages: the present age and the age to come. Christ and the apostles announced that the age to come had arrived in Christ (Mark 1:15). Christians live today in both ages. They have eternal life now, through being in Christ (John 3:15; 17:3), but will enter into its fulness in the glory to come (John 12:25).

The Bible does not discuss the Greek philosopher Plato's belief that time and eternity are completely different from each other. Such a belief suggests that there is no passing of time in eternity. In other words, past and future do not exist there. The Bible teaches that God is eternal in the fullest sense of the word. That is, God is without beginning and without end (Ps. 90:2; 102:27; 1 Tim. 6:16) and he is not limited by time (2 Peter 3:8).

Eunuch

The basic meaning of the Hebrew word is 'court official'. As some courts in ancient east Asia used castrated men for such officials, the word took on a second meaning of 'a castrate' (e.g. Isa. 56:3-5). We should not assume that all court officials were castrates, especially in Israel, because godly Israelites would have abhorred the practice of castration in view of Deut. 23:1.

In Matt. 19:12, Jesus mentions 'those who make themselves eunuchs'. He does not mean they castrated themselves, but that they chose to lead celibate lives for the sake of God's kingdom.

Evangelist

The word means a herald who announces good news on the authority of the king. In the New Testament an evangelist, therefore, is one who explains and argues for the gospel (good news) to people on the authority of Christ, especially to those who have not heard it before. In the New Testament the whole church evangelized (Acts 8:4; Phil. 1:27; 1 Peter 3:15) but some showed a particular God-given ability for this work (Eph. 4:11).

Apostles such as Peter and Paul had the gift of evangelism as they announced the gospel and planted churches. Philip, who was one of the seven (Acts 6:5) was called an evangelist (Acts 21:8), no doubt to distinguish him from the apostle of the same name. Examples of Philip's work are found in Acts 8. Paul also told Timothy to do the work of an evangelist (2 Tim. 4:5).

Evil

The Bible often contrasts evil with good. Evil behaviour is the result of rejecting God (Jer. 7:26). Evil can mean doing wrong, is a habit (Jer. 13:23) and shows a lack of understanding (Jer. 4:22). Evil acts come from sinful desires (James 1:13-15). People are therefore responsible for their sin, because they are responsible for their desires.

The Evil One is Satan who sinned first and tempted the first man and woman to sin (Gen. 3; 1 John 3:8). He is the leader of the evil spiritual forces (Eph. 6:12). Christ defeated evil and the powers of evil on the cross (Col. 2:15).

The word 'evil' is also used to mean pain and suffering. This suffering is the result of sinfulness (Gen. 3:17,18; Rom. 8:19-23) although each person's suffering is not necessarily linked to personal sin (Luke 13:2,4; John 9:3). The main lesson of the book of Job is that the righteous may suffer and the wicked may prosper in this life because evil has entered the world through sin.

God is not the cause of moral evil (sin), but he is the ultimate cause of physical evil (suffering). Even in Job's case, Satan had to get permission to harm him (Job 1:12; 2:6). Although suffering may often not be directly related to sin, God does bring evil in this life to the wicked (Isa. 1:20).

In the end, God will bring evil on all evildoers (John 5:29). With this final defeat of sin, both kinds of evil (sin and suffering) will be abolished for ever from the new heaven and earth (Rev. 21:1-8).

Excommunication

Excommunication is the exclusion of a church member from the membership of a church and from its privileges such as communion. For Old Testament background see Lev. 13:46; 17:4. The actual word does not appear in Scripture, but the practice is clearly taught.

Christ gave instructions about discipline in the church. First, the person wronged must talk with the wrongdoer. Next, two or three witnesses are to be consulted. If this is unsuccessful, the church must deal with the matter. If the church is ignored by the sinner, then - and only then - does excommunication take place (Matt. 18:15-17).

Paul repeats Christ's teaching. There must be warnings (Titus 3:10), witnesses (1 Tim. 5:19,20) and the whole church must meet in Christ's name to decide on any excommunication. 1 Cor. 5:1-8 is an important passage on excommunication. In v. 5 and also in

1 Tim. 1:20 Paul speaks of delivering a person to Satan. This must mean temporarily putting that person outside the fellowship of the church.

Excommunication is only for serious faults which include such things as sexual immorality (1 Cor. 5:6) and divisiveness (Titus 3:10) and heresy (Gal. 1:8).

The purpose of excommunication is to purify (1 Cor. 5:5) and restore the offender (2 Cor. 2:5-8), and also to stop the sin from spreading by warning the other members (1 Tim. 5:19,20).

The practice of excommunication became widespread after New Testament times, though not always done in a biblical manner.

Exile (noun and verb)

Exiles [noun] are those who are forced to live away from their home country. God told the Israelites that persistent rebellion against him would lead to their being exiled [verb] (Deut. 28:63; Isa. 5:13). This happened to the people of the northern kingdom of Israel in 722BC when they were taken to Assyria (2 Kings 17:23) and Nebuchadnezzar exiled leading people from Judah in stages up to the fall of Jerusalem in 587BC.

Through the prophets (e.g. Jer. 29:10), God promised to end Judah's exile and some Jews started to return to Jerusalem in 538BC.

Exodus

Exodus is a Greek word meaning 'a going out'. In the Bible it refers to the Israelites going out of Egypt where they had been for 430 years. The exodus marked the birth of Israel as a nation, when God redeemed his people by his grace (Exod. 6:6; Deut. 7:7,8; 2 Sam. 7:23).

The Greek word is translated 'departure' in Luke 9:31 and 2 Peter 1:15.

Expiation

Expiation is clearing guilt by paying something, such as a fine, or offering a sacrifice. Christ expiated sin by dying on the cross. His sacrifice was the payment or means by which God forgives sin.

Although expiation is a biblical teaching, the word does not have enough in its meaning to explain the whole Bible truth. Expiation does not include the idea of appeasing the offended deity. Some teachers prefer 'expiation' in verses such as Rom. 3:25 and 1 John 2:2, but the Greek word means 'propitiation'.

See Propitiation.

Faith

No one can be a Christian without faith. Unbelief is the great evil and unbelievers stand condemned by God (John 3:18). Sinners are put right with God through faith alone, not by any good deeds they may have done (Gal. 2:16). And Christians live by faith in Christ (Gal. 2:20).

Biblically, faith is conviction that God exists, that he is completely reliable, and will do everything he has promised (Heb. 11:6). Faith is an inner certainty about things heard (Rom. 10:17; Heb. 11:1). This leads believers not to be self-reliant but to trust completely in God's mercy (Eph. 2:4-8; Ps. 51:1). Their whole life is governed by their faith in God (Rom. 1:8,12; Gal. 5:5; 2 Tim. 1:5).

Most important of all, faith is trust in a person: in God (Prov. 3:5) and in his Son Jesus Christ (John 14:1; Acts 16:31). This leads to trusting what God says in his Word (Ps. 119:41) and to believing things about Christ (Rom. 10:9).

True faith leads to obeying God. There is a wrong kind of faith which is no more than mere talk. This is when people agree in their minds with Christian teaching, but show no change in their lives. Even demons have this kind of faith (James 2:18-24). True faith must lead to a life of obedience (Eph. 2:8-10; Heb. 11), the reason for which is simple. True faith is giving oneself to God, agreeing that his prescribed way of living is the only true way.

The New Testament also talks of 'the faith'. This is the teaching about God, Christ, and the Christian life, that Christians believe (Acts 6:7; Gal. 1:23). The first kind of faith (personal trust in God) must include the second kind of faith (holding as true the teaching that God has revealed to his people in his Word).

Fall

The fall is the name we give to the events described in Genesis 3 when Adam and Eve disobeyed God by eating the forbidden fruit. The fall was from perfection to sinfulness, fellowship with God to the wrath of God, and from life to death. The effects of the fall spread to the whole human race descended from Adam and Eve (Rom. 5:12) and to creation itself (Gen. 3:17,18). Christ secured the ultimate reversal of the effects of the fall by his death at Calvary (Rom. 5:12-21; 8:19-23).

Family

Old Testament Hebrew society was based on families. The families of the patriarchs (Abraham, Isaac and Jacob) were independent of society around them. The family consisted of the patriarchs' wives, their children, and their sons' wives and children. The servants were also included (Gen. 14:14).

Jacob's twelve sons became the leaders of the twelve tribes of Israel. By the time of the exodus, the tribes had divided into clans, and clans were divided into families (Exod. 6:14; Num. 1:2). An illustration of this structure is found in Josh. 7:16-18 where Achan is from the tribe of Judah, the clan of Zerah and the household of his grandfather Zimri.

The family unit continued to be important throughout the Old Testament (1 Kings 8:1; 2 Chr. 35:4) including after the exile (Neh. 7:5). This is also shown by the importance put on family lists of ancestors (1 Chr. 1-8).

In the New Testament, Christ taught that loyalty to him is more important than loyalty to one's family (Luke 14:26). His teaching may even split families, between believers and unbelievers (Luke 12:53). This only applies when there is a choice to be made between following Christ and following one's family. In all other cases, Christ and the apostles taught loyalty and honour in the family (Matt. 1919; Mark 7:9-13; John 19:25-27; Eph. 6:1-3; 1 Tim. 5:4).

In the New Testament, therefore, the family continues to be very important. The first loyalty of Christians is to Christ and his people, the family of God (Luke 8:21; Eph. 2:19; 1 Peter 4:17).

Fasting

In the Bible, fasting means going without all food and sometimes drink as well (Esth. 4:16). It does not mean avoiding some kinds of food and eating others.

Before the exile, there was one annual fast, the Day of Atonement (Lev. 23:26 - 'deny yourselves' means fasting). Later, other fasts were added (Zech. 8:19; Esth. 9:31). Jewish writings tell us the four fasts in Zech. were linked to disasters in Jewish history. In addition to the annual official fasts, there were times of special fasting, both by individuals and by larger groups.

Fasting includes a humble waiting on God, and also encourages self-control. It enables the people fasting to devote themselves to God. It can express grief (1 Sam. 31:13; Neh. 1:4), repentance (1 Kings 21:27; Jonah 3:5), desire for God's help when in serious difficulty (2 Sam. 12:16; Ps. 35:13), before a difficult journey (Ezra 8:21), or before a task (Esth. 4:16). It could be a preparation for a revelation from God (Exod. 34:28; Dan. 10:2,3).

Some Israelites thought fasting would force God to help them, despite their unrighteous lives (Isa. 58:3-5) but true fasting must be linked to a righteous life (Isaiah 58:6-14).

Strict Pharisees fasted every Monday and Thursday (Luke 18:12). John the Baptist's disciples fasted (Mark 2:18) but the only time we read of Christ fasting was in the desert before his ministry began (Matt. 4:2). This showed his willingness to depend on the Father. Jesus did not command regular fasting but expected his disciples would fast after he left them. While he was on earth it was a time of joy, not of fasting (Mark 2:18-20). Jesus also taught that fasting must be done in secret (Matt. 6:16-18).

Fasting is mentioned in Acts 13:2,3 before Barnabas and Paul were sent on a mission, and in Acts 14:23 when elders were chosen for churches. On those occasions, fasting showed an openness to Christ's leading. In 2 Cor. 11:27 Paul's fasting meant that he did not have money for food.

Father

Fathers held a special place of honour and authority in Old Testament days. This was especially true of the patriarchs in Genesis. The father could even put a seriously erring member of his family to death (Gen. 38:24). His daughters were under his authority until they were married, when they came under their husbands' authority (cf. Num. 30:3-8).

The word 'father' can also mean ancestor, especially founder of a nation (John 8:39) or dynasty (2 Kings 22:2). It was also a term of respect given to a spiritual father, as Elisha to Elijah (2 Kings 2:12) and King Jehoash to Elisha (2 Kings 13:14). Revered leaders of the nation were also sometimes called fathers (Acts 7:2).

Jesus told his disciples not to yearn for the title father. This was because no Christian has a special rank and spiritual authority over others, for God is the Father of all Christians (Matt. 23:9). Paul was not disobeying Christ when he called himself father of the Corinthians (1 Cor. 4:15) and Timothy his son (1 Tim. 1:2). He was not seeking for a title and rank. He meant that through his preaching these people had been converted; they were his spiritual 'children'.

Fatherhood of God

The most characteristic way that Christians think of God is as Father. Christ called God 'Father' and taught his disciples to pray: 'Our Father'. The opening greetings of all Paul's letters mention God as Father. The word 'Father' does not imply maleness in God — for God is spirit, and not male or female in the human sense. The word is meant to convey the sense of relationship. (See God).

The Old Testament sees God as Father of the nation of Israel (Exod. 4:22; Deut. 32:6; Hosea 1:10). He is father because he made Israel

(Mal. 2:10; Isa. 64:8). It also brings out the covenant relationship between God and his people, including the responsibilities each party has to the other (Isa. 1:2; 63:15-17; Mal. 1:6).

There are exceptions to the Old Testament view of God as Father of the nation. The Davidic king is spoken of as a son of God (2 Sam. 7:14; Ps. 2:7). God is also Father of the fatherless (Ps. 65:5) and of those who fear him (Ps. 103:13).

Christ taught that fatherhood is part of God's character. Earthly fathers are a poor copy of our Father in heaven. He cares for his children (Matt. 7:11). The close relationship between Jesus and God the Father was shown in his use of the word 'abba' and his disciples also used this word of God. (See Abba).

Christ is Son of God in a special way. He is Son equally eternal as is the Father (see Heb. 1:2,3). Christ never linked himself with his disciples to talk about 'our Father' but said 'my Father and your Father' (John 20:17). Christ is God's Son by nature. We are God's children by adoption (Rom. 8:15) and by being born again (John 3:3; 1 Peter 1:23).

Each Christian can call God 'Father'. The Spirit shows us that we are God's children (Rom. 8:14-17). Nowhere are we told that God is Father of everyone. In fact, Christ said that those who rejected him had the devil as their father (John 8:44).

Being a child of God is a privilege, but there are responsibilities too. Christians are to show that God is their father by being like him (Matt. 5:45).

Fear

Fearing God is a reverence which comes from a right view of God's holiness. It is God-given (Jer. 32:40), the beginning of wisdom (Ps. 111:10), and makes people hate evil and do good (Prov. 8:13; Job 2:3). It is true religion.

This true fear of God must not be confused with the slavish fear that pagans have for their gods. We must tremble before the awesomeness of God, yet he is our loving Father who cares for us (Matt. 10:28-30). Christ frees us from all wrong kinds of fear (Ps. 118:6; Matt. 28:5; John 12:15).

Sin and judgment also make people afraid of God (Gen. 3:10; Acts 24:25; Rev. 6:15,16). Sometimes it leads to faith in God (Acts 16:30). Indeed, fear of God is a mark of those who have faith (Acts 9:31, cf. Rom. 3:18).

There is a right fear of human beings, which is a true regard for those in authority (Rom. 13:1-7; 1 Peter 2:18). The wrong kind of fear, however, can lead to being unfaithful to God (Isa. 57:11). The best way not to be afraid of people is to have a proper fear of God (Matt. 10:28).

In Gen. 31:42,53, 'Fear of Isaac' is a name for God. God is the one who is to be feared, and is therefore referred to as 'the Fear'.

Feasts

The Old Testament feasts were days or longer periods of joyful thanksgiving to God. Mixed with the joy were sacrifices offered for the forgiveness of sin.

The authorised feasts are listed in Lev. 23. These are the sabbath (v. 3), the passover (vv. 4-8), firstfruits (vv. 9-14), weeks or pentecost (vv. 15-22), trumpets (v. 23-25), the day of atonement (vv. 26-32) and tabernacles (vv. 33-43).

After the exile, the feast of Purim was added (Esth. 9:18-32). Between the Old and New Testament periods, another feast was begun. This marked the purification and rededication of the temple in 164BC by Judas Maccabaeus after the Greek ruler (Antiochus Epiphanes) had desecrated it three years earlier. This eight day feast was the feast of lights, also called the feast of dedication (John 10:22).

Fellowship

See Communion.

Firmament

The Hebrew word literally means something that has been beaten out. From that, it comes to mean an expanse: the atmosphere in which the birds fly (Gen. 1:20), or the heavens in which the sun, moon and stars shine (Gen. 1:14-18).

First day of the week (Lord's day)

The words 'Lord's day' appear only in Rev. 1:10. It means Sunday, the day dedicated to the Lord Jesus Christ, who rose from the dead that day. The resurrection revealed him as Lord (Rom. 1:4). In the second century, which was not long after Revelation was written, the Lord's Day became an official name for the special day of worship among Christians. Paul assumed that the Corinthians would meet on that day (1 Cor. 16:2). Later, Paul took communion at Troas on a Sunday, the first day of the week (Acts 20:7).

Revelation was written to the seven churches in Asia Minor (Rev. 1:4). In Asia Minor there was an Emperor's Day, which seems to have been observed early each month. The name Lord's Day may well be an example of Christian defiance against the worship of the emperor. Instead of the Emperor's Day, they celebrated their Lord's Day.

Firstfruits

The Israelites were not allowed to eat anything from a new harvest until the firstfruits were offered to God (Lev. 23:17). This showed that the whole harvest belonged to God, who accepted a token gift from the best of the firstfruits (Exod. 23:19). These firstfruits went to the priests for their use (Num. 18:13).

The New Testament uses firstfruits as a picture showing the promise of what is to come. Thus Christ raised from the dead is the firstfruits of many who will rise from the dead (1 Cor. 15:20,23), and the Holy Spirit is the firstfruits of the blessings that wait for Christians in heaven (Rom. 8:23).

Flesh

Flesh has different meanings in the Bible. Human (Gen. 40:19) and animal (Lev. 6:27) bodies are made of flesh. Flesh can also mean the body itself (Job 19:26). 'One flesh' means the union between husband and wife (Gen. 2:24). 'Your flesh and blood' means your family (Judg. 9:2). A heart of flesh (Ezek. 11:19) is a heart that truly loves God, in contrast with a heart of stone, which stubbornly ignores God. 'All flesh' is all mankind (Joel 2:28; Zech. 2:13).

Sometimes the word flesh is used to contrast the weakness and ignorance of human beings with the power and wisdom of God (Ps. 56:4; Matt. 16:17). The New Testament (AV) also uses it to mean sinful nature (Rom. 8:5; Gal. 5:16,17) but it does not always mean that. Christ coming in the flesh means coming with a human nature (John 1:14; 1 John 4:2). The body he gave as a perfect sacrifice is his flesh (John 6:53) in the same way as our bodies are made of flesh (1 Cor. 15:39).

Forgiveness

Forgiveness is the cancellation of a debt. It is to act as if a fault or sin had never happened. When God forgives sins, he removes the obstacle which was destroying that person's relationship with God. Forgiveness is a complete forgetting of sin (Ps. 103:12; Jer. 31:34).

Forgiveness is part of God's character (Exod. 34:6,7; Neh. 9:17; Dan. 9:9). He is a God of grace who is willing to forgive, not an unwilling God we have to force into forgiveness.

God's forgiveness is not automatic. One of the Hebrew words for 'forgiveness' carries with it the idea of atonement. We can also see the necessary link with atonement in the connection between forgiveness and sacrifice for sin (Lev. 4:20,31,35).

There must also be penitence. In the Old Testament, people often thought that offering a sacrifice was enough to make sure that God was on their side. The prophets condemned this view (Is. 1:10-17; Micah 6:6-16). To be forgiven, sinners first had to admit their sin and guilt before God (Jer. 3:12,13; Is. 57:15) and must change their whole style of life (Ezek. 33:11).

The New Testament teaches us that Christ can forgive sins (Mark 2:5,7,10) and it is for the sake of Christ (Eph. 4:32) and through his atoning work on the cross (Matt. 26:28; Eph. 1:7) that we are forgiven. Forgiveness is not earned in any way. Rather, it is completely unmerited (Matt. 18:23-27; Rom. 3:22-24).

Christ and his apostles also taught that the forgiven sinner must forgive others (Matt. 6:14,15; Col. 3:13). Not to forgive others for faults is a way of despising God's far greater forgiveness of us (Matt. 18:28-35).

Frankincense

A milky coloured resin obtained by cutting the bark of certain trees, apparently produced in Arabia (Is. 60:6). It had a strong smell and was used in the tabernacle incense (Exod. 30:34), with the meal offerings (Lev. 2:1; 6:15). The fragrant smoke rising heavenward was symbolic of prayerful worship being given to God. It was also used in a purified form on the shewbread (Lev. 24:7) and in wedding processions (S. of S. 3:6), expressive of joy. Frankincense was one of the gifts given by the magi to the infant Jesus (Matt. 2:11) as a symbol of worship.

Fullness

Some think Paul uses the word in Col. 1:19 to combat false teaching. This false teaching is that supernatural powers live between the world and God. If God and the world wish to talk to each other, they must go through these powers as a mediator. All of these powers together are called 'the fullness' and Christ was only one of these powers. If this was the popular teaching in Paul's day, then Paul is correcting it in Col. 1:19 by saying that instead of many powers mediating between God and the world, there is only one - Christ. Christ is the fullness, the totality, of supernatural powers mediating between God and the world.

Paul is opposing a heresy in Colossians. However, this false teaching appears as Gnosticism in the century after Paul and there is no evidence that it existed before then. Also, Paul does not seem to be opposing the use of the word 'fullness' by false teachers. It is better to interpret Col. 1:19 with 2:9, that is, that Paul is saying that in Christ all of God's attributes and deity dwell in a visible form. Christ is more than just a supernatural mediator. Christ is God.

In Eph. 1:23, the word fullness could refer to Christ or to the church. According to Greek grammar, both are possible, but by far the most likely is the church. This being so, it could mean that the church in some way completes Christ, or that Christ fills the church. Again, the Greek grammar supports the first of these views, that the church completes Christ. This does not mean that Christ's nature is defective and needs the church to make him complete. Rather it means that in his love Christ sees himself as incomplete without the church, as a bridegroom is incomplete without his bride (Eph. 5:32), or a shepherd without his sheep (John 10:11-16). The end of Eph. 1:23 prevents any thought of Christ as having an imperfect nature needing the church to complete it.

In Eph. 3:19; 4:13, Paul desires the church to be filled with God in Christ, and because of that, to show full Christlikeness.

Gentile

A Gentile is anyone who is not a Jew. The Hebrew plural originally meant 'nations', but as the Jews were aware of their special position as the people of God, the word began to mark out those who did not belong to the Jewish race. After the exile, the Jews struggled to keep their heathen neighbours from spoiling their religious purity. By New Testament days, this had led to the word Gentile being a term of scorn and hatred (Acts 22:22, 'this word' — i.e. 'Gentiles').

The Old Testament, however, looked forward to the time when Gentiles would be included in God's kingdom (Is. 55:5; Mal. 1:11). This happens in Christ, where the distinction between Jew and Gentile is no longer important (Gal. 3:28; Eph. 2:11-22).

Generally, non-Jewish Christians are still called Gentiles in the New Testament. An exception is Eph. 4:17 where Gentiles refers to those who are outside the family of God (non-Christians).

Glory

In Hebrew the word glory comes from the word 'to be heavy'. The Hebrew people connected glory with things that are big, important, or valuable. Human beings can have a glory (Is. 8:7) but without God it is shortlived (Is. 16:14; 1 Peter 1:24).

God's glory is terrifying in its power and splendour. The Bible compares it with a terrible storm or volcano (Exod. 24:17; Ps. 29:3; Hab. 3:3-15), or a brilliant light (Exod. 34:29-35; Mark 9:2-8). No human being can stand before it. Even Moses could not see God's face (Exod. 33:18,23) nor go into the tabernacle when God's glory filled it (Exod. 40:35).

There is also grace in God's glory! The ark (cf. 1 Sam. 4:21) and the temple (1 Kings 8:10,11) show that God's glory has come to live with people. God shows his glory by his graciousness, as well as by awesome display. When Moses asked to see God's glory, God showed it by displaying his character as a merciful and just God (Exod. 33:17-34:7).

Christ shows God's glory the most clearly. He is all-powerful, God living with people, and God's self-revelation. Glory surrounded his birth (Luke 2:9), his ministry (Mark 9:2-8; John 2:11), his death and resurrection (John 12:23) and will surround his return (Mark 13:26).

The salvation that a glorious Christ brings must be glorious also (2 Cor. 4:4) and because God lives in his people (1 Cor. 3:16) the church also shares in God's glory (1 Peter 4:14). Indeed, through their work for God, his people show God's glory to the world (Matt. 5:16; Rom. 15:8,9; 1 Cor. 6:20). Then, when Christ comes in his glory, the church will shine with the glory of God (Rev. 21:11). See Shekinah glory.

God

God is the eternal Spirit who created and rules the universe. The word 'God' shows the kind of being God is, in the same way as 'human' shows what kind of being we are.

God's personal name was revealed to Moses as Yahweh (Exod. 3:15), translated in English as 'LORD'. The Bible teaches that there is only one true God; all other gods are worthless idols (Isa. 44:4-20; Jer. 10:10; 1 Tim. 1:17). As God is the only God, he has all wisdom and power (Job 12:13; Isa. 2:12-18; Rom. 16:27).

There is only one true God, yet he is Father, Son and Spirit. The Father is God (1 Peter 1:3), the Son is God (John 1:1) and the Holy Spirit is God (1 Cor. 2:10,11).

The Bible sometimes talks about God's eyes, hands, nostrils, but these are only ways to help us think about someone we cannot really understand. God is spirit (John 4:24) and invisible (1 Tim. 1:17). Because he is pure spirit, he is without a body. The Son of God, however, took human flesh and is thus the visible image of the invisible God (Col. 1:15).

God created everything that exists except himself (Gen. 1:1; Heb. 11:3). He is separate from all creation and beyond our understanding (Isa. 55:8,9). He alone is eternal, without beginning and ending (1 Tim. 6:16). As creator, he owns everything (Ps. 24:1) and is the source of life (Gen. 2:7; John 1:4).

He is also a personal God. He can have a relationship with other persons, such as human beings. He can speak, listen, and love, unlike pagan gods. He reveals himself to people (Heb. 1:1) and has a will and a plan for his creation (Eph. 1:11).

God shows himself to people as the holy God, full of glory (Isa. 6:3). He is the righteous Judge (2 Tim. 4:8) who tolerates no sin in his presence (Hab. 1:13; Isa. 59:2; Rom. 1:18). At the same time, he is the loving Father of those who belong to him and do right (Ps. 103:13). He is able to be righteous Judge and loving Father because he planned before the world began an atonement (1 Peter 1:20) for those he chose in Christ (Eph. 1:4; Rom. 8:29,30).

Only this God is worthy of worship (Matt. 4:10).

Godliness

Godliness is the proper respect and devotion that is God's right to receive. God gives it to human beings by his power (2 Peter 1:3) through their knowing the truth of the gospel (Titus 1:1). True godliness means holy lives (2 Tim. 3:5). Godliness, therefore, is a right attitude to God which leads to a right behaviour before God.

The 'mystery of godliness' (1 Tim. 3:16) is the teaching which shows how Christian devotion and behaviour comes from the Person of Christ.

Golgotha

The place just outside Jerusalem where Jesus Christ was crucified. The word comes from the Aramaic word for skull. The name Calvary comes from the Latin word for skull. We cannot be sure exactly where Golgotha was, nor do we know why it was called The Skull.

Mentioned in Matt. 27:33; Mark 15:22; John 19:17.

Good

The biblical words for 'good' basically mean something which contains value, or is of benefit. Examples showing these are the gold of Havilah, which had special value (Gen. 2:12), and the trees of Eden which were beneficial as food (Gen. 2:9).

A proper understanding of goodness must start with God. God is of infinite worth and worthy of our worship (Ps. 118:1). He is the source of all our benefits. Only God is truly good (Mark 10:18). This means more than that God does what is good. Good is what God is. Goodness does not exist outside of God. God is morally perfect and generous, the standard by which we measure goodness, and the source of all that is good.

Because God is good (Ps. 100:5), what he does is good (Gen. 1:31; Ps. 119:68). Every good thing comes from God (James 1:17). In God's providence, he does good to every creature (Psalm 145:9; Acts 14:17).

The gospel is the good news (Luke 2:10) about salvation through Christ (Heb. 10:1). Those who believe the good news are God's children, who may ask for good things from their Father in heaven (Matt. 7:11). God works everything for his children's good (Rom. 8:28) including the pain of discipline (Heb. 12:10).

Because God's commands are good (Ps. 119:39), obeying them is the good way and leads to blessing (Deut. 6:18; 1 Tim. 2:3; Titus 3:8). Christians are called to do good works (Eph. 2:10). Failure to do so shows that a person does not know God at all (Titus 1:16).

Because only God is good, only those who know God and have a good (redeemed) nature can do true good (Matt. 12:33-35). Others may even call evil good and good evil.

The phrase 'good or evil' is a Hebrew way of including everything in a particular context (Num. 24:13; 2 Sam. 13:22). Another Hebrew idiom is 'it is good' which means 'I agree' (1 Sam. 20:7; 2 Kings 20:19). 'A good eye' shows generosity (Prov. 22:9).

Gospel

Gospel means good news. It is a New Testament word but it relies on the Old Testament. The Old Testament announced the gospel will come: the New Testament announces that God's promises to Abraham (Gal. 3:8) and the prophets (Rom. 1:2) have been fulfilled.

The good news is that the kingdom of God has come (Matt. 4:23; 24:14). The good news is about Christ (Mark 1:1; 2 Cor. 4:5). The gospel is not only about God (1 Thess. 2:8), it is actually God at work saving by his power those who believe (Rom. 1:16). All these point very clearly to the gospel being part of the sovereign rule of God.

The church is commanded by Christ's sovereign authority (Matt. 28:18) to preach the gospel to everyone (Mark 16:15). The gospel is a sacred trust (1 Tim. 1:11) which must be preached (1 Cor. 9:16). It is God's truth but not everyone can see that truth (2 Cor. 4:4). The proper response to the hearing of the gospel message is to repent (Mark 1:14) and believe the good news. Without faith, the gospel does not save (Heb. 4:2).

The whole Bible is about Christ and therefore the gospel is in the whole Bible (Luke 24:27). To think of the gospel message as only contained in Matthew, Mark, Luke and John is not correct.

Grace

To understand this word is the key to understanding the Bible. True religion is not a matter of obeying rules or having mystical experiences, but of experiencing God's grace. The idea of free grace is found throughout the Bible, even when the actual word is not used.

The main Hebrew word for grace suggests something that a superior being does for an inferior (Gen. 33:8). It is a favour shown to someone. It is free because the person who receives it does not deserve it and because the one who gives it is in no way obliged to do so.

The election of Israel as God's people was an act of God's grace (Deut. 7:7,8). In the same way, salvation in the New Testament is God's gift (Eph. 2:8) given to those who do not deserve it (Rom. 5:8; 6:23) or even ask for it (Rom. 5:10). Everyone has sinned (Rom. 3:9-20) and deserves God's wrath (Rom. 1:18) but God gives righteousness through the death of Christ as a free gift (Rom. 3:21-26).

It is important to emphasize that God's grace comes because of Christ (John 1:17). Grace is a major theme in the Old Testament as well as the New, but the basis of it all is Christ. The way we receive the gracious benefits of what Christ has done for sinners is through faith (Eph. 2:8).

No one can earn God's favour by obeying his laws (Gal. 2:16). Christians are under grace, not law (Rom. 6:15). This does not mean that they can sin as much as they like. God's free grace is to release believers from their slavery to sin in order that they can obey God (Rom. 6:16-18). God gives them a new heart and the Holy Spirit leads them to live righteous lives (Ezek. 36:26,27; Rom. 8:9; Gal. 5:16-25).

Grace is also used to describe various abilities in the churches (Eph. 4:7) or the effectiveness of the witness of believers for Christ (Acts 4:33). Their abilities to work for Christ all come from God who works in all members (1 Cor. 12:4-6), both to build up the church (v. 7) and to enable them to live godly lives (2 Peter 1:3).

Grain offering

Also translated as meat, cereal and meal offering. This offering is described in Lev.2:1-16; 6:14-23. It was given in the form of crushed and roasted new grain (2:14), fine flour mixed with oil, incense and salt (2:1,13), or as special cakes [wafers] (2:4) which could be cooked in various ways (vv. 4-7). Part of the offering was burnt as a gift to God. The rest belonged to the priest and his family (2:2,3; 9,10) who ate it in the tabernacle or temple courtyard (6:16).

The Hebrew word is also used in a non-religious sense of gifts or tribute to a superior person, such as a king (1 Sam. 10:27; 1 Kings 4:21). This helps us to understand that the grain offering is a present to God in order to secure his goodwill. In other words, it is a propitiatory sacrifice. (See Propitiation).

The Hebrew word is also used for sacrifices in general (Gen. 4:4,5; 1 Sam. 26:19).

Guilt offering

The guilt offering was very similar to the sin offering. The only difference was that guilt offerings were made where the sinner also had to pay for whatever had not been done, or had been lost or damaged, plus an extra fifth of the value (Lev. 5:14-6:7; 7:1-10).

Hades

In classical Greek literature, hades was the underworld or the kingdom of the spirits of the dead. The Greek translation of the Hebrew Old Testament used it to translate sheol. The same Greek word is translated as hell in the following references in the Authorised Version: it mostly means the grave or death (Acts 2:27,31) and can also be a picture of something deep in the earth (Matt. 11:23 where it is contrasted with the skies). Christ declares that he has the keys of it (Rev. 1:18).

See Hell.

See also Sheol.

Hallelujah

Hallelujah is Hebrew for 'Praise Yah'. Yah is the shortened form of Yahweh, the name for God. Hallelujah occurs twenty-four times in the Psalms - always, except for Ps. 135:3, at the beginning or end of the psalm. This suggests that it was a call to temple worship.

The word is also found in Rev. 19:1-6 where it is the theme of the song that the redeemed in heaven sing.

Hate, Hatred

Hatred is the opposite of love. It is a feeling of intense dislike, or even repulsion, for someone or something. Whereas love draws people together, hatred drives them apart.

God commanded the Israelites not to hate one another (Lev. 19:17). They were to love even fellow Israelites who hated them (Exod. 23:5). Christ said that this love should be shown to all enemies (Matt. 5:43,44).

Hatred is sin (Gal. 5:19,20), except when evil is the object of the hatred. God hates evil (Isa. 61:8; Zech. 8:17), evil-doers (Ps. 5:5) and sinful worship (Amos 5:21). The godly will hate evil also (Ps. 97:10; 139:21; Rev. 2:6).

There seems to be a contradiction between Old and New Testaments. The Old Testament saints hated evil people (Ps. 139:21) yet Christ said believers should love their enemies (Matt. 5:43,44). In the New Testament 'hate' means that believers should hate evil people in the sense that they should separate from their evil practices (2 Cor. 6:17), but love them by doing good deeds to them (Prov. 25:21,22; Luke 6:27; Rom. 12:20).

Jesus says that his disciples should hate the members of their families (Luke 14:26). This is not real hate, which would disagree with teaching found in other parts of the Bible. Jesus sometimes exaggerated (Matt. 7:3; 19:24; 23:24) as did other Jewish teachers, in order to emphasize a truth. Our Lord means that love for him must be greater than our love for even our nearest family. This interpretation is proved by comparing Luke 14:26 with Matt. 10:37-39.

Head

Today we often link the head with thinking, but in Bible days people did not. They saw the head as the highest and most prominent part of the body. Also, they noted that without the head there can be no life. In the Bible, the head is a picture of leadership and authority (Exod. 6:14; Isa. 7:8), of height (Ps. 24:7) and of the source of life. When the head is removed, there can be no life (1 Sam. 17:51; Matt. 14:8).

Christ as head has all authority (Eph. 1:22). The picture of Christ as head of his body the church has even more meaning. In addition to authority, it shows the close union between Christ and his church whereby he is the source of her energy, life and growth (Col. 2:19; Eph. 4:15).

Heart

The word heart in the Bible does not often mean the physical organ. It can mean the centre of anything (Exod. 15:8), but it mainly points to a person's inner nature, or whole being (Ps. 9:1). It can mean the emotions, such as joy (1 Sam. 2:1), love (2 Sam. 14:1), grief (Neh. 2:2), fear (Gen. 42:28) or courage (2 Sam. 17:10). It can mean the mind (Luke 2:19), capable of memory (Deut. 4:9), understanding (1 Kings 3:9). It can mean the will (2 Chr. 12:14) which can decide for the right (Gen. 20:5) or be evil (Jer. 17:9; Matt. 15:19). A hardened heart (Exod. 10:1) is one unable to decide for the right. The stubborn heart must be broken (Ps. 51:17) or replaced with a new heart (Ezek. 18:31) which God gives (Ezek. 11:19).

Heaven

Heaven is the place where God dwells (Matt. 5:45) along with the angelic beings (Mark 13:32) and where true believers will one day live (1 Peter 1:4). Christ has returned to heaven (Acts 1:11) where he acts as high priest (Heb. 4:14) for his people (1 John 2:1) and where he reigns as Lord (Acts 2:33-36; 17:24; Heb. 1:3).

The Bible looks forward to a new heaven and a new earth (Isa. 65:17; Rev. 21:1). This will be a renewed creation where everything will be done in God's holy way, and without sin.

Hebrew

The name Hebrew comes from Eber (Gen. 10:21,24). The name is only used of Abraham (Gen. 14:13) and the Israelites in the Bible, but at least in Abraham's time it must have included other Semites.

In the Old Testament, the term Hebrew is mainly used when distinguishing the chosen nation from other peoples. For example, it describes the Israelites in Egypt (Exod. 2:13), is found on the lips of Israel's enemies (1 Sam. 4:9) or is used by any of the Israelites to explain their nationality (Jonah 1:9).

Early in history, therefore, the meaning of the word 'Hebrew' narrowed from a group of Semites to the Israelites. By the time of the New Testament, it had narrowed further to mean a Jew who was not influenced by Greek culture (2 Cor. 11:22; Phil. 3:5; cf. Acts 6:1).

Hell

The Greek word for hell is Gehenna, which comes from the Hebrew name for the Valley of Hinnom just outside Jerusalem. A shrine called Tophet was built there, where children were sacrificed to the Ammonite god Molech. This practice was hated by God (2 Kings 23:10). Jeremiah said in punishment for this evil, the valley would become a graveyard (Jer. 7:31,32). Later, the valley became the town rubbish dump.

Because this valley was a place of death, burning and decay, Jewish writers between the Old and New Testaments used it as a symbol for the place where the wicked are punished. The New Testament takes this for its teaching on hell.

Hell is the place of unending torment symbolized by a fire that cannot be put out (Mark 9:44), or a lake of burning sulphur (Rev. 20:14), although hell is not a kind of furnace. Hell is also described as a place of deepest darkness (2 Peter 2:17), which it could not be if it were simply a place of flames. The fire and the darkness are pictures of something far more horrible — being separated from God (2 Thess. 1:9).

The Bible's teaching on hell is terrifying, showing the awfulness of sin. By contrast, the Bible also teaches the wonder of God's mercy and love which saves sinners from hell. Some people say that the teaching on hell was invented by the early church and was not part of Christ's gospel of love. This is easily answered by noting that the Greek word for hell (Gehenna) appears twelve times in the New Testament, all but one of which (James 3:6) are in the Gospels, spoken by Christ. The rest of the New Testament has plenty of teaching on hell but different Greek words are used. For example, 2 Peter 2:4 where the fallen angels wait for God's punishment.

Heresy

The Greek word means 'a choice'. Classical Greek literature uses the word for a philosophical school someone may choose to follow. The Greek word is used in this sense of party or sect in the New Testament. It is used of the Sadducees (Acts 5:17), the Pharisees (Acts 15:5) and even of Christians by outsiders (Acts 24:5). There is no thought of these being separate from Judaism, but rather of them being parties inside the Jewish faith.

The same Greek word is used of parties or divisions inside Christian churches (1 Cor. 11:19, AV). Paul disapproves of the divisions because they come from people's sinful natures, not from the Spirit (Gal. 5:20, factions). There should be harmony and unity in the churches, not groups such as the rich keeping themselves and their help from the poor (1 Cor. 11:20).

The heresy in 2 Peter 2:1 is a serious error in doctrine. That is the meaning of the word today. Those who keep to the faith will have nothing to do with heretical teaching, or its teachers (2 John 10,11). One who teaches heresy is a heretic. See Titus 3:10.

Herod

Herod the Great appears in the accounts of Christ's birth. He had Edomite blood but was made king of the Jews by the Roman Senate in 40BC and reigned as a loyal friend and ally of the Romans until his death in 4BC.

He was a suspicious person and this led him to wipe out the rival pure Jewish claimants to the throne, the Hasmonaean family. This included his own wife and later their two sons. He executed another son, his eldest, a few days before his own death.

Herod tried to become a friend of the Jews but was unsuccessful. In 19BC he started work on a lavish temple, which is the temple mentioned in the Gospels and Acts. He was a Jew by religion but also built temples elsewhere to pagan gods.

He left his kingdom to three of his sons. Archelaus (Matt. 2:22) had Judea and Samaria until AD6, when he was deposed to prevent a revolt by his subjects. Philip (Luke 3:1) had the land north east of Palestine. Antipas had Galilee and Peraea.

Herod the Tetrarch, or Antipas, is the Herod in the Gospels during Christ's ministry. The son of Herod the Great, he reigned over Galilee and Peraea from 4BC to AD39. He married a daughter of King Aretas IV who is mentioned in 2 Cor. 11:32. He divorced her to marry his half-brother Philip's wife, Herodias. John the Baptist denounced this and was beheaded (Mark 6:14-28). Later, King Aretas revenged himself by waging war against Antipas in 36AD. His nephew Agrippa told the Roman emperor that Antipas was plotting against Rome. Antipas was deposed and sent into exile in AD39.

Herod the king, or Agrippa, appears in Acts 12. He was the son of Aristobulus, one of the Hasmonaean sons that Herod the Great executed and was therefore Herod the Great's grandson. He was reared in Rome but the Emperor Gaius Caligula gave him the territory north east of Palestine. After he had his uncle Antipas deposed, Galilee and Peraea were added to his territory in AD39. His sudden death is described in Acts 12:21-23.

King Agrippa appears in Acts 25 and 26. He was the son of Herod the king. When his father died, he was thought too young to succeed to the kingdom. He later received the title of king from the Roman emperor, Claudius, with the territories north east of Palestine. His kingdom was enlarged in AD56 and after the Jewish War. He died in AD100.

High place(s)

A high place can simply be a mountain top (Micah 1:3) but generally it is a place of worship, in particular, by sacrifice. Often these places were on hills, but not always. Tophet was in a valley (Jer. 7:31) and town gates sometimes had high places (2 Kings 23:8).

Canaan had these shrines before the conquest under Joshua. The Israelites were told to destroy them, complete with their idols (Num. 33:52). Only at the one place that God would choose should the Israelites offer their sacrifices (Deut. 12:4-6).

The high places remained and helped to corrupt Israelite religion, which became similar to the Canaanite religion (2 Kings 17:9-12). Even good kings did not necessarily destroy them (2 Chr. 20:33) but the great reforming kings Hezekiah (2 Kings 18:4) and Josiah (2 Chr. 34:3) acted against them.

Between the destruction of Shiloh about 1050BC and the building of Solomon's temple over eighty years later, high places were the only places that Israelites could use for sacrifices (1 Kings 3:2). Samuel used them (1 Sam. 9:13) and God appeared to Solomon at one (1 Kings 3:4,5). After the temple was built, high places were only showing the influence of pagan worship, with the single exception of 2 Chr. 33:17.

High Priest

All unblemished men descended from Aaron were made priests by the law of Moses. The head of the tribe also had special responsibilities as high priest. He entered the Most Holy Place alone once each year to represent the nation on the Day of Atonement (Lev. 16). When he entered that place, he wore the special garments which included the breastpiece bearing the names of the twelve tribes and the Urim and Thummim which were used for making decisions (Exod. 28).

The kings of Israel were able to dismiss the high priest and appoint another (1 Kings 2:26,27,35; 12:31). This was against the law of Moses as the priesthood was hereditary and not a political appointment.

The letter to the Hebrews makes it clear that the work of the high priest was a picture of the salvation work of Christ (Heb. 7:23-8:6). The Old Testament priest was a shadow of which the reality is Christ.

Hin

A pot used as a liquid measure. It was one-sixth of a bath, probably about 3.67 litres. For an example of its use, see Num. 15:5.

Hittites

This Indo-European race invaded the central part of the land south of the Black Sea around 2000BC. The people they conquered were Hattians and the Hittites were named after them. After a period of city states, the Old Kingdom emerged about 1800BC. It raided the Amorite kingdom of Babylon about 1560BC but this success was followed by anarchy. About 1480BC, King Telepinus ended this with his law-making.

Soon afterwards, the Hittite empire expanded south and east. It reached its greatest importance under Suppiluliumas I who reigned about 1380-1350BC. By 1200BC, the empire had collapsed under pressure from people migrating from the west. This period was followed by twenty-four Hittite city states, seven of which are of interest in the Bible as they were in Syria.

The empire's southernmost part was Lebanon. Hittites are found in Palestine in the Bible but these are more likely to be people who had moved from the Hittite empire to Palestine.

Hittites are also called sons of Heth (Gen. 27:46) after their ancestor (Gen. 10:15). David had Hittites among his leading men (1 Sam. 26:6; 2 Sam. 23:39). The last reference to a Hittite is in Solomon's reign (2 Chr. 8:7). No doubt those who were left were absorbed into the nation of Israel.

Holy Spirit

The Holy Spirit is the third Person of the Trinity. His power carries out the Father's plans in the world. He is a person, not just a force. Christ talked of him as 'he', not 'it' (John 15:26). A force cannot speak (Acts 1:16), teach (John 14:26), as the Holy Spirit can; neither can a force be told lies (Acts 5:3) or be grieved (Eph. 4:30). The Holy Spirit, therefore, must be a person.

The Hebrew and Greek words for 'spirit' are the same as the words for 'breath' and 'wind'. The breath of God acts in Gen. 2:7 and Ps. 33:6. The wind is a sign or illustration of the Spirit (Ezek. 37:9; John 3:8; Acts 2:2). Like the wind, the Spirit is powerful; it cannot be seen, nor controlled, by human beings.

The Spirit in the Old Testament. The Holy Spirit carried out God's plan in creation (Gen. 1:2; Ps. 104:30). He also gave special abilities to certain people so that they could do God's work, such as making the tabernacle (Exod. 31:3), leading Israel (Judg. 3:10) or doing acts of strength (Judg. 14:6). People prophesied through the Spirit (Num. 11:29; 1 Sam. 10:6; Micah 3:8). In individuals, the Spirit brought humility, purity, steadfastness and joy to godly people (Ps. 51:7-12).

The Spirit in the life of Christ. God promised to send a special person having the Spirit in a special way (Isa. 11:2; 42:1-4). This was Jesus Christ, the Son of God. The Holy Spirit was at work in his forerunner, John the Baptist (Luke 1:15), as well as at the incarnation (Luke 1:35), baptism (Matt. 3:16), ministry (Luke 4:14,18) and resurrection of Christ (Rom. 1:4).

The Spirit in the mission of Christ. Our Lord told his apostles that he was going back to heaven, but he would send the Spirit in his place. The Spirit's task is to glorify Christ (John 16:14) and to talk about him (John 15:26). By showing Christ to the world, he convicts it and shows its guilt in regard to sin, righteousness and judgment (John 16:7-11). This mission of showing Christ and the gospel to the world is the Spirit's work, but this does not mean that Christ's disciples need not do anything. They too must tell people about Christ (John 15:27; Matt. 28:18-20). The Spirit is the Counsellor, or Helper, of the church, not its slave (John 16:7). The church obeys the command to evangelize and baptizes in the name of the Father, Son and Holy Spirit. This formula recognizes the part that the Spirit plays in the great mission of Christ.

The Spirit in the church of Christ. As we have seen, the church has a central place in the Spirit's work of mission. Pentecost was the day when the Spirit came upon the church, giving her power to preach Christ. He also teaches the church about Christ (John 14:26) and gives her members various abilities to help the church grow strong and do her work properly (1 Cor. 12:7-11). Church leaders must be filled with the Spirit (Acts 6:3). Indeed, the Spirit chooses people for particular tasks and the church should obey the Spirit by separating these for the ministry (Acts 13:2, cf. Eph. 4:11-13).

The Spirit in the Christian. The work of the Spirit in the life of Christians is part of his work in mission and in the church. It is all one work. The missionary work of the Spirit leads him to give new life to all Christians (John 3:5). The Christians are then baptized, to show that the Spirit has made them part of the church (1 Cor. 12:12). Thus all three aspects of the Spirit's work — in mission, in the church and in individuals - are united.

The Spirit adopts Christians into the family of God's people and assures them that they do indeed belong to God (Rom. 8:15,16). The Spirit is a seal and a guarantee, showing that God treats them as his children and that the full salvation he has promised will indeed be given in due time (Eph. 1:13,14).

The Spirit helps Christians to worship (Phil. 3:3), which includes prayer (Rom. 8:26,27). He guides (Acts 13:4; 16:6-10; Gal. 5:16-18). He gives special abilities to use within the church (Eph. 4:7) and makes the Christian more like Christ (Gal. 5:22-25; 1 Peter 1:2).

The Spirit and the end of the age. The climax of mission is the eternal glory in the new heaven and new earth, when the church will be presented to Christ as his holy bride. The Old Testament linked the pouring out of the Spirit with the end time (Joel 2:28-32) and Peter said this was fulfilled at pentecost (Acts 2:16-21). The end time, therefore, started when Christ returned to heaven and will continue until the final resurrection when all the church will also be in heaven with Christ. Just as Christ's resurrection was through the Spirit (Rom. 1:4), so will the Christian's be (Rom. 8:11; Gal. 6:8).

The Spirit and the Scriptures. We have already seen that the Spirit spoke through the Old Testament prophets. The written word of God was also the work of the Spirit, as he inspired men to write (2 Peter 1:21; Heb. 10:15). In addition, the Spirit interprets the Bible's teaching to Christians (1 Cor. 2:14).

Holy, Holiness

The word 'holy' can describe a day of the week (Gen. 2:3), a place (Exod. 3:5), objects used when worshipping God (Num. 4:4), a fast (Joel 1:14), priests (Lev. 21:5), all God's people (Exod. 19:6; 1 Peter 2:9), the Scriptures (2 Tim. 3:15). Most importantly, it is used of God (Ps. 99:3; Rev. 4:8).

A thing is holy when it is set apart for God and separated from everything common (Ezek. 42:20) or profane (Lev. 10:10). Once dedicated for God's use, it must not be used in any other way (Exod. 30:31-33). Even the censers used for an offering in Korah's rebellion which made God angry had to be used afterwards only for God's use. They had been set apart to God and were holy (Num. 16:38).

Being set apart for God must lead to moral uprightness. The call to holiness is often in the form of a call to obey God's commands (Lev. 19:1-37; 1 Thess. 4:3; 1 Peter 1:14-16). Only those who are pure, keeping themselves from sin, may approach the holy God (Ps. 24:4; Heb. 12:14).

In the full meaning of the word, only God is holy. The Father (John 17:11), the Son (Acts 3:14) and the Spirit (Matt. 1:18) are each called holy. God's holiness makes things and people dedicated to him holy. God, being holy, is different from his creation (Isa. 40:25), including mankind (Hosea 11:9). To experience his holiness brings a feeling of great fear (Exod. 3:5,6). Even sinless angelic beings cover themselves in reverence as they talk of his holiness (Isa. 6:2,3). Sinful people, however upright, despair (Isa. 6:5; 64:6) yet God in his powerful holiness saves people (Isa. 52:10) to make them holy (Eph. 1:4).

The word 'saints' means holy people. All Christians are called saints in the New Testament (Phil. 1:1) because they are set apart to serve God (Eph. 1:4; Rom. 12:1). God's holy nation (1 Peter 2:9) consists of the sum total of all saints.

Holy of holies — Most holy place

This was a cubic room in the tabernacle and later in the temple. A curtain separated it from the larger room called the Holy Place (Exod. 26:33). This curtain was torn at the crucifixion (Luke 23:45).

The Most Holy Place held the ark of the covenant which symbolized God's presence. On the ark was the atonement cover where propitiation was made once each year on the Day of Atonement. Only the high priest could enter and even he was only allowed to do so on this special day. He had to offer a sin offering for himself and his family before he could atone for the sins of the people (Lev. 16). This was a picture of what Christ did on the cross. As the real high priest, he offered his own blood and entered the real Most Holy Place, where God is enthroned (Heb. 9:1-14).

Homer

A donkey load. It was a measurement used for cereals, and was probably about 220 litres. For an example of use, see Lev. 27:16.

Hope

To hope is to expect something good to come in the future (1 Cor. 9:10). Some of our human hopes may be disappointed (Acts 16:19) but Christian hope is different. The Christian hope is a confidence that knows that what we hope for is a certainty (Rom. 5:5; Heb. 11:1), because our hope is not based in ourselves but in the God of hope (Rom. 15:13) and because of Christ in us (Col. 1:27).

But what is it that Christians wait for with such confidence? Almost always, Christian hope looks to what will happen after this life, such as the resurrection from the dead (Acts 23:6), complete righteousness (Gal. 5:5), God's glory (Rom. 5:2). It can also mean God fulfilling his promises in this life, even when things seem beyond hope (Rom. 4:18).

Although hope looks beyond this life, it has a strong effect now. Pagans are without God and therefore without hope (Eph. 2:12), but in the trials of life the Christian hope acts as an anchor, giving us security (Heb. 6:19). Hope protects us in our fight against evil (1 Thess. 5:8) because it makes us more concerned to become in this life what we will be in glory, that is, like Christ (1 John 3:2,3). Also, once we understand what hope we have as believers, our attachment to the things of this life disappears (Heb. 13:14), making us more willing to serve Christ whatever the cost.

Hosanna

This Hebrew word was shouted by the crowd when Jesus entered Jerusalem on Palm Sunday (John 12:13). It means 'please save' and is a quotation from Ps. 118:25. To the crowds, the word may not have meant more than an expression of religious excitement but later the disciples understood the real significance of this event, coming as it did only a few days before the crucifixion (John 12:16).

Host

The word host basically means an army (Judges 4:2). It is used of God's spiritual army (Josh. 5:14), the angels in heaven (1 Kings 22:19) and the heavenly bodies (Deut. 4:19). The Hebrew word is also used to mean service (Num. 4:23).

One name for God is LORD of Hosts. It is first used in 1 Sam. 1:3, near the end of the Judges period. From the basic meaning of 'an army', we can see that 'LORD of Hosts' shows the power of God and his authority as ruler over all the universe. The Greeks used their word for 'almighty' to translate 'LORD of Hosts'.

Humility

Humility is a virtue (Prov. 15:33). Only the humble receive grace from God (1 Peter 5:5). The word 'humble' is closely linked in the Bible, and especially in the Old Testament, with affliction and poverty. Humility often comes as the result of affliction.

Christ is the supreme example of humility. He stooped down from his divine grandeur to save sinners (Phil. 2:5-8). Christians should follow him by putting others first (Phil. 2:3,4). There is a false humility to avoid (Col. 2:18,23) but Christians must clothe themselves with true humility which will forgive and love in a genuine way (Col. 3:12).

God will exalt all those who are truly humble but will force humility on the proud (Matt. 23:12).

Hymn

Basically a hymn is a song which praises God. Singing was an important part of worship in the Old Testament (Psalms, 1 Chr. 25) and in the New Testament (Matt. 26:30; 1 Cor. 14:15; James 5:13). They were expressions of joyful worship (Ps. 95:1) and ways of teaching the faith (Col. 3:16). The phrase 'had sung a hymn' (Matt. 26:30) is, literally, 'they hymned' and may refer to Ps. 113-118 which were sung at the passover.

Hypocrite

Hypocrite comes from a Greek word meaning someone who acts a part on a stage. It then came to be used as someone who pretends to be what he or she is not. Jesus called the Pharisees of his day hypocrites, because they were inconsistent: what they appeared to be was different from what they really were. They appeared to be upright godly men, but Jesus saw their blindness (Matt. 23:16) and their self-righteousness (Matt. 6:2). Peter's play-acting, however, was an attempt to cover up what he really believed (Gal. 2:13).

Idolatry

The Bible opposes idolatry, without any compromise. Worshipping idols is not an alternative to true faith in God, but a poisonous delusion which is an attack on God. The Old Testament shows a struggle with idolatry by the chosen people of God from the beginning of Israel's history to the exile.

Idols are made by people and can do nothing (Isa. 40:19,20). They are worthless, and they make their worshippers worthless too (Jer. 2:5). They defile their worshippers (Ezek. 22:4), deceiving them and leading them astray (Zech. 10:2). Israel's history shows clearly how idol worship leads to moral decay.

The God of Israel is Lord over all the nations (Isa. 41:1-4) and will not allow worthless and degrading idols to steal what is rightly his (Isa. 42:8). The first two commandments forbid both the worship of other gods and making images for worship. The Israelites were unique among all the nations of their day in that their true religion did not have any image of God

The New Testament repeats the teaching of the Old. Idolatry is a deviation, the result of rejecting the true God (Rom. 1:21-23). Idols are made by people (Acts 17:29), and have no reality at all (1 Cor. 8:4). They are able to do nothing (Rev. 9:20), yet at the same time, evil spiritual forces lie behind them (1 Cor. 10:19,20) and they lead to moral decay (Col. 3:5).

Idols, meat offered to

In New Testament days, part of a pagan sacrifice was offered to the god and the rest was eaten either in the temple or at home as a religious meal. Social invitations to dinner sometimes were described as at the table of a god. Pagan worship affected a great deal of social life in Gentile towns and this caused Gentile Christians many problems. Should they attend public festivals, which included pagan rites? If they wanted to practise a trade, they were forced to belong to a guild, but pagan worship was included. Meat on sale in market places was sometimes offered first to idols. The churches had many poor members and pagan temples sometimes gave free meals to the poor.

These problems were especially difficult in Corinth. Paul devotes 1 Cor. 8-10 to answering their questions. There were two groups in the church with opposing views. One group stressed Christian freedom, saying that idols were nothing and that attending a feast in a pagan temple was no more than a social occasion, not a religious one (8:4,10). Some non-Christian Greeks also did not believe in these gods and attended temples for the same reason. The other group in Corinth believed that there was a reality of some kind behind the idols and were very careful not to eat anything which may have had any form of pagan ritual performed on it.

In chapter 8, Paul agrees that idols are nothing, but some Christians with a pagan background still thought of idols when they ate certain foods and this hurt their consciences. It is better, said Paul, for the Christians with strong consciences to stop eating meat than to harm their fellow believers. Chapter 9 expands this theme of foregoing one's rights for the sake of others, with Paul using himself as an example.

Chapter 10:1-13 argues against the view that baptism and communion prevent evil influences in idolatry. The Israelites in the desert went through the waters of the Red Sea (? a picture of baptism) and ate manna (? a picture of communion), yet fell into idolatry and its associated immorality. God judged them severely.

Paul's conclusion comes in 10:14-11:1. Keep away from idolatry. Do not join in worship at a pagan temple, as that links you to demons. Eat meat sold in the market and join pagan friends for social meals without asking questions about the meat, because even if it were offered to idols, they are nothing, and God owns all creation. However, when someone tells you that the meat has been offered to idols, don't eat it if that action will make a fellow believer distressed.

Rev. 2:14 repeats the ban on pagan ceremonies and the immorality that went with them.

Image - the image of God - Imago Dei

An image is more than a likeness to something or someone. An image is a representation. This could be on a coin (Matt. 22:30), or a statue used in worship (Rom. 1:23). In the case of idols, whatever was represented was often thought to be present in the image.

Man was made in God's image (Gen. 1:27). This means both that mankind depends on God for their existence and that people are somehow like God. This likeness cannot be in appearance, because God is Spirit and has no physical body. Rather it is seen in the ruling over creation as God's representative (Gen. 1:26), in righteousness and holiness (Eph. 4:24) and ability to know God (Col. 3:10). This image gives people a great dignity (Gen. 9:6) although it has been badly damaged by the fall. Salvation in Christ restores that image (Col. 3:10).

Christ is the image of God (2 Cor. 4:4). This means that he represents God and God is present in him (Col. 1:15). This makes him different from Adam. Adam was like God, but was not God. Christ is like God, and is God. In Christ, all God's fulness dwells (Col. 1:19; John 14:9). God's purpose is that believers be 'conformed to the image of his Son' (Rom. 8:29).

In Hebrews 1:3 a different Greek word for image is used. The idea is of a die which stamps out an impression, such as on a coin.

All the features of the image and the die correspond exactly. God is invisible, but Christ shares his nature and therefore shows us exactly what God is like. Christ is equal to the Father in his essence.

The phrase 'the image of God' often appears in its Latin form - imago Dei.

Immanuel

This Hebrew word means 'God with us'. It appears in a prophecy of (Isa. 7:14; 8:8) and in Matt. 1:23 as a name for Christ).

The background to Isaiah's prophecy is a coalition between Syria and the northern state of Israel against Judah (Isa. 7:2). King Ahaz was troubled by this but Isaiah told him to trust God. After Ahaz refused to ask for a sign, Isaiah spoke of a supernatural event when a virgin would have a son, Immanuel (v. 14). The God who was with them would defeat the coalition.

Matthew says that the birth of Christ fulfilled this prophecy (Matt. 1:23). In a far greater way than in Ahaz's day, God will bring salvation through Christ, who is God with us.

Inheritance

The Old Testament view of inheritance starts with God. He promised a land to Abraham (Gen. 12:4-7) and fulfilled that promise (1 Kings 8:36). The land belongs to God and the Israelites are tenants (Lev. 25:23). It was divided among the tribes by lot (Josh. 18:10) and these were divided among the clans, families and individuals. The lot was used not because they were leaving the distribution to chance, but through his control of the lot God allocated the land (cf. Prov. 16:33). The land was given with the condition that the people obeyed God (Deut. 4:1, 25-31).

Inheritance of the plots of land was by legal right. The land was divided into equal portions. The eldest son had two, the remaining sons had one each (Deut. 21:16,17). If the dead man did not have any sons, then a strict order of inheritance was laid down (Num. 27:8-11; 36:1-9). If the man's wife was still alive, the dead man's brother should marry her and their son would legally be the dead man's son and heir (Deut. 25:5-9; Ruth 4:10).

Because the land was God's, an inheritance could not be transferred to another family or tribe. Boundary stones must not be moved (Deut. 19:14). In cases of poverty, the land could be sold but the next of kin could redeem it, or the seller could redeem it if he later had enough money (Lev. 25:25-27). Even if the land were not redeemed, it had to be returned in the jubilee, free of charge. What was really sold were the crops, not the land (Lev. 25:13-17). This law did not apply to houses in walled cities.

The tribe of Levites did not have part of the country given to them as an inheritance. God was their inheritance (Deut. 18:1,2). They benefited from the tithes (Num. 18:21). Levites, however, were given certain cities (Num. 35:2) and these were always redeemable and had to be returned in the jubilee (Lev. 25:32-34).

The New Testament develops the teaching of the Old. Sonship becomes more important. Christ is the true heir of God's inheritance as God's Son (Mark 12:7; Heb. 1:2). Christian believers share in this inheritance through adoption as sons (Rom. 8:17). They become sons and heirs not because they can trace their physical descent from Abraham but because they share the faith of Abraham (Gal. 3:7-9,29). Gentiles are therefore fellow-heirs with Jewish believers (Eph. 3:6) and men and women are equal heirs (1 Peter 3:7).

The inheritance is no longer the land of Canaan, but what Canaan symbolized — the kingdom of heaven (Matt. 25:34; Heb. 11:9,10,16). This inheritance is reserved in heaven for the believer (1 Peter 1:4). Christians will enter into this fully at the second coming of Christ, when the new heavens and new earth replace the present world (Matt. 5:5; Rev. 21:7). In the meantime, believers have a foretaste of this inheritance in the Holy Spirit who is the guarantee of our inheritance (Eph. 1:14).

Inspiration

This important word appears in 2 Tim. 3:16 where all Scripture is said to be inspired by God. Some translate this verse as saying that Scripture breathes out God, or that God breathes through the Scriptures. This would imply that God uses the Scriptures to speak to us today. This is true, but the text says more than that. The real meaning of the word is that God breathed out Scripture. The words of the Bible, in the original, were the very words that God wanted to be spoken. This agrees with the New Testament's treatment of the Old Testament, where what men had written is also seen to be what God is saying (Heb. 3:7; 4:3). Also, the smallest detail of each word is important (Gal. 3:16).

The doctrine of inspiration does not mean that God dictated the words for the people to write. Rather, as each man wrote according to his God-given character, insight and purpose, God was breathing through him to ensure that these human words were also the unchangeable Word of God.

In both Hebrew and Greek the words for 'breath' and 'Spirit' are the same. The breath of God is often a figure of speech for his creating power (Job 33:4; Ps. 33:6). The word 'inspiration' shows that the Spirit's work included the inspiration of Scripture.

Israel

Jacob, Abraham's grandson, was given the name Israel by God after the wrestling at Penuel. Israel means 'God struggles', or, 'he struggles with God'. God said: 'You have struggled with God and with men and have overcome' (Gen. 32:28).

The nation of Israel was descended from Jacob through his twelve sons. Often 'Israel' means all the twelve tribes, but after the nation split under Rehoboam and Jeroboam, the ten tribes of the north took the name Israel in contrast to the tribe of Judah (1 Kings 12:16-20) in the south.

Jannes and Jambres

Paul speaks of Jannes and Jambres as men who resisted Moses (2 Tim. 3:6-8). Although these names are not in the Old Testament, we know from other writings that they stand for the Egyptian magicians in Exod. 7 and 8.

Jealousy

Jealousy is a very strong emotion (Prov. 27:4). It is a desire for something. It can be directed towards something that is rightly ours, where we will not accept others taking it away or even sharing it. Often this relates to marriage. A jealous husband will not accept an adulterer sharing his wife (Num. 5:14).

God is a jealous God and will not share his place in people's lives with idols (Exod. 34:14). He is Israel's husband (Jer. 3:14) and their mixing of true worship with idolatry was adultery (Hosea 3:1; Ezek. 23:37).

Godly people may have a right jealousy when they have a zeal for God and godly purity (Ps. 69:9; 2 Cor. 11:2). When the jealousy is directed towards something that is not rightly ours, it is a sin (Gen. 30:1; 37:11; Gal. 5:20).

Jehovah

The Hebrew language was written without vowels. God's name was written as Yhwh (Gen. 6:3). The Hebrew consonants are the same as those of the verb 'to be' (in its older form) and in Exod. 3:14 God called himself the 'I am'. The phrase refers not only to his eternal existence, without beginning or end, but to the fact that he is dependent on nothing and no-one for his existence. Such a God was in complete contrast to heathen gods.

In order to help the public reading of the Bible, some Jews called the Mas(s)oretes started writing vowels over and under the consonants. They did this from AD500 to AD1000.

Because God's name was thought too holy to pronounce, the Jews said 'Adonai' (my lord) every time Yhwh appeared. The Mas(s)oretes wrote the vowels of Adonai (a-o-ai) with the consonants Yhwh.

About AD1100, people started to mix the two words, the consonants Yhwh with the vowels for 'my lord'. The result was Jehovah. However, older Greek texts point to the pronunciation Yahweh being far more likely.

When the consonants Yhwh appear in the Hebrew, the English Bible translates as 'LORD' or 'the LORD'. It translates Adonai as 'Lord' or 'the Lord'.

Jerusalem

Built high in the hills of Judah, Jerusalem's history goes back at least to Abraham's time (Gen. 14:18 - Salem is most likely Jerusalem, cf. Ps. 76:2). It was called Jerusalem long before it became an Israelite city and the name means 'city of peace' (cf. Heb. 7:2). Joshua defeated a coalition led by the king of Jerusalem (Josh. 10) but although Jerusalem was taken (Judg. 1:8), the Israelites did not keep control of the city (Judg. 1:21).

The Jebusites controlled Jerusalem until David defeated them (2 Sam. 5:6-8). The name Zion appears here for the first time. David made it his capital city (2 Sam. 5:9,10) and brought the ark of God there (2 Sam. 6). It was an ideal choice for a capital as it was situated on the borders of Benjamin and Judah. This prevented tribal jealousies between David's tribe and the tribe of his predecessor Saul.

From that time, Jerusalem became the centre of the Jewish faith. Solomon built his temple there on Mount Moriah (2 Chr. 3:1; cf. Gen. 22:2) and the other two temples which followed were also in Jerusalem. It was called the holy city (Isa. 52:1) and exiles longed to be there (Ps. 137).

In the New Testament, Jerusalem was the place where Jesus the Messiah was rejected (Matt. 23:37). It was a symbol of the legalism of the Jews (Gal. 4:25). The apostles also saw that the Old Testament Jerusalem, the holy city where God dwelt in his temple, is a picture of a more important reality — heaven (Gal. 4:26; Heb. 12:22; Rev. 21:2).

Jesus Christ

Jesus Christ is the theme of Christian preaching (1 Cor. 1:23). He is the one whom true Christians seek to follow in every aspect of their lives. Through faith in Christ sinners are saved from sin.

Christ is the Son of God, the second Person of the Trinity. Through him all creation was made and now holds together (John 1:3; Col. 1:15-17). He became a man known as Jesus of Nazareth, who was born of a virgin, spent time in teaching and healing, died for the sins of his people, rose again from the dead and is now in heaven at God's right hand. He will come again to judge the world and to take his people to heaven with him (Phil. 2:6-11; 1 Thess. 4:13-17; John 5:24-30). He reversed Adam's sin on behalf of his people (Rom. 5:12-19); he is the last Adam, the second man (1 Cor. 15:45,47), the head of his body, the church (Col. 1:18-20).

The name Jesus comes from the Aramaic form of 'Joshua' and means 'salvation': Christ means 'anointed' and is the Greek equivalent of the title 'Messiah'.

Christ, therefore, was originally a title, meaning 'God's anointed man'. Teaching about the Messiah did not mean so much to the Gentiles and the word Christ became more like a name than a title. The meaning of the word Christ was still important, however, and was used by both Gentiles and Jews.

The years on the Christian calendar are supposed to be numbered from the birth of Christ. However, this was not calculated until long after the New Testament era and a mistake was made. Jesus was born during the reign of King Herod, who died in 4BC. Jesus, therefore, was born around 7BC.

John the Baptist

John was born around 7BC, about six months before Jesus Christ was born to Mary. He was a younger relative and was born of priestly parents (Luke 1:26,36). When he grew up, he lived in the desert before starting his prophetic ministry as Christ's forerunner (Luke 1:17,80). He preached to the Jews about sin and judgment, telling them that they should show they had repented by being baptized. Some asked if he claimed to be the Messiah but he replied that he was the Messiah's forerunner (Luke 3:1-18). In addition to preaching and baptizing in the Jordan valley, he spent some time in Aenon, which was in Samaritan country (John 3:23).

John denounced Herod Antipas for divorcing his wife and marrying his brother-in-law's wife. Herod put him in prison and later beheaded him (Mark 6:17-29).

During his time in prison, John showed uncertainty about Jesus. Jesus reassured him (Matt. 11:2-6) by pointing out the signs of the Messiah (cf Isa. 35:5,6; 61:1-3). When John's disciples returned, Jesus told the crowd that John was indeed his forerunner and was the greatest Old Testament man, the Elijah promised in Mal. 4:5,6. The Bible clearly says that because he came before Christ, John did not have the privilege that the least member of the kingdom of heaven now has (Matt. 11:2-19). John knew nothing of Calvary, the resurrection or pentecost (Matt. 13:16,17).

Jot and Tittle

The jot stands for the smallest letter in the Hebrew alphabet, a letter which is not even necessary sometimes in the spelling of a word. The tittle is a small stroke of the pen which distinguished one letter from another.

In Matt. 5:18 and Luke 16:17, these words mean that the law stands so firm that not even the slightest part can be taken away. This shows how important God's law is. Christ does not say that the law is no longer relevant. He gives it a deeper significance by fulfilling it (Matt. 5:17).

Joy

On a few occasions, the word joy means simply a feeling of gladness that any person may have (Ps. 104:15; Prov. 15:20). Mostly, however, it is a sign of the people who trust in God. The Old Testament festivals (Deut. 12:6,7) and other times of worship (2 Sam. 6; Ps. 100:2; Neh. 12:43) were happy times, with singing, dancing and shouting in celebration of God and what he had done. Crowds worshipping together (Ps. 42:4) and individuals on their own (Ps. 43:4) did so with joy.

Christ brought joy from the time of his birth (Luke 2:10), through his ministry (Luke 13:17) and entry into Jerusalem (Luke 19:37) to his resurrection (Luke 24:41) and ascension (Luke 24:52). The New Testament church was also full of joy (Acts 13:52; 1 Thess. 5:16).

Spiritual joy is not merely a human emotion stirred up from inside the believer. God gives it (Ps. 16:11; Rom. 15:13). Christ (John 15:11) and the Holy Spirit (1 Thess. 1:6) join with the Father in giving joy. Spiritual joy comes from being in God's presence (Ps. 16:7-11; Jude 24) and seeing him at work, especially in salvation (Neh. 12:43; Acts 8:8,39).

Although this joy is God's gift, it does not come automatically. The faithful are told to rejoice in the Lord (Ps. 95:1; Phil. 4:4). This joy brings strength (Neh. 8:10) but sin takes away joy, which is restored only after confession and repentance (Ps. 51:12).

Joy fills a person to overflowing (2 Cor. 8:2). It is great joy (2 Chr. 30:26) making people shout (Ps. 118:15) and leap in the air (Luke 6:23). In fact, it is beyond words to describe it (1 Peter 1:8).

But although believers may have abundant joy now, greater joy awaits them. To enter the kingdom of heaven will be to enter the joy of the Lord. Both Old and New Testaments see something of this future joy (Isa. 55:12; Rev. 19:7). This future joy enables the Christian, like Christ (Heb. 12:2), to endure suffering now (Matt. 5:12; 1 Peter 1:6-8). Trials also help to make Christians stronger in their faith, which should make them rejoice (James 1:3).

Jubilee

The people of Israel were told to let their land rest every seventh year as a sabbath. On the seventh such sabbath year, that is, the forty-ninth year, on the Day of Atonement, the trumpet was to be blown through the land (Lev. 25:9). The next year, the fiftieth, was the jubilee. The name 'jubilee' comes from the Hebrew word for 'ram'. The trumpet was made from a ram's horn.

Like the sabbath year, the jubilee was a time for the land to rest (Lev. 25:11,12). Debts were already cancelled on the last day of the sabbath year (Deut. 15:1) but now in the jubilee the land had to be returned to its original owners (Lev. 25:10,13,28). Israelite slaves and hired workers were to be released (vv. 39-43, 47-55).

The jubilee can be seen to have had two main purposes. It would reduce poverty and prevent the power of big landowners, but more importantly, it would show that the land belonged to God and was allocated to the Israelites by him as a sacred trust.

See Inheritance.

Judah

Judah was Jacob's fourth son (Gen. 29:35). He was a natural leader (Gen. 37:26; 43:3-10; 44:16; 46:28) and his father said that his descendants would take a leading role in Israel (Gen. 49:10).

The tribe of Judah settled in the south of the promised land. They were active in the whole nation at the start of the judges period, providing Israel with their first judge, Othniel. Their contact with the more northern tribes did not seem to continue very strongly and by Saul's day they were numbered separately from the rest of Israel (1 Sam. 11:8). This seems to show that the later split in Israel had its roots in the judges period, probably because of pressure from their enemies preventing much contact.

The second king of Israel (David) came from Judah. His son Solomon also reigned over the united kingdom, but after Solomon's death the kingdom split into two states, Israel in the north and Judah in the south (1 Kings 12).

The promise of the kingship passed from the tribe of Judah (Gen. 49:10) to the family of David (2 Sam. 7:16) to the great King, Jesus Christ, descendant of David (Luke 2:4).

The name Judah comes from the Hebrew word for praise (see Gen. 29:35).

Judge

A judge today is someone who listens to court cases and decides what the law of the land says about it. The Old Testament judges did more than that. The Hebrew word for judge means a person who governs, leads, or saves the people. In addition to hearing cases brought before them, they made sure that society was just - in other words, that God's covenant was upheld. The judges would punish the guilty, rescue the innocent, ensure that weaker members of society were treated in a fair way, make laws, administer government and even lead the people against armies oppressing them.

People in Old Testament times had laws but did not see themselves as ruled by laws so much as ruled by their seniors. It was these senior people who made the laws. The great Judge is God

(Gen. 18:25; Ps. 96:13). As Judge, he gave his laws to Moses. The Hebrew judges represented God, to ensure that his will as shown in the covenant was carried out (Exod. 18:15; Deut. 1:17). In the New Testament Paul teaches that earthly authorities are appointed by God to represent him (Rom. 13:4).

In patriarchal days, the head of the family administered justice (Gen. 38:24). Later, Moses judged Israel and at Jethro's advice delegated the easier cases (Exod. 18:24-26) to other men. This practice was continued in Canaan (Deut. 16:18) with the priest, the main judge, deciding the difficult cases (Deut. 17:9).

Between the times of Joshua and Saul, God sent judges to rescue Israel from the attacks of other people and to administer justice in the land. The great achievements of each judge showed that God's Spirit was given for their tasks (Judg. 3:10; 6:34; 11:29; 14:19).

Under the monarchy, the king was the main judge (2 Sam. 15:2; 1 Kings 3:16-28). Judges continued to work after the exile (Ezra 7:25).

Judgment

Moses told the Israelites before they entered Canaan that God would punish them if they disobeyed him (Deut. 28:15-68). Later, the prophets said that the heaviest punishment, exile, would soon be on them as God's judgment (see Day of the LORD). The prophets often looked beyond Israel and Judah and spoke of God's judgments on the surrounding nations. Daniel foretold a worldwide judgment, when the righteous would be delivered and the wicked punished (Dan. 7:26).

Christ and his apostles continued this teaching. The Judge is God who acts through Christ (2 Tim. 4:8; Acts 17:31). He judges what people have done (Rev. 20:13). Those who know God's written law will be judged by that, but those who do not will be judged by the knowledge of right and wrong that everyone has (Rom. 2:12-16).

No ordinary human being has lived up to God's standards (Rom. 3:23). God could declare everyone guilty. Only Christ lived a perfect life and died on the cross for the sins of his people (1 Peter 2:22-24). Escaping a guilty verdict, therefore, depends on our attitude to Christ (John 5:24).

Judgment is after death (Heb. 9:27) at the second coming of Christ (John 5:24-30). Everyone will stand before God's judgment throne (2 Cor. 5:10) but the believer will have nothing to fear (1 John 4:17). Judgment is a time of deliverance for the faithful but a time of punishment for sinners (2 Thess. 1:5-10; Rev. 6:10).

God's verdict depends on whether people have faith in Christ, so unbelievers are already condemned (John 3:18) as long as they remain in unbelief. The only way to escape condemnation is by faith in Christ (Rom. 8:1).

Judging

Christ (Matt. 7:1) and the apostles (Rom. 2:1; James 4:11) condemned the judging of other people. They referred to critical attitudes which point out other people's faults and fail to see their own. Such judging always sees itself in the right and others in the wrong (Rom. 14:4). These people fail to see that God is the true Judge.

Churches should judge members who persist in sin (Matt. 18:15-18; 1 Cor. 5). This is not a self-righteous critical attitude, but discipline by the whole church for the good of the church and the sinner. Paul also says that churches should judge disputes between members and that believers should not go to the secular courts.

Christ also taught that people should exercise wise judgment when thinking about him (John 7:24) and what is happening around them (Luke 12:57). Christians should be those who think about things carefully and are not easily deceived. All judgments should agree with what God says is true (John 8:16).

Justice, Righteousness,

Justice and righteousness are closely linked and are treated together here. A just person does what is right. God's righteous character causes him to act justly.

God is the Judge of all the world (Gen. 18:25). Everything he does is just and right (Deut. 32:4; Ps. 145:7; Rev. 15:3). What he wants above everything else in his people, even before worship, is justice (Amos 5:21-24; Micah 6:8).

People are just when they do things in God's way (Gen. 18:19). They serve God (Mal. 3:18), obeying his law (Ezek. 18:19; Rom. 2:13). People from different nations or different periods of history have various ideas of what is just and right, but the Bible teaches that true justice is always the same. This is because justice is based in God and his law. Those who do not know God can only be just and right as they obey the law that God has written in their hearts.

One of the main Hebrew words for justice means 'acting according to a standard'. This standard may be weights and measures (Lev. 19:35,36) but in the Bible the principal standard is the law of God. This standard would ensure that everyone is treated in the same way, whether they are rich or poor (Exod. 23:2-9; Deut. 16:18-20).

Justice punishes the guilty (Luke 23:41; Acts 28:4). God's judgment against sinners is shown in his wrath (Rom. 2:5). But justice also restores the rights of the righteous and even avenges them (2 Sam. 15:4; Ps. 103:6; Rev. 7:10). God's justice has a saving, as well as a condemning, side. His justice saves the righteous and the penitent (Isa. 1:27).

But although people's lives could be called just and righteous (Phil. 3:6), in the full sense of the word no one is righteous before God (Rom. 3:10). Our most righteous acts are as filthy rags to him (Isa. 64:6). God gives a righteousness to those who repent of their sin and come to Christ in faith (Rom. 3:21 - see Justification).

Justification, Justify

The word justification was used in law courts. When a judge declared that an accused person was not guilty, he justified that person. The word means to acquit, to declare a person to be righteous.

Except when it is used by Paul, justification in the Bible means that a person is innocent or righteous. Psalm 51:4 means that God is in the right when he condemns the sinner. Elihu (Job 32:2) and God (Job 40:8) accuse Job of putting himself in the right even when it meant putting God in the wrong. James uses the word in the same way (James 2:24). James means that people are shown to be righteous (godly) by what they do.

Some think that Paul and James disagreed about justification. What these people fail to notice is that James uses the word in the usual way, whereas Paul makes it a technical word to show the way God saves sinners. James is not saying that we earn our salvation, but that we show that we are saved by what we do (James 2:18). Paul uses the word to show how we become righteous in the first place. He agrees with James that those who have faith will show it by good works (Gal. 6:10: Eph. 2:10; Titus 2:11,12).

The way Paul uses justification is the same as other biblical writers but with one very important exception. In Paul's writings, people are justified not because they have proved themselves to be innocent (or righteous) but by a free gift of God's grace (Rom. 3:24). God declares people to be not guilty despite their sin, because he gives them a righteousness they have not earned (Rom. 3:21). God can do this justly, because Christ atoned for sin, bearing the punishment that God's justice demands should be given to the guilty (v. 24-26).

Paul teaches, therefore, that it is not by obeying God's law that we are justified by God (Gal. 3:11). Measured by that standard, we are guilty. It is only in Christ (1 Cor. 6:11; Gal. 2:17) that we are justified and we receive God's acquittal through faith in Christ (Rom. 5:1; Gal. 3:24).

Kenites

The Kenites were part of the people of Midian. They were in Canaan in Abraham's day (Gen. 15:19). Moses married a Kenite woman from a family in the southern part of the Sinai peninsula. (See Num. 10:29 and compare with Judg. 1:16). After the conquest, some Kenites settled with the tribe of Judah (Judg. 1:16) but were still distinct from them much later (1 Sam. 30:29). The Rechabites (1 Chr. 2:55; Neh. 3:14) were Kenites.

The word Kenite means 'smith'. As copper is found in their region of the Sinai peninsula, they no doubt worked with this metal.

Kidneys

The kidneys of a sacrificed animal were sometimes offered separately with other parts (Exod. 29:13; Lev. 3:4). This was probably because the fat that surrounded the kidneys was thought of as a delicacy reserved for God.

In Job 16:13 and Lam. 3:13 arrows are said to have pierced the kidneys. This would imply that a soldier was shot from behind, where there was little protection. The meaning is that God had surrounded them and overcome them.

On other occasions, kidneys are a symbol for a person's innermost being (Ps. 73:21). This may have arisen because the kidneys would be the last member of an animal to be reached when pulling it apart.

Kin, Kinsman

The family unit was always important to the Israelites. The closer two people were related to each other, the closer was the bond between them. On the other hand, all Israelites were brothers (Deut. 1:16; Acts 7:2) because all were descended from the patriarch Israel.

The nearest relative had special responsibilities. If a man died without children, his brother should marry the widow to give the man a legal heir (Deut. 25:5-10). The nearest relative was expected to buy back property or people sold because of poverty (Lev. 25:25, 47-49) and put to death a murderer (Num. 35:19).

See Family.

See also Inheritance.

King

In Israel, the kings took over the civil government from the judges. Their tasks were similar to those of the judges - that is, to ensure that justice was kept in the land (Ps. 72; Jer. 33:15). They were not allowed to do the work of a priest (1 Sam. 13:7-14; 2 Chr. 26:16-20).

Like all leaders in Israel, the king represented God. God would choose him (Deut. 17:15). God's prophets (1 Kings 19:16; 2 Kings 9:6) or priests (2 Chr. 23:8-11) anointed the king. In Psalm 2 God, the King in heaven (v. 4), anoints the human king in Jerusalem (vv. 2,6). This King is God's Son (v. 7; 2 Sam. 7:14). This refers in the first place to the Davidic king, but the complete fulfilment is in David's greatest Son, the Lord Jesus Christ (Acts 4:25-26; Heb. 1:5).

Unlike the judges, kings normally passed their position to a son. This did not seem to happen in Edom (Gen. 36:31-39) and many of the kings of the northern kingdom of Israel seized the throne by force. In Judah, God promised David that his descendants would keep the throne stable for ever (2 Sam. 7:16-19).

Samuel resisted the people's call for a king at first. God said that they had rejected him as King, but that Samuel should nevertheless do as the people asked. Samuel pointed out that the kings would oppress the people in order to gain wealth and splendour (1 Sam. 8). The law in fact did allow the people to have a king, but stated that he should not seek wealth and splendour (Deut. 17:14-20).

Kingdom of God

God is King. All the Bible teaches this but the Gospels in particular talk about the kingdom of God. Matt. 13:11 and Mark 4:11 report the same incident but Matthew refers to the kingdom of heaven and Mark calls it the kingdom of God.

Teaching in the Old Testament

God rules over all creation (Ps. 97:1). In a special way, he reigns over his people Israel (Isa. 43:15) who are a kingdom of priests to God (Exod. 19:6). The Old Testament saw God's kingdom as present in its day, but it also looked forward to a greater and future kingdom which would last for ever (Dan. 7:14).

Teaching of John the Baptist

John told his hearers that the promised kingdom had almost arrived (Matt. 3:2). They should repent because this kingdom would bring judgment (Matt. 3:10).

Teaching of Christ and the apostles

The kingdom has come. Like John, Jesus preached that people should repent because the kingdom was near (Mark 1:15). He also said a little later that it had arrived in him. The fact that he was casting out devils showed that Satan's defeat was beginning (Matt. 12:28).

A new type of kingdom. Jesus rejected the world's idea of a kingdom (Matt. 4:8-10). His kingdom is entirely different (John 18:36) where service, not lordship, is the way (Matt. 20:25-28). It is important that we understand that the kingdom is God at work saving his people (Matt. 13); it does not mean people at work changing society. The kingdom is where God rules.

The subjects of the kingdom. Only those who are born again enter the kingdom (John 3:5). They must become as little children, turning away from their sins and humbly begging for mercy (Matt. 18:2,3).

In the kingdom, God's subjects obey their King (Matt. 5:19). They must lead righteous lives (Matt. 6:33; Rom. 14:17). They must stop doing sinful things (Gal. 5:19-21) and instead do good to all for the sake of their King (Gal. 6:10; Matt. 5:16). All true Christians are in the kingdom of God and seek to serve their King in every part of their lives.

The kingdom is yet to come. Although Jesus said that the kingdom had come in him, he also taught that it had not come in its fullest sense. Satan is defeated but is still fighting against God. Not all mankind accepts God's rule in Christ. Jesus Christ is coming again in glory. That will be a day of judgment (Matt. 25:31-46) and all creation will then bow before Christ as King (Phil. 2:11). God, Christ and the people of God will rule for ever (Rev. 22:3-5).

Our Father in heaven, may your kingdom come!

Knowledge

To the Hebrews, knowledge was not simply being aware of facts. Knowing something or someone also included a right relationship with whatever was known. This relationship resulted in some activity. Knowledge and activity were linked in Hebrew thought.

Knowing the loss of children (Isa. 47:8) is to feel the pain of a lost relationship. When an animal knows its master (Isa. 1:3) it experiences a relationship where the master cares for it and in return it works obediently for the master. Because Israel did not live obediently to God, they did not 'know' God. The right activity did not follow what they learned of him. Jer. 4:22 speaks of this. The Israelites refused to accept God's claim on their obedience.

God's knowing a person and having a relationship with that person is the doctrine of election. God knew Jeremiah before he was conceived (Jer. 1:5). God chose him before his birth for the task of prophet. Paul uses the word 'know' in the Hebrew way when he says that God foreknew his elect (Rom. 8:29).

People gain some knowledge by listening to teaching (Prov. 1:1-4) or by meditation (Eccl. 1:12-18), but the fullest knowledge comes from God (Prov. 2:6) and from having a right attitude to him (Prov. 1:7).

Hebrew thinking continues in the New Testament. To know the truth (1 Tim. 2:4) is not simply to know facts (cf James 2:19), but is to respond to the gospel of truth by trusting in God.

The New Testament speaks against false knowledge (1 Tim. 6:20; Col. 2:8). Some pagan cults at that time claimed to give their followers a special, secret knowledge. Right knowledge comes from God alone. Paul opposes the Christian church at Corinth where claims to have knowledge led to disruptions in the church (1 Cor. 8:1).

The spiritual gift of the word of knowledge (1 Cor. 12:8) is the ability to teach spiritual things.

Lamb of God

This is the title given by John the Baptist to Jesus (John 1:29,36). The picture of Jesus as the lamb also appears in other parts of the New Testament, especially in Revelation.

John says that the Lamb of God takes away the sin of the world. He may have been thinking about the sin offering of Lev. 4:32. He probably also had in mind the lamb sacrificed at the passover (Exod. 12:3) and the Lamb of Isa. 53:7. John was concerned to teach that Jesus was God's Lamb for the sins of people of all nations (the world) and so different from the lambs offered by Israelites for the sins of Jews only (John 11:52).

Lamp, Lampstand

Lamps in Bible times were usually made from clay and burned olive oil soaked up by a wick. Their design had developed over the centuries from a simple bowl-shape to a moulded design with a long spout and a hole in the main body of the lamp for pouring in the oil. Lampstands held these lamps.

Lamps are also used as symbols in the Bible. The tabernacle had a seven-branched lampstand in the Holy Place (Exod. 25:31-40; 26:35). David was called the lamp of Israel (2 Sam. 21:17) and God was called David's lamp (2 Sam. 22:29). God's Word is a lamp (Ps. 119:105) but the lamp of the wicked is snuffed out (Job 18:5; Proverbs 13:9). John the Baptist was a lamp (John 5:35) and the churches are lampstands (Rev. 1:20). The Spirit of God is seven lamps (Rev. 4:5).

Lamps give light, showing things in the dark or showing people the way. Lamps therefore are an obvious symbol for leadership such as God's Word leading the godly in the right way to live (Ps. 119:105), or men as leaders of their people (2 Sam. 21:17) and churches showing people Christ and his ways (Rev. 1:20). Lamps are also an obvious symbol for truth and the blessings that come from God (Prov. 20:27; Ps. 18:28).

Landmark

Landmarks were stones which showed the boundaries of a plot of land owned by an Israelite. Because this land was an inheritance given by God, landmarks were not to be moved (Deut. 19:14; Prov. 22:28). If they were moved, this was a sign of wickedness (Job 24:2; Hosea 5:10).

Law

The Hebrew word in the Old Testament means 'instruction'. The same word is used in Exod. 35:34 to mean teaching a craft, and in Prov. 3:1 the instruction a father gives his son.

The law, then, is God's instruction. This instruction is given to those with whom he has made a covenant by his free grace. For example, Exod. 20:2 shows that God is Israel's Redeemer. The law that follows set out the Israelites' obligations under this covenant of promise (see also Gal. 3:16-22).

God teaches his people how they should live by his law. All parts of their lives are covered. This law can be the written code he gave through Moses (Deut. 30:10), instruction given through a prophet (Isa. 1:10; 8:16), or the eternal and unchanging will of God (Ps. 119:89-91).

God's law is God revealing his will to his people. The godly person, therefore, delights in it (Ps.1:2). It gives God's people life, makes them wise, and fills them with joy (Ps. 19:7-9). Their great desire is to obey it (Ps. 119:34).

In the New Testament, the law can be the law given through Moses with the obligation to keep it (Gal. 3:17), the first five books of the Old Testament (Luke 24:44), or the whole of the Old Testament (Rom. 3:19; note the previous verses are quotes from Psalms, Ecclesiastes and Isaiah). It can also mean God's will for mankind (Rom. 2:15), or a way to earn God's pleasure by obeying the written law of God (Gal. 3:11).

The New Testament says that Christians are no longer under law (Rom. 6:14). The law here is a way of salvation, involving the necessity to become a Jew and keep the Old Testament rituals. This law was fulfilled in Christ. Our not being under God's law does not mean that we can ignore it completely. God's will is still important. Christians should obey God's will, which is God's law (1 Cor. 9:21; 1 John 2:3).

There is no essential difference between God's law in Old and New Testaments. In both cases, God saves his people by his grace. This grace is completely undeserved. But God's people are saved in order to serve him by following his instructions.

Lawyers

Lawyers appear in the New Testament, especially in the Gospels. They were also called 'scribes'. They were originally experts in Old Testament law, but by the time of Christ there were numerous extra traditions taught by Jewish teachers. There were lawyers in the Sanhedrin which tried Christ (Luke 22:66).

Legion

The main Roman army was divided into legions. Officially a legion was 6000 men, divided into 10 cohorts of 6 centuries of 100 men. In practice they were often smaller, perhaps 4800 men in all. This led the demon-possessed man to call himself Legion, because of the number of demons in him (Mark 5:9). Jesus also talked about twelve legions of angels that he could call on if he wanted to be rescued from the cross (Matt. 26:53).

Levi

Levi was the third son of Jacob (Gen. 29:34) and the founder of the priestly tribe of the Levites.

Levi was also another name for the apostle Matthew. He is called Matthew in Matt. 9:9,10 but Levi in Mark 2:14 and Luke 5:27-29.

Levirate

See Marriage.

Levites

The tribe of Levi was descended from Levi, Jacob's third son. When Moses came down from Mount Sinai to find the Israelites worshipping the golden calf, the Levites answered his call: 'Whoever is for the Lord, come to me' (Exod. 32:26). Because of this act of zeal, God gave them a special place in his ministry (Deut. 33:8-11). They took the place of the first-born males who were set apart when God killed the Egyptian first-born (Num. 3:12,13).

The three families of Levites were given different tasks in the tabernacle (Num. 4). They were also in charge of the music (1 Chr. 6:31,32). They could not act as priests because that was reserved for the descendants of Aaron (Num. 18:7).

Unlike the other tribes, the Levites did not have an area of Canaan for themselves. Instead, they had cities and land within the territories of the other tribes (Num. 35:1-5). The tithes given by the Israelites were to be given to the Levites (Num. 18:21).

Lie, Lying

Satan is the father of lies (John 8:44). In the Garden of Eden, the serpent accused God of lying (Gen. 3:4). That is impossible, for God is the God of truth (Ps. 31:5). People who lie show that they are the children of Satan. Even their worship is called a lie (Rom. 1:25).

The children of God hate lies (Prov. 19:22), recognising that lies are part of the old, sinful life they have left behind (Col. 3:9). When Ananias and Sapphira told a lie to the church, Peter said that they lied to the Holy Spirit (Acts 5:3,4).

The ninth commandment forbids telling lies about other people (Exod. 20:16). All attempts at deceiving people are condemned in Lev. 6:2,3. Sometimes God-fearing people deceived evil people in order to stop their wickedness (e.g. Exod. 1:19; Josh. 2:4,5). This, however, does not lessen the wickedness of lies in all other cases.

Life

God is the living God (Num. 14:28) in contrast with idols (Ps. 115:4-8). He is the Lord of life, for he is its source (Gen. 1:20; 2:7; Ps. 36:9) and the one who gives life and takes it away (Deut. 32:39). When we say that God is alive, we do not simply mean that he exists. We mean that he does powerful things (Josh. 3:10; Jer. 10:10; Heb. 4:12). There is no hint of death, or any weakness, in him. He is immortal (1 Tim. 6:16).

This understanding of God as the source of life helps us to a biblical view of life. First, life is seen in terms of activity (Gen. 7:21; Ps. 69:34; Acts 17:28). By contrast, death is a total lack of movement. Even things that are not alive can be described as living, such as moving water (Gen. 26:19 - literal translation 'living water'). See John 4:11.

Life in the Old Testament is something that is full of health and energy. The same Hebrew word for life is used for wild animals when they are contrasted with quieter domestic livestock (Gen. 7:14: Hebrew literally is 'living creatures' and 'beasts'). Wild animals show greater energy, and therefore have more life.

A person who is ill, weak, or threatened with death is not fully alive. True life is full of blessings (Prov. 3:16). Abimelech was a dead man because of his sin. In other words, God was threatening to take away his life (Gen. 20:3). Adam was no longer fully alive after his sin because for the first time death cast its shadow over him (Gen. 2:17; 3:22). On the other hand, those who recover from illness become alive again (Num. 21:8; Ruth 4:15 [literally, 'a restorer of life']; Ps. 30:2,3).

Life comes from God. True life therefore comes only to those who live in a proper relationship with God (Deut. 8:3). The righteous have life, whereas the wicked have death (Prov. 11:19). God's people receive life by obeying his Word (Deut. 30:11-20; Ps. 119:92,93).

The New Testament shows that true life is life in Christ (John 1:4; 10:10). This spiritual life is contrasted with ordinary life, which is not true life (1 Tim. 6:19). Spiritual life is eternal life, given to those who are born again (John 3:3) and is experienced now (John 5:24). Those who are not born again are dead in sin (Eph. 2:1,2; 4:18) but rebirth means that believers share in Christ's resurrection life now (Rom. 6:4). God's Spirit lives in Christians, giving them this full life in Christ. The Spirit is also a guarantee of the life to come (2 Cor. 5:5). This life to come is not a mere continuing to exist, but a life full of a quality that is at present unknown to us. There will then be no sickness, sadness or death (Rev. 21:4). Spiritual life is the most important thing that a person can have (Job 2:4; Mark 8:37).

Light

God's first act in creation was to make light (Gen. 1:3). Many people have worshipped the sun because it brings light and life, but Genesis 1 shows that light is something separate from the sun. The sun was not created until the fourth day (vv. 14-19). Even the names sun and moon are not mentioned in the chapter, thus lowering their dignity and showing even more clearly that God made them. They should not be worshipped as if they were gods (cf. Job 31:26-28).

Our eyes need light in order to see (Ps. 38:10; Matt. 6:22). Light can also mean life (Ps. 56:13) and to see the light (Job 3:16) is to be born alive. When a person sees the light of someone's face, it means he has that person's acceptance and goodwill (Job 29:24). This includes God's acceptance (Num. 6:25; Ps. 44:3).

Light is a symbol for salvation (Ps. 27:1; Isa. 49:6), joy (Ps. 97:11), truth (John 3:21), love (1 John 2:9-11), or simply what is good (Isa. 5:20; Eph. 5:9). In other words, light is all that comes to the godly from God.

God is light (Ps. 27:1; 1 John 1:5) and he lives in light so bright that human beings cannot approach it (1 Tim. 6:16). This means that God is all that is holy and righteous. His holiness is so pure that there is no hint of darkness in him (1 John 1:5).

Christ is light (Isa. 9:2; John 1:9; 8:12). Those who belong to him are the children of the light (Eph. 5:8). By obeying his Word (Ps. 119:105) they walk in the light (Isa. 2:5; 1 John 1:7) and give light to the world (Matt. 5:14).

Darkness stands for all that is against God, such as sin and sin's results - suffering and death. Christians have passed from darkness to light (1 Peter 2:9) and should therefore live as in the day time (1 Thess. 5:4-8). The present age is a time of night, that is, when sin seems to rule, but the dawn, that is, Christ's Second Coming, is near (Rom. 13:11-14).

Lion of the Tribe of Judah

This title of Christ appears in Rev. 5:5. The thought is Jacob's words to Judah in Gen. 49:9,10. Jesus was from the tribe of Judah and a descendant of king David. Like the tribe of Judah and king David, Christ has fought courageously and conquered, as would a lion. The enemies that Christ conquered were sin, death and Satan.

The power of a lion to conquer is also used as a picture of God's judgment in Isa. 38:13; Lam. 3:10; Hosea 5:14; 13:8.

Log

A liquid measure found only in Lev. 14:10. It probably held about 1.8 litres.

Longsuffering

God is longsuffering (Exod. 34:6). The meaning is that he would be right to be angry, but he holds back his anger for a while. This gives sinners time to repent (Rom. 2:4; 2 Peter 3:9).

God's people should also be longsuffering (James 5:10). Longsuffering is part of the fruit of the Spirit (Gal. 5:22). Christians face difficulties and people who oppose them, but rather than becoming angry, they should endure with patience.

Lord, LORD

A lord is someone who has power over others. Sometimes the thought of master or owner is included. 'Lord' may be little more than a title of respect given to a stranger (Gen. 19:2; John 11:21; Acts 16:30). 'Lord' was also used by wives of their husbands (Gen. 18:12), slaves of their owners (Gen. 24:12) and of people in authority (Gen. 40:1; 1 Sam. 1:15; 16:16).

God is called LORD. This uses the word in its fullest meaning, showing God's sovereign power. After the Old Testament was completed, the Jews out of respect for the name of God would read aloud 'my Lord' when Yahweh was written. The Greek translation of the Old Testament used the word Lord for the divine name and many translations do the same today.

On a few occasions, the title Lord when given to Christ is simply a term of respect (Matt. 8:2; John 4:11). Examples of an obvious intention to copy the Old Testament's use of Lord for God when talking about Christ can be found (Acts 10:36; John 20:28; Jude 4 — see that the word Lord is used in the next verse for God). This also occurs when the New Testament quotes the Old Testament. In the places where Lord means God in the Old Testament, it means Christ in the New Testament (Isa. 40:3, cf. Matt. 3:3; Ps. 34:8, cf. 1 Peter 2:3).

Lord's Day

See First Day of the Week.

Lots

Lots were used in Old Testament times to find God's will on various matters (Prov. 16:33). These matters included choosing the goats on the Day of Atonement (Lev. 16:8-10), finding a guilty person (Josh. 7:14), dividing the promised land between the tribes (Josh. 14:2), deciding which families should supply provisions for the temple (Neh. 10:34). Other nations also used lots to decide government matters (Esth. 3:7), for dividing spoil (Obadiah 11) and for finding the guilty person (Jonah 1:7).

It is not known exactly how a lot was taken, except that it was thrown in some way. The lot may have been a pebble.

In the New Testament, lots were cast to decide which soldier would receive Christ's garment (Matt. 27:35). The apostles cast lots to find Judas' successor, but after pentecost we do not read any more about lots. From that time, Christians listen to the Spirit for guidance, as he gives them understanding of Scripture teaching.

Love

Love has a wide range of meanings, depending on who is loving and what is loved. It can be the love of a married couple (1 Sam. 1:5; Eph. 5:25), parents for their children (Gen. 22:2; 25:28), a man for his friend (1 Sam. 18:1), a servant for his master (Exod. 21:5), a man for his favourite food (Gen. 27:4), the greedy for wealth (Eccles. 5:10), the wicked for evil (Ps. 52:3), the righteous for truth and peace (Zech. 8:19).

God loves his chosen people, and this is not because of anything lovable in them (Deut. 7:8). Because God loves them, he saves them (Deut. 4:37; John 3:16). Love can be very strong in mankind, but God's love is much greater, endless in its power and size (Isa. 49:15; Eph. 4:18,19). Love is so much part of God's being that John wrote: 'God is love'. The deepest expression of that love was in sending his Son to die for sinners (1 John 4:7-10).

A special type of love exists between the Persons of the Godhead. Christ was God's beloved one (Mark 1:11; John 3:35; Col. 1:13). Christ loved God and told others to do the same (Mark 12:30).

God commands his people to love him (Deut. 6:5). This love includes devotion to God (Jer. 2:20 and delight in being in his presence (Ps.16:11; 42:1,2). However, love to God is not genuine unless there is obedience. God's people show their love for him by their obedience (Deut. 6:5-9; 1 John 5:3), and obedience is the way that God tests our love (Deut. 13:3).

God's people should love other people. In the Old Testament, this is love for the neighbour (Lev. 19:18), who would normally be a fellow Israelite. In the New Testament, the mark by which outsiders know that people are Christians is their love for each other (John 13:34; 1 John 3:11).

Christians should also love all who are in need (Luke 25-37). They should do good to all, but especially to those who are Christians (Gal. 6:10). They should even love their enemies and those who persecute them (Matt. 5:44). Like their love for God, their love for their fellows should not stop at feelings, but should lead to doing something to help (1 John 3:16,17).

Like all Christian virtues, love comes from God (1 John 4:7). God loved his people while they were still his enemies (Rom. 5:8-10) and hated him (John 15:18). Christians love God and other people because they have first experienced God's love themselves (1 John 4:19), are taught by God to love (1 Thess. 4:9) and have the Spirit of God in them giving the ability to love (Gal. 5:22).

Of course, this does not mean that those who are not Christians are not able to love. But they cannot love God in the way that God demands because this love wants only to live for God and to obey him. And unbelievers cannot love their fellows in the way that Christ loved his people, for true love is love in the power of God's Spirit.

Love Feasts

This term appears only in Jude 12 but the New Testament refers to the practice elsewhere. A love feast was a fellowship meal which during the period when the New Testament was written was part of the Lord's Supper.

The original Lord's Supper was a full meal, the passover, which was immediately followed by Christ passing around the bread and wine which symbolized his body and blood (Mark 14:17-26). In the New Testament church, this practice of a meal ending with the eucharist continued (Acts 2:46; 20:11).

Paul had to correct the rich members at Corinth who misused this fellowship meal. At the Lord's Supper they gorged themselves while the poor looked on and went hungry (1 Cor. 11:21,22,33,34).

Peter wrote about false teachers who thought that being free from the law meant they could indulge themselves, and they did so at the love feasts (2 Peter 2:13).

See Communion.

Loving-kindness

The Hebrew word 'cheseth' (loving-kindness) means a kindness given because of love shown to someone who is to be pitied. This feeling of kindness leads to a kind act (see Ps. 103:4).

A popular view is that 'cheseth' means loyalty to a covenant. God's 'cheseth' therefore means his mercy given because he is bound to them by his covenant. However, 'cheseth' does not always mean loyalty to a covenant. There are several instances in the Hebrew Bible where it is used where there is no hint of a covenant (e.g. Ruth 3:10; 1 Kings 20:31).

In any case, although God shows mercy because he has promised mercy in his covenants with people, it is not true that his covenant comes first. He had mercy on his people first in love, and it was that mercy which led to his making his covenant with them.

Lucifer

This name comes from the Latin Vulgate translation of Isa. 14:12, which is copied by some older translations of the Bible. The Hebrew name means 'shining one' and the Latin Lucifer means 'light-bearer' or refers to the planet Venus. In heathen religions at the time, Venus was personified into the god Ishtar.

The meaning of Isa. 14:12-15 is that the king of Babylon (v. 4) sees himself as glorious and powerful, even godlike, but he was going to have a great fall. The mountain (v. 13) is Mount Zaphon where the pagan gods were thought to live.

Some ancient interpreters applied Isa. 14:12 to Christ's description of Satan's fall (Luke 10:18) and said Lucifer was Satan. This goes against the clear statement that the king of Babylon is meant. Also, Satan's fall from heaven was not followed immediately by a full lack of power and death as Isa. 14:12-15 shows.

Calling oneself the Morning Star is an example of great pride. Only Christ has the true right to that name (Rev. 22:16).

Lust

This word sometimes appears in the New Testament as a sin (1 Peter 4:3). The Greek word originally used means any kind of strong desire. The desire can be good or bad. It is used in a good sense in Luke 22:15; Phil. 1:23; 1 Thess. 2:17. However, when the desires are against God's will, they are sinful.

Strong desire is not sinful in itself. It is only sinful if the thing desired is sinful.

Lycaonia

This was part of the Roman province of Galatia in Asia Minor. It was inhabited by the Lycaones, who had their own language. The word only appears in the New Testament in Acts 14:6,11.

Magi (wise men)

'Magi' was originally the name of a tribe of Medes. They were a priestly tribe who were interested in studying the stars. The name Magi then became used for other priests among the Medes and Persians. There were similar people a little earlier in Babylon (Dan. 1:20).

It is possible that the Magi of Matt. 2:1-12 came from a similar group, but we cannot be sure. All we know for certain is that they came from east of Palestine and studied the stars.

Magic, Magician

Magic is using supernatural or occult methods to find out something (as in divination), or to influence events or people. Spells, charms and suchlike are often used in magic. In the Bible magicians are found at work in Egypt (Gen. 41:8; Exod. 7:11), Canaan and surrounding areas (Num. 22:7; Deut. 18:14), Babylon (Isa. 47:9-13; Dan. 2:2), Israel (Micah. 5:12; Ezek. 13:17-23) and in the New Testament (Acts 8:9).

The Bible is always against the use of magic (Lev. 19:26). The law of Moses put the death penalty on the practice (Exod. 22:18; Lev. 20:27). Jezebel (2 Kings 9:22) and Manasseh (2 Kings 21:6) who were perhaps the two most corrupt rulers in Israel, encouraged witchcraft and magic.

The fact that the Bible strongly opposes the use of magic shows that there is a supernatural reality behind it, which is at enmity to God.

Malice

This word appears in some lists of sins in the New Testament (e.g. Col. 3:8; Titus 3:30) and in other places. It can mean wickedness in general, but more often means a desire to do harm to others.

Mammon

The original Greek word means wealth, or profit. The word does not necessarily have a bad meaning. Seeking after wealth for oneself cannot mix with true religion. You cannot serve God and mammon (Matt. 6:24).

The word also appears in Luke 16:9,11,13.

Man

Man is a part of nature. God created mankind along with all the other parts of nature (Gen. 1) and he used the dust of the ground to make Adam (Gen. 2:7). At the same time, mankind is above nature, for Man alone was made in the image of God (Gen. 1:27). [By Man in this article, mankind - male and female — is meant.]

The Bible presents Man as a united being. We read of his spirit, soul, body, mind, flesh, will, emotions, conscience, but these are not to be thought of as parts of Man which can be separated from the other parts like building blocks. These are all different ways in which the whole person is seen or acts. Man's spirit, for instance, refers to the whole person in relation to God (Rom. 8:16), flesh refers to his weakness (or sinful nature - Gal. 5:19) in contrast to God's power and purity (Ps. 78:39). Man is always this whole being, although his body will be changed to a resurrection body from the earthly body which returns to the ground (1 Cor. 15:35-49).

The Bible does not define the phrase 'the image of God'. It cannot mean that Man looks like God, because God is Spirit (John 4:24) and is therefore invisible (1 Tim. 1:17), without a body. However, the Bible does show how the image of God is seen in Man.

In Gen. 1:26-30 God's image in Man gives authority over the rest of nature. Man, of course, is still under God's rule (1:28; 2:17). He rules and subdues nature as God's representative, that is, in the way that God wants it ruled. Mankind may use creation for their own needs, such as food (Gen. 1:29; 9:3), clothing (3:21), farming (Exod. 23:12), transport (Matt. 21:1-7). They must care for creation (Gen. 6:19,20; Exod. 23:5; Deut. 25:4). Cruelty is not godlike behaviour.

The image of God is seen in righteousness and holiness (Eph. 4:24). God is holy and Man was made holy. Man was pure in everything he thought, said or did, and he had a special relationship with God. Adam's one desire was to please God. That should be the desire of every human being.

This is close to what Col. 3:10 says about the image of God being seen in knowledge. This knowledge is the knowledge of God and includes communion with God (Gen. 2) and obedience to his commands.

Sin, however, spoiled the image of God in Man. Nature was affected by Man's sin. It is no longer under Man's rule (Heb. 2:8); rather Man is under nature's rule, for it brings hardship, disease and death (Gen. 3:17-19). Also, Man is no longer righteous and holy, but sinful. He no longer knows God (Matt. 11:27) but makes his own gods instead (Rom. 1:21-25) and makes up his own rules as to what is right or wrong (Rom. 10:3).

Christ is the true image of God in a way that Adam never was. Not only is Christ in control of nature (Heb. 2:8; Mark 4:41), righteous and holy in all he does (Heb. 4:15) and knows God perfectly (John 10:15) but he also shares the nature of God (Heb. 1:3).

By their being in Christ, the lost image of God in sinners is restored. They are made new and sin is defeated in them through their faith in Christ (Eph. 4:20-24). This makes Christ the new Adam, the first Man in the renewed humanity. Just as being part of the first Adam through our natural birth makes people sinful and brings death, being part of the new Adam through faith, or the second birth, brings sinners righteousness and life (Rom. 5:12-21; 1 Cor. 15:20-22,45). Also, just as the fall of Man spoiled nature, so the salvation of Man through Christ will bring a new heaven and a new earth, a restored creation (Rom. 8:18-21; Rev. 21:1).

Manna

God first gave the Israelites manna six weeks after they left Egypt. He continued to send it until they reached Canaan forty years later. It came with the dew each morning except the Sabbath and melted in the sun's heat. It was in the form of small white wafers and tasted like honey (Exod. 16:31).

Each Israelite had one omer (about 2.2 litres) of manna each day except on the day before the Sabbath when two omers were collected. However much they collected, they had no more and no less than one omer each.

When they first saw manna, the Israelites asked, 'What is it?' They called it manna because the Hebrew word for 'what' is 'ma'.

By means of the manna, God taught his people obedience (Exod. 16:28-30) and dependence on himself and his Word (Deut. 8:3). Jesus said that manna was a picture of himself, except that those who have Christ as the bread of life live for ever (John 6:49-58).

Man of lawlessness, Man of sin

Some Greek manuscripts of 2 Thess. 2:3 read 'man of sin'; others 'man of lawlessness'. Lawlessness is probably the correct reading, but there is no real difference between the two readings. Sin is lawlessness (1 John 3:4).

Man of lawlessness is Paul's name for the anti-Christ found in John's letters (1 John 4:3). There is a similar teaching in parts of Revelation and Paul's portrayal of the anti-Christ has in it hints of the Old Testament (Isa. 14:13,14; Ezek. 28:2; Dan. 7:7-26; 8:9-12; 11:30-32).

Paul says that the man of lawlessness will appear just before Christ's second coming. He will oppose the true God and set himself up as God (2 Thess. 2:4). He will even do miracles using Satan's power (2 Thess. 2:9).

Like John, Paul saw the work of anti-Christ already in the world as he wrote his letter (2 Thess. 2:7). There are many today and indeed have been through the whole of history who have opposed God and set themselves up as god in his place. But the final conflict between Christ and anti-Christ is yet to come, because the anti-Christ has not yet appeared. See Anti-Christ.

Marah

Marah is the Hebrew word for 'bitter'. The Israelites gave this name to the first camp they set up after crossing the Red Sea because the water there was bitter (Exod. 15:23).

The name by which Naomi wanted to be called after she returned from Moab is the same basic word (Ruth 1:20).

Market, Market place

In the Old Testament, a market was the part of a town where trading was carried out. The word in the New Testament means the place of assembly. In addition to trading, children would play there (Luke 7:32), men would look for work (Matt. 20:3) and people would greet each other (Matt. 23:7).

In Gentile towns, market places were often influenced by the Greek and Roman culture. They were wide, paved streets with sheltered places for walking on each side. Magistrates would judge (Acts 16:19) and philosophers and religious teachers would dispute there (Acts 17:17,18).

Marks

Various marks are placed on people in the Bible. Some of these are literal marks that can be seen; others, not visible, are symbols of a deeper mark in a person's life.

God put a mark on Cain (Gen. 4:15). We do not know where it was, or what it was like, but obviously it would be noticed. God put it there to protect him from retribution.

The marks in Lev. 19:28 seem to be tattoo marks. No doubt they were forbidden because they had pagan or magical associations.

A mark was placed on the forehead of the righteous in Ezek. 9:4,6. In Revelation, a similar mark is called a seal, or the name of Christ (7:3; 14:1; 22:4). These are not physical marks but symbols of the fact that Christ has marked his elect. This inner mark gives them protection from judgment.

The mark of the beast in Rev. 13:16,17 appears to be a parallel to the mark of the righteous. Again, it is best not to think of this as a literal mark but a symbol that the behaviour and characters of people show that they belong to the power symbolized by the beast of Rev. 13:11.

Paul said he bore 'the marks of Christ' — sometimes called 'stigmata' (Gal. 6:17). Several different theories have been put forward to explain what Paul meant by the phrase. The most obvious theory is that he meant the scars where he had been whipped and stoned. These scars were won while he was doing the work of Christ which showed his devotion to the gospel and to his Lord and Saviour.

Marriage

God created mankind as male and female (Gen. 1:27) who were to live together as man and wife (Gen. 2:24). Marriage is not just a private matter between two people, but the union must be recognized by the society around them. The couple need to accept each other in a public ceremony, and the society around must respect the sacredness of that marriage bond.

God included marriage in his creation of mankind for three main purposes: having children (Gen. 1:27), companionship (Gen. 2:18) and the regulation of sexuality (Gen. 2:24). Note that 'one flesh' (1 Cor. 6:16) includes sexual union. But 'one flesh' means more than that: it also means the oneness of the relationship between man and woman at a deeper level. The sexual aspect is a symbol of that deeper unity and also helps towards that bond.

In Old Testament times, another important aspect of marriage is that children carry on the family name and receive the family inheritance (Num. 27:4). A law in Mesopotamia allowed a barren wife to give her female slave to her husband in order to have children through the slave. The child was legally the wife's child. Examples of this occur in Gen. 16:2; and 30:3. Leah went beyond this law (Gen. 30:9) because she already had children when she received more through her maid.

Although this practice was legal and therefore accepted in Abraham's and Jacob's culture, the Bible does not give its approval to it. Instead, a man had to die before anything was done about his name and inheritance. If he died childless, his widow married his brother or another close relative and their first child was legally the dead man's heir (Deut. 25:5-10; cf. Ruth 4:17). The name 'Levirate marriage' was given to this custom. Levirate comes from the Latin word 'Levir', meaning brother-in-law. Gen. 38:8-10 shows that this type of marriage existed before Moses and the law in Deuteronomy.

The culture in Bible times assumed that marriage was normal and to remain unmarried was exceptional (Jer. 16:2; Matt. 19:10-12). Polygamy (a man having more than one wife) is not forbidden in the Old Testament but it is clear that God's intention was for a one man, one woman, union. God made only one woman for Adam (Gen. 2:22). The Bible shows that polygamy leads to trouble in the family (Gen. 16:1-6,12; 30:1; 1 Sam. 1:6). The law forbade the king to have a large harem (Deut. 17:17) and when this law was ignored, trouble occurred (1 Kings 11:1-8). God's pattern for marriage, therefore, is a union of two people.

Marriage is a life-long partnership. Moses' law allowed for divorce (Deut. 24:1-4) but Christ made it clear that this law was given to protect the woman from the results of sin (Matt. 19:8). God's intention is that the marriage should continue until one of the partners dies. Then the surviving partner is free to remarry (1 Cor. 7:8,9; 1 Tim. 5:14).

Married people have sexual relationships only with each other. Adultery (sexual intercourse when at least one person is married to someone else) is a very serious sin (Gen. 20:3; Exod. 20:14; Lev. 20:10). Sexual activity between two unmarried people is also sinful. Deut. 22:14 shows that the bride at her first wedding is expected to be a virgin. Deut. 22:25-29; 2 Sam. 13:11-13 show that physical union should take place only after marriage and within marriage.

In Bible times, marriage was usually arranged by the husband's parents, but sometimes by the wife's (Ruth 3:1; 1 Sam. 18:21). On a few occasions we find a husband choosing a bride (Gen. 34:4,8; Judg. 14:2) and Rebekah was asked whether she would go with Abraham's servant (Gen. 24:58). People in certain relationships were not allowed to marry each other (Lev. 18).

When choosing partners, it was important to make sure that the relationship would help to promote godliness. Gen. 6:2 shows ungodly unions. Abraham (Gen. 24:3,4) and Isaac (Gen. 28:1,2) on the other hand were careful to ensure that Isaac and Jacob married women who would be worthy of their God. Paul taught that believers should only marry other believers (1 Cor. 7:39).

Before a marriage took place, the couple were betrothed. This was done before two witnesses and was almost as binding as marriage. The betrothed couple were sometimes called husband and wife (Deut. 22:23,24; Matt. 1:19) and the betrothal needed a divorce to break it (Matt. 1:19).

Gifts were made at the time of betrothal. A marriage present was given by the groom to the bride's family (cf. Gen. 24:53; 29:20). It acted as compensation for the family who gave up their daughter and helped to seal the covenant between the two families and join them together. The dowry was the bride's father's gift to the bride or groom (Gen. 24:59,61 - servants; Judg. 1:15 - land). The groom gave the bride a present, often jewelry or clothes (Gen. 24:53).

At the wedding, the bride wore special clothes and jewels (Ps. 45:13,14; Isa. 51:10; Rev. 21:2). The groom wore a garland (Isa. 51:10) and the guests also wore festive clothes (Matt. 22:11,12). Royal brides had maids attending them and probably other brides had them too (Ps. 45:13,14; possibly Matt. 15:1). The groom had his companions (Judg. 14:11; Matt. 9:15).

On the evening of the wedding, the groom and his friends processed to the bride's house and he brought her to his own or his parents' house for the wedding supper. The procession included singing, music and dancing (Jer. 7:34). Sometimes the wedding supper was held at the bride's parents' house (Gen. 29:22).

During the wedding supper, the husband covered the bride with the skirts of his clothes (Ruth 3:9; Ezek. 16:8). This showed that she was his alone, and also under his protection. The couple covenanted to be faithful to each other (Prov. 2:17; Mal. 2:14).

Before the wedding, a bridechamber was prepared. The parents (Gen. 29:23) or sometimes friends escorted the couple to this room where the marriage was consummated. A blood-stained cloth was shown later to prove that the bride was a virgin (Deut. 22:14-21). The festivities would then continue for a week or so (Gen. 29:27), with music and song (Ps. 45; 78:63) and joking, such as riddles (Judg. 14:12).

The relationship between God and Israel (Isa. 62:5) and Christ and the church (Eph. 5:25-27; Rev. 21:2) were pictured as a marriage. Israel and the church were the brides.

Medes, Media

This Indo-Aryan people had settled in what is now north-west Iran by the ninth century BC. Assyrians raided their country for horses, and later had some control over the Medes. Sargon I of Assyria deported some Israelites to Media in 721BC (2 Kings 17:6).

The Medes joined the Scythians and Cimmerians in a rebellion in 631BC. Later they allied with the Babylonians, defeating Nineveh in 612BC and the last traces of the Assyrian Empire 610-609BC.

While Babylon became dominant west of the river Tigris, the Medes enlarged their empire to the east and north of Babylon. Their empire stretched from south-east of the Black Sea to what is now Afghanistan. In 550BC the vassal king, Cyrus the Persian, revolted and took over the empire. His family was related to the Median princes and he gave the Medes positions of authority. Their customs and laws were combined with those of the Persians.

Mediator

A mediator tries to restore a good relationship between two parties who are alienated from each other.

Although the word mediator does not appear often in the Bible, the idea is an important one and often occurs. The Old Testament prophets and priests, for example, were all mediators between God and his people.

Moses was the most important Old Testament mediator. He stood between God and Israel to receive and explain the covenant and the laws. But there is a far greater Mediator than Moses, and that is Christ (Heb. 8:6). Christ is the only Mediator between sinful people and the holy God (1 Tim. 2:5) and has dealt with the state of war between sinners and God by making peace by his death on the cross (Col. 1:20). He continues to mediate for Christians, as all prayer and worship is directed to God through Christ.

Meditation

Biblical meditation means 'filling the mind with thoughts about God, his works and his Word'. We must not confuse this with what meditation means in other religions and in some traditions of Christianity.

Old Testament saints meditated on God's law in order that they might obey it (Josh. 1:8; Ps. 1:2; 119:48,78,99). They also meditated on what God had done in the past (Ps. 77:12-20) to give them hope for his help in the present (vv. 1-9). Other subjects of meditation are God's acts in creation (Ps. 104, note v. 34), his promises (Ps. 119:148), his unfailing love (Ps. 48:9). As well as being a path to obedience and hope, meditation is itself an act of worship (Ps. 19:14; 104:34).

One Hebrew word translated 'meditate' means 'a low sound'. The same word is used of a lion growling over its prey (Isa. 31:4) and a dove's moaning (Isa. 38:14). No doubt people read God's law aloud to themselves. This emphasizes that God's Word is central in meditation. In fact, the saints meditated on God's law day and night (Josh. 1:8; Ps. 1:3; cf Deut. 6:6-9). Meditation does not have to be aloud. In Ps. 39:3 it is obviously silent, because David speaks aloud after his meditation.

Another Hebrew word for meditation means 'considering a matter in one's mind'. Meditation does not simply repeat words of Scripture but thinks carefully about them. Two words used with meditate in the Psalms are 'remember' and 'consider' (Ps. 77:3,6; 119:45; 143:5). [In Hebrew poetry, a thought is often repeated using different words. In such a couplet, the parallel words have the same meaning.] Meditation, then, is a careful consideration of God's Word, finding out what it means, and how it affects our lives. Our memory of other parts of Scripture and our experiences in the past, help us in our thinking.

We do not often find the word 'meditate' in the New Testament. However, Christians are told that their minds are renewed (Eph. 4:17,18,23) and this renewal of their minds leads to a changed life (Rom. 12:2). Believers should set their minds on heavenly (Col. 3:2) and excellent things (Phil. 4:8). They should work hard with their minds in order to know how to live holy lives.

Meekness

The Old Testament word is the same as the one for someone who is poor and afflicted, who learns how to endure trials patiently and humbly. Meekness is this patient endurance which will not hit back at people or circumstances which are against them. For example, Moses did not resent his brother and sister when they spoke against him (Num. 12:1-3).

Christ was meek and gentle (2 Cor. 10:1). Meekness refers to a person's inner attitude; gentleness refers to the outward acts which arise from a meek attitude. Christ's meekness was his inner calm in the face of opposition, having no resentment in his heart.

Christians too are to be meek people (Col. 3:12). They can trust God who guides everything in their lives, however painful, for their good. Although a meek person is outwardly gentle, this calmness comes from a great inner strength. For the Christian, this strength comes from the Holy Spirit (Gal. 5:23).

Melchizedek

This king of Salem (Jerusalem) met Abram after Abram defeated the king of Sodom and his allies (Gen. 14:18-20). 'Melchizedek' means 'King of Righteousness'. He was priest of God Most High.

In Ps. 110 David says, 'The LORD said unto my Lord' (v. 1) ... 'Thou art a priest for ever after the order of Melchizedek' (v. 4). Mark 12:35-37 makes it clear that David's 'Lord' is Christ. So it is Christ who is a Priest for ever after the order of Melchizedek.

Hebrews takes up the Melchizedek reference (5:6,9; 6:20 and particularly chapter 7). The writer shows that Christ's priesthood was not of the old order of Aaron. Those priests inevitably died (v. 23). Christ's priesthood is eternal, because it is patterned on the priesthood of Melchizedek.

Melchizedek, of course, was not an eternal being. He was a man. But he appears in Scripture as eternal because he has no recorded parentage, date of birth or day of death (v. 3). It was vital for these facts to be known about an earthly priest (cf. Nehem. 7:63,64). God purposely withheld these facts about Melchizedek so that he would appear to be an eternal being and therefore a type of Christ the eternal priest 'who is made, not after the law of a carnal commandment', i.e. not according to the laws which appointed earthly priests, 'but after the power of an endless life' (Heb. 7:16).

Mene, Mene, Tekel, Upharsin

These are Aramaic words which were written on the wall at Belshazzar's feast (Dan. 5:25). Aramaic is a language close to Hebrew and was spoken widely in western Asia. It was the language of diplomacy and commerce. We do not know why the Babylonians could not read the words (vv. 7,8). Perhaps it was in a script used in western Asia but not in Babylon. Or the letters may have been unusual on purpose so that the readers needed God's help to understand them.

The words mean 'numbered, numbered, weighed and divided'. (The U of Upharsin means 'and'.) When Daniel gives the meaning, he gives the singular form of Pharsin, which is Peres. He uses this word also as a pun on the name Persian.

Some people have pointed out that the words could also be read as three different weights — mina, shekel and half-shekel. This may be so, but it does not help with the interpretation which is clearly given in Dan. 5. Daniel's statement that the Babylonian empire is to be divided did not mean that the Medes and Persians would have distinct parts. The idea is that the Babylonian empire would be destroyed by the united power of the Medes and Persians.

Mercy

God is the father of mercies (2 Cor. 1:3). This means that all mercy comes ultimately from God. He shows mercy to those who fear him (Luke 1:50), especially by saving them from their sin (Eph. 2:4,5). God does not show us mercy because we deserve it (Titus 3:5) but only because he decides freely to give it (Exod. 33:19). He shows mercy because he is a merciful God and not for any other reason. His mercy is part of his electing love.

When people ask God for mercy, they understand that they have a need that they cannot supply for themselves. They fully depend on the one who can meet that need — God. Believers may pray for mercy knowing that God will give it (Heb. 4:16).

When Christians realise that God is merciful to them, they also must show mercy to others (Luke 6:36). In fact, they can also be assured that they will receive God's mercy as they in turn are merciful to those who need their help (Matt. 5:7).

Christ showed mercy during his ministry on earth (Mark 10:47-52). By his death on the cross he became the merciful high priest (Heb. 2:17).

See Grace.

See also Loving Kindness.

Mercy-Seat

This was a slab of pure gold placed on top of the ark in the tabernacle (Exod. 25:17). On top of this at each end was a solid gold cherub, facing towards the middle (vv. 18-20).

The Hebrew word comes from the same root as the word for atonement. This makes the mercy-seat the place of propitiation. Blood was sprinkled on the mercy-seat on the Day of Atonement (Lev. 16:14). God spoke to Moses above this place of atonement.

Some people think that the root meaning of the Hebrew word means 'to cover' and therefore say that the mercy-seat was simply a covering or lid with no further significance. There is no evidence that the Hebrew word is used to mean simply a cover. The Hebrew words KPR (cover) and Kapporeth (mercy-seat) and Kippur (atonement) are all connected in meaning. Certainly, KPR is not just a cover but means 'to propitiate' in the sense of covering over sin against the wrath of God.

See Atonement.

Mesopotamia

Mesopotamia is a Greek word meaning 'between the rivers'. In some Bible versions, it is used to translate the Hebrew for the two rivers of the Arameans — today's East Syria and North Iraq. The New Testament Mesopotamia includes all of Iraq. Examples of use: Gen. 24:10; Acts 2:9.

Messiah

The Hebrew word from which we get 'messiah' means 'anointed one'. The Messiah is the man promised in the Old Testament whom God chose to be King and Saviour of his people, and Conqueror and Judge of the nations.

This promise goes back to the beginning of history. Immediately after the fall, God said that an offspring of Eve would defeat Satan (Gen. 3:15). The result would be a return to the peace and prosperity of Eden (cf. Isa. 11:6-8; Amos 9:13-15). The Messiah or Christ is therefore the last Adam (Rom. 5:12-19; 1 Cor. 15:45-49). 'Messiah' and 'Christ' have the same meaning.

Shortly before he died, Moses predicted that a prophet like him would rise from Israel (Deut. 18:15). God sent many prophets to Israel but none equalled the greatness of Moses (Deut. 34:10). Moses laid the foundation of worship and law for the new Israelite nation in Canaan. The later prophets called the nation back to Moses' teaching, although they looked forward to something better, a new covenant (Jer. 32:36-41). The Messiah brought in this new covenant and is therefore that prophet who Moses promised would come (Acts 3:22-26; Heb. 3:1-6).

The Messiah is not only a second and greater Adam and a second and greater Moses, but also a second and greater David. Jacob said that God's King would come from the tribe of Judah (Gen. 49:10).

David was from Judah and God promised him that his descendants would rule for ever (2 Sam. 7:11-16). David's family ruled for nearly 500 years until the exile, but the Israelites expected the Messiah to be a king who would be more like David in his conquering power and godliness. This Messiah would defeat all opposition and rule over the nations (Ps. 2). His rule would bring righteousness and would last for ever (Ps. 45:4-7). Jesus Christ is this Son of David (Matt. 1:1-17; Heb. 1:8).

The Old Testament prophets look forward to this second David (Ezek. 34:23). Sometimes he is called the Branch of David (Jer. 23:5) or the Branch (Zech.3:8). Isaiah talks of a servant who will not only reign (Isa. 42:1-4) but will also suffer for his people (Isa. 50:4-9). This element of suffering is very important if we want to understand how Christ understood his messiahship. Daniel, on the other hand, speaks of a glorious person, the Son of Man, who is worshipped by the nations over which he rules for ever (Dan. 7:13,14). Jesus quotes from these verses when he describes his Second Coming in Mark 13:26; 14:62.

The Jews looked forward to their Messiah but did not acknowledge him when he came. Despite this, the Christian message is that Jesus is the Messiah, the Son of God (Matt. 16:16).

See Christ

Millennium

In Rev. 20:1-6 we read of a thousand years where Satan is bound and the saints are raised from the dead to reign with Christ. Revelation is a difficult book to understand because it is full of symbols. Different teachers have different views on how the book should be understood. This has led to three main views on the thousand years' reign (the millennium).

Millennialism says that the reign is a literal one. Christ will come again, will bind up Satan and reign on earth for a thousand years with the raised saints. Then Satan will be released for a while, but will be defeated. After that, the judgment will take place and eternity follow. This view is sometimes known as 'Pre-millennial'.

A-Millennialism sees the thousand years as symbolic. It is a picture of the church age, that is, the time between Christ's ministry and his second coming. There will be no literal thousand years' reign on earth after Christ's coming, but judgment and eternity will follow straightaway. The binding of Satan took place at Christ's first coming to earth when Christ defeated Satan on the cross. The resurrection of the saints (Rev. 20:4) either stands for the Christians' new life in Christ, or for their life with Christ in heaven after martyrdom, in the case of those who are martyred.

Post-Millennialism also sees the thousand years as symbolic and, like a-millennialism, says that Christ's coming will immediately be followed by judgment and eternity. They see the millennium as God at work in the church age, when the kingdom of God will be set up through the preaching of the gospel. Society will become so Christian that the earth will enjoy a golden age, which will be followed by the Second Coming.

Miracles

A miracle is the result of God working in nature in a special way. Miracles are part of his self-revelation to mankind, to nourish faith in his intention to save. Some miracles are unusual. One boy's lunch does not normally feed five thousand people; people do not normally walk on water; lame people do not normally get up suddenly and dance; dead people do not normally become alive again. Those miracles could be called supernatural because they are above what is normal or natural. In fact, they contradict what is normal. Other miracles do not necessarily contradict what is normal. The disease God sent on the Philistines in 1 Sam. 5:9; 6:4,5 seems to be bubonic plague which is a terrible disease spread by rat fleas, giving tumours to those who are infected. This instance is a special use by God of what is normal in nature.

The created world belongs to God. He made it (Gen. 1), he owns it (Ps. 24:1), he keeps it going (Ps. 104:27-30; Col. 1:17) and he will renew it at the end of this age (Rev. 21:1). Scientists tell us that things happen on earth because of what they call the laws of nature. A stone falls to the ground not because a spirit throws it there but because of the law of gravity. Everything natural that happens has a cause and that cause is also a part of nature. Malaria is caused by a bacterium which gets into the body through a mosquito bite.

Christians agree with this, but they add that God made the laws of nature and works in them. Rain is caused naturally by changes in the air pressure but it is also true that God sends the rain (Job 38:22-30; Matt. 5:45) because God controls all creation. However, certain of his acts have a special meaning which is connected with his plan to save. These events are what we call miracles.

Three main words are used to describe miracles. The first means a powerful act - found, for instance, in Ps. 106:8; Acts 2:22. God is a mighty God (Isa. 9:6) and he does mighty things. These may be awe-inspiring, such as commanding the storm to stop (Mark 4:41), or it may be that God's power is seen in his working through weak people (2 Cor.12:9). The Greek word for 'power' in this verse is the same as for 'miracle' in other parts of the New Testament.

The second word is 'wonders' (Exod. 15:11; Rom. 15:19). Miracles cause amazement, especially when they are supernatural.

The third word is 'signs' (Isa. 7:11; John 2:11). God does not do miracles for their own sake. Christ refused to be just a wonder-worker (Matt. 12:38,39). God's miracles point to some truth that he wants to say. Christ's signs, for instance, show that he is the one promised in the Old Testament (Matt. 11:2-6), the Christ, the Son of God (John 20:30-31). The fact that God's miracles are not just to make people amazed but are to teach something is shown by Acts 2:19, which is a quote from the Old Testament. The word 'wonders' is always linked with the word 'signs'.

A miracle is God acting in a powerful and amazing way, telling us something about himself. But we must not think that all wonders and signs are God at work. God's enemies sometimes do wonders (Exod. 7:11; Matt. 7:22; Rev. 13:13). As with everything else, the proper test is whether the message with the miracle confirms God's Word (Deut. 13:1-5).

God has a message for us when he does miracles. Obviously, therefore, faith is important. Miracles help to strengthen faith in God's intention to save. Gideon's faith, for example, was strengthened by the miracle of the fleece (Judg. 6:36-40). John recorded Christ's miracles for the same reason (John 20:30,31).

Faith, however weak (Mark 9:23,24), must come before the miracle. Seeing a miracle will not lead unbelievers to faith but rather it will harden them against God (Exod. 8:32; John 12:37). When unbelievers see a miracle, they try to find some natural reason for it so that they do not need to believe in the supernatural (Mark 3:22).

This helps us to understand why Jesus did only a few miracles in Nazareth (Mark 6:5). The unbelief of the Nazarenes did not make Jesus unable to heal, but it made miracles the wrong thing for him to do. Without faith to understand the message that the miracle taught, such miracles would have been no more than meaningless signs. Jesus would not do that. Such miracles would only have hardened the people's hearts against the gospel.

Another point to consider is the fact that the supernatural miracles did not happen throughout the whole of biblical history. God sent them at critical points in the history of his plan of salvation. The two most critical times in the history of God's plan of salvation are the exodus of Israel from Egypt and the ministry of Christ. Even in Christ's ministry, we find that miracles are almost entirely absent during the week before the crucifixion. We also find miracles in the days of Elijah and Elisha, when the northern kingdom was most likely to reject God; and we also find them in the days of the apostles when the New Testament church was being established. There are a few other miracles in the Old Testament but there were also long periods when no miracles were performed.

Moab

Moab was the son of Lot by his eldest daughter (Gen. 19:37). The Moabites settled in the plateau east of the Dead Sea before the exodus (Exod. 15:15). Sihon, king of the Amorites, pushed them back to the river Arnon southwards. The Arnon flows into the middle of the eastern side of the Dead Sea.

Balak the Moabite king tried to stop the Israelites when they passed through his land but he did not succeed (Num. 22-24; Judg. 11:17). God told Moses not to attack Moab (Deut. 2:9) but because they hired Balaam to curse Israel, no Moabite could afterwards go into the tabernacle (Deut. 23:3).

A later king of Moab, Eglon, ruled over Jericho and that area of Israel for eighteen years until Ehud killed him (Judg. 3:12-30). Saul fought the Moabites (1 Sam. 14:47). David sent his parents to Moab for safety (1 Sam. 22:3,4). One of David's ancestors was a Moabite (Ruth 1:14; 4:13-22).

When David became king, he conquered Moab (2 Sam. 8:12). Probably Moab broke free again after Solomon's death, when Israel divided into two nations. An inscription written by Mesha, king of Moab, tells us that Moab was conquered by Omri, king of the northern state of Israel. Mesha gained Moabite freedom after Ahab's death (2 Kings 1:1; 3:4-27). With others, Moabites attacked Judah at about this time (2 Chr. 20). Later, Assyria subdued Moab but when the Assyrian empire fell, Moab was again free. They raided Judah (2 Kings 24:2), but the Babylonians under Nebuchadrezzar conquered them. After the Babylonians, Moab country was controlled by Persians and Arabs, and Moab ceased to exist as a nation. Moabite people were, however, still found in Ezra's day and Nehemiah's day (Ezra. 9:1; Neh. 13:23).

Moab's main god was Chemosh. 2 Kings 3:27 shows that Moabites sacrificed their children to this god.

Molech

This god was worshipped by the Ammonites and was particularly denounced in the Old Testament because of the practice of sacrificing children to it (Lev. 20:1-6; 2 Kings 23:10; Jer. 32:35). The Phoenicians and other peoples in northern Canaan also worshipped Molech and practised child-sacrifice. The name means 'the one who rules'. The Hebrew name would normally be melek, but the name was combined with the vowels of the Hebrew 'bosheth' (shame) to make molek.

Money-changers

When Jews in New Testament times paid money to the temple — for example, the half-shekel tax (Exod. 30:13) — they had to pay it in a coin from Tyre. This Tyrian shekel was the nearest available to the old Hebrew shekel. The Jews would normally have Greek or Roman coinage and would bring their coins to the money-changers in the temple courts to exchange them for the acceptable Tyrian coins. The money-changers made a charge for this. Jesus ejected the money-changers from the temple (Matt. 21:12; Mark 11:15; John 2:15).

Month

For the Hebrews each month started at the sunset after the thin crescent of the new moon was first visible. As each month lasted either 29 or 30 days, extra months had to be added to ensure that the year started in the spring, and not before. We do not know how they added a month to a year.

In the Bible, the months are numbered: e.g. the second month (Num. 1:10, the tenth month (Esth. 2:16). Months also had names. We only know the names of four of the Hebrew months, but after the exile, Babylonian names were used.

Special offerings were made at the beginning of each month (Num. 28:11-15).

Month No.	Hebrew Name	Babylonian Name	Modern Name
1	Abib	Nisan	March - April
2	Ziw	Iyyar	April - May
3		Siwan	May - June
4		Tammuz	June - July
5		Ab	July - August
6		Elul	August - September
7	Etanim	Tiari	September - October
8	Bul	Marheswan	October - November
9		Kislev	November - December
10		Tebet	December - January
11		Sebat	January - February
12		Adar	February - March

Moses

Moses was born into the tribe of Levi but was brought up as the adopted son of an Egyptian princess. The Egyptians by this time oppressed the Israelites and made them slaves building store cities for the Pharaoh. When Moses was forty years old, he tried to help his fellow Israelites but ran away to Midian because people knew that he had killed an Egyptian for beating an Israelite. In Midian he married the daughter of a Midianite priest and looked after sheep.

Forty years later, God sent Moses back to Egypt to lead Israel out of that country to go to Canaan. Pharaoh only agreed to the Israelites leaving Egypt after ten plagues had devastated Egypt. Pharaoh then changed his mind and sent an army to recapture them, but the Israelites escaped by miraculously crossing the Red Sea on dry ground.

Moses then led the Israelites for a further forty years while they wandered in the Sinai desert. Early in that period, God gave Moses the law at Mount Sinai, with instructions for making the tabernacle and its furnishings. Moses died on Mount Nebo just before the Israelites entered Canaan under Joshua's leadership.

Moses was one of the most important men of the Old Testament. His importance can be seen by the fact that he spoke to God face to face (Num. 12:6-8) and that he, with Elijah, appeared with Christ during the transfiguration (Mark 9:4). This importance is particularly because of his role as the law-giver and it is as law-giver that he is mainly mentioned in the New Testament.

The Books of Moses — Genesis to Deuteronomy — are often called 'The Law'.

Most High

This name for God can appear on its own (Ps. 9:2) or be linked with another name for God (Gen. 14:19; Ps.47:2). In the Bible it always refers to the true God, the God of Israel, but the name is also known to have been used by other Canaanite peoples for the highest god in their religions.

The name Most High shows God as supreme. He is above all other gods who are nothing but worthless idols. He is supreme over all creation.

Mother

Children should give their mothers equal respect to their fathers (Exod. 20:12). The Bible gives mothers a high standing and expects that they should be obeyed (Gen. 28:7; Eph. 6:1). When she is in need, her children should care for her (1 Tim. 5:4). When a man marries, however, his relationship to his mother takes second place to his relationship with his wife (Gen. 2:24).

The Bible sees the mother as one who comforts her children (Isa. 66:13). She also teaches them (Prov. 31:1) and disciplines them (Zech. 13:3).

Murder

In the law of Moses, murder is any unlawful killing of a person except when it was accidental (Num. 35:11,22-25). No distinction is made between a murder which is planned in advance and a murder committed on the spur of the moment because of a sudden passion or after provocation.

The seriousness of the crime comes from it being an attack on the image of God (Gen. 9:6). In the Bible, the death penalty is the only punishment for murder.

Myrrh

An oily, yellowish-brown resin from a small tree found in the Arabian Desert and other parts of Africa. Myrrh was used in the holy anointing oil (Exod. 30:23). It was also used for perfuming clothes (Ps. 45:8) and beds (Prov. 7:17). The Magi gave myrrh to the infant Jesus (Matt. 2:11). It was offered to Christ mixed with wine to relieve his pain on the cross, although he refused to take it (Mark 15:23). Nicodemus used myrrh at Christ's burial (John 19:39). Myrrh came to be used as a symbol of death (Matt. 2:11).

Name

In the Bible, a person's name is more than a means of identification. The name describes the person. The person and name are so closely linked that they can be thought of as being the same.

Superiors gave names to their inferiors. Mothers (Gen. 29:32) and fathers (Gen. 21:3) named their children. Conquering kings named their vassals (2 Kings 24:17). The act of giving a name showed that the person who was named did certain things or had certain duties and responsibilities towards the giver of the name.

Rachel called her second son Ben-oni (Gen. 35:18), showing the relationship between them — that of mother and child. The name means 'Son of my sorrow'. He brought sorrow to her when he was born, because she died. His father, however, thought of the boy in a different way. The child was the son of his favourite wife and was therefore precious to him, as later events confirmed (Gen. 42:33-44:34). Jacob called Ben-oni, Ben-jamin, which means 'Son of my right hand' (Gen. 35:18).

Names may give the circumstances of the person's birth (Ben-oni above, 1 Chr. 4:9), or even the national situation (1 Sam. 4:21). Sometimes the name was a prophecy (Isa. 8:1-5, the name means 'Quick to the plunder, swift to the spoil', Hosea 1:4-9). Other names expressed a hope that they might give some benefit (Gen. 5:29; 29:34). Nabal (fool), seems a strange name to give a child (1 Sam. 25:25). Perhaps an ancestor was foolish and the name passed on (cf. Luke 1:61), or perhaps the name was given as an example of something to avoid.

Changing a name brings a change in a person's dignity or function. God changed Abram and Sarai's names to Abraham and Sarah not long before Isaac was born (Gen. 17:5-8,15,16). God was showing them that their status had changed. They were now to be the founders of his chosen race. A new name may show a change of situation - being saved (Isa. 62:2; 65:15) or being condemned (Jer. 20:3).

Another link between a name and status is found in Phil. 2:9-11. Christ's name is above every other name. His dignity, authority, power is above any other person's, whether human or angelic.

A person and name are so closely linked that one way of saying someone was dead was to say his name was cut off (Deut. 7:24; Josh. 7:9). Also, people did not really know someone until they knew his name (Judg. 13:6).

Sharing a name, on the other hand, brings people close together. A wife shares her husband's name (Isa. 4:1). Jeremiah pleads with God to save Israel because the nation bears God's name. God and his people are closely related (Jer. 14:9).

When a person comes in another's name that other person is reckoned to be present in his representative (1 Sam. 25;9). When someone comes in the Lord's name, God is present in his representative (1 Sam. 17:45-47, cf. v. 37). Likewise, meeting in Christ's name secures his presence (Matt. 18:20).

The phrase 'to call on God's name' (Gen. 4:26; 12:8; 1 Kings 18:24), means to use his name in worship. But calling on God's name also means calling on God himself because God and his name are the same. As the people call, God is present with them. In the same way, a house for God's name is a house for God (Deut. 26:2).

A name tells us something about the person. Revealing a name reveals the person. The mysterious beings who refused to give their names to Jacob (Gen. 32:29) and Manoah (Judg. 13:18) refused to reveal themselves. They remained strangers. This means that when God revealed his name to Moses (Exod. 3:15), it was an act of grace. He showed himself and made knowing him possible.

The point of Exod. 3:15 is not that God told Moses a name that was never known before for Abraham knew this name (Gen. 24:7). But now God revealed the meaning of his name to Moses (v. 14). The patriarchs knew that God was all-powerful (Exod. 6:6-8), but now God's people knew he was eternally the same. Another name for God is found in Exod. 34:14. His name is Jealous which reveals that he is jealous.

From what we have seen, it follows that statements like 'the name of God comes' (Isa. 30:27) means 'God comes'. It therefore means that God, in all his glory and power, comes!

Nazirite

In Old Testament times, men or women who wanted to make a special vow could do so by becoming Nazirites. The name comes from the Hebrew word which means to separate, to consecrate.

Nazirites had to abstain from wine and anything connected with grapes. They did not cut their hair, nor were they to approach a dead body. Nazirites bound themselves to their vow for a set length of time, after which they made an offering. The details of the law are found in Num. 6. For an example, see Judg. 13:1-5.

Nebuchadrezzar - Nebuchadnezzar

Nebuchadrezzar was the son of Nabopolassar, who founded the Babylonian empire in 625BC. Nebuchadrezzar, as crown prince, led the Babylonian armies against Egypt in 606BC and defeated Pharaoh Necho II at Carchemish (2 Kings 23:29). Hearing of his father's death, he then returned to Babylon to claim the throne (605BC).

King Jehoiakim of Judah was his vassal for three years (2 Kings 24:1). In 601BC Nebuchadrezzar's army suffered heavy losses in battles against Egypt. Nebuchadrezzar returned to Babylon to rebuild his army while Jehoiakim rebelled. In 597 he was back in Judah, removed Jehoiakim's son Jehoachin from the throne and made Zedekiah king instead (2 Kings 24:17). He also took away the temple treasures.

A rebellion in Babylon in 595/4 raised false hopes in Palestine (Jer. 28:1-4). Nebuchadrezzar quickly crushed it and Zedekiah assured him of his loyalty. Zedekiah openly rebelled in 589BC, no doubt with Egypt's support. In January 588, Nebuchadrezzar's army surrounded Jerusalem and also captured other strong places in Judah. Egyptian armies marched against him (Jer. 37:5) but the Babylonians drove them back. In July 587, Nebuchadrezzar breached the wall of Jerusalem and the state of Judah came to an end. Nebuchadrezzar showed no mercy to Zedekiah (2 Kings 25:7).

In 568BC Nebuchadrezzar's army made a punitive campaign against Egypt. This made the Egyptians stop interfering in Babylon's empire and the two powers had friendly relationships until Babylon fell.

Nebuchadrezzar reigned until his death in 562BC. He retained his power throughout his life but Babylon declined after his death.

Nebuchadrezzar restored and enlarged the city of Babylon. One tenth of the city held temples, public buildings and private houses, and the remainder was parklands and gardens. A strong wall surrounded the city.

Necho

Necho II was Pharaoh of Egypt c610-595BC. In 609BC he marched his army into Syria to help Assyria against Babylon. He did this to keep a balance of power in western Asia. Josiah king of Judah fought against Necho at Megiddo (2 Kings 23:29,30). Josiah was killed and the delay in Necho's plans led to the defeat of Assyria and the continued rise of Babylon.

Egypt claimed Palestine as its own, but in 605BC Nebuchadrezzar of Babylon drove the Egyptians back to Egypt. In 601BC Nebuchadrezzar marched against Egypt and both sides suffered great losses in an open battle. This may have been the reason why Jehoiakim revolted against Babylon (2 Kings 24:1).

Needle's eye

Jesus said, 'It is easier for a camel to go through the eye of a needle than for a rich man to enter the kingdom of God' (Mark 10:25). The rabbis in Jesus' day used similar pictures. It means that something is very difficult and does not happen very often. The Jews were fond of exaggeration. See Matt. 7:3 for another example of exaggeration in use.

Some people think that the needle's eye was a small door. There is no evidence for this suggestion.

Negeb

Negeb is Hebrew for 'dry'. The Negeb is the southern part of Palestine, with its northern boundary near the southern end of the Dead Sea. It is a desert area and has less than 8 inches of rain a year.

Oaths

A person who swears on oath calls God as witness that he is telling the truth (Exod. 22:11), or that he will do something (Num. 30:2) or not do something (Gen. 21:23). Sometimes there are conditions which free a person from his oath (Gen. 24:8; Josh. 2:17-20). Oaths were used in law courts (Exod. 22:11), to make agreements (Gen. 212:22-24), to bind someone always to agree to the truth of something (Gen. 21:27-31), by kings to ensure loyalty (Ezek. 17:13,14), between friends (1 Sam. 20:42), to affirm faithfulness to God (2 Chr. 15:14).

Oaths had to be kept (Josh. 9:20). Whoever swears an oath asks God to act against him if he breaks it, and God will do so (Zech.5:3,4). Breaking oaths breaks the third commandment (Exod. 20:7) and perjurers are listed in 1 Tim. 1:10 with other sinners.

Some people in the Old Testament swore oaths by pagan gods (Jer. 5:7; Amos 8:14). This was an insult against God and was one reason for the exile (Jer. 12:14-17).

God swore oaths (Gen. 22:16; Ps. 89:3). His word on oath is no different from his word without an oath: both are unbreakable. However, it did strengthen faith in his word when things seemed to go wrong (Heb. 6:17).

In Matt. 5:33-37 Jesus speaks against the teaching on oaths by the rabbis. They said certain oaths such as those sworn in the name of God were binding but others such as those sworn 'by heaven' or 'by earth' were not. Oaths 'by Jerusalem', they said, were nothing unless the swearer faced Jerusalem. Christ's answer was that all oaths are 'by God', even oaths 'by one's head', which meant 'May I die if ..'. Because all oaths were 'by God', all were binding.

The rabbis implied by their teaching that you need not tell the truth, or keep promises. In fact, sometimes oaths hid lies, as Peter showed (Matt. 26:72-74). Jesus said that his disciples should have a righteousness which is better than that of the Pharisees (Matt. 5:20). This better righteousness includes always speaking the truth and keeping promises. If people always did that, there would be no need to swear oaths to strengthen what they say.

Christ's teaching does not mean that Christians should refuse to swear oaths if required to do so by the authorities. He opposed the wrong use of oaths. Christ's teaching did not stop Paul from swearing oaths in his letters (2 Cor. 1:23; Gal. 1:20).

Obedience

Hearing and obeying arc closely connected in the Bible. It is not enough to hear God's teaching: we must obey it (Matt. 7:24-27; James 1:22).

Mankind's first duty is to obey God. All was well in the Garden of Eden until Adam disobeyed God. Then sin entered the world (Gen. 3). Obeying God is more important than worshipping him (1 Sam. 15:22). In fact, if we disobey God, he will not accept our worship, however lavish it may be (Isa. 1:10-17; Micah 6:6-8). The difference between believers and unbelievers is that believers obey God and the gospel (Acts 6:7; Rom. 6:17) whereas unbelievers do not (2 Thess. 1:8).

God has given authority in the family (Eph. 5:22; 6:1), the churches (Heb. 13:17) and the state (Rom. 13:1-7), and Christians should obey those in authority. Paul also told slaves to obey their masters (Eph. 6:5). The modern equivalent to that situation would be workers, who should obey their supervisors.

Obeying those who have proper authority over us is part of obeying God. However, if they command something that God forbids, Christians should obey God rather than those rulers (Acts 5:29).

Officers of the church

The organisation of each church in the New Testament is not the same in every detail. At Jerusalem, we find apostles and elders (Acts 15:2) with James taking a leading position (Acts 12:17; 15:13). There were also prophets (Acts 11:27) and the seven men chosen to serve (Acts 6:1-6). We do not read of elders in Antioch, but prophets and teachers set apart Barnabas and Saul (Acts 13:1-3). At Philippi there were bishops and deacons (Phil. 1:1).

Despite these differences, we do find a general pattern. The position of eldership is found throughout the New Testament, although elders are also sometimes called bishops or pastors. Paul appointed elders for the churches he founded (Acts 14:23) and told his assistants to do the same (Titus 1:5). James (James 5:14) and Peter (1 Peter 5:1), as well as Paul, mention elders. Apart from the possible exception of James at Jerusalem, no one man was the leader of a church until the second century, that is, after the New Testament was completely written.

Ointment

This was widely used in biblical times. It was used for various cosmetic reasons (S. of S. 1:3), and also to anoint kings (1 Sam. 10:1), the sick (James 5:14) and the dead (Luke 23:56). A special oil used in the tabernacle was holy, and not to be copied for personal use (Exod. 30:23-33).

When kept in alabaster containers (Matt. 26:7), the ointment improved with age. After several years, such ointment could become very valuable (Mark 14:5). Three hundred pence was a whole year's wages for a labourer).

Omer

A small bowl and a measure. It is only found in Exod. 16:16 where it measured the amount of manna collected. It was probably about 2.2 litres.

Parable

Most of the parables are in the first three Gospels but there are a few in the Old Testament (e.g. 2 Sam. 12:1-4). Rabbis often told parables in Jesus' day. Our Lord was therefore using a method of teaching which was familiar to his hearers, though sometimes unpopular (Matt. 13:10; John 16:29).

Parables tell a story of everyday things or events, to teach a moral or religious lesson applicable to a certain situation. They are not allegories. In an allegory, each detail of the story has a meaning of its own. The details in a parable do not. They are only parts of the story which are included to make the whole realistic, and teaching one main truth. There may be other subsidiary truths taught by the story.

The parable of the workers in the vineyard (Matt. 20:1-16), for example, tells about the grace of God. We learn that God rewards us not according to what we have done but according to his generosity and kindness. We learn that it is wrong to compare what we have done for the Lord with what others have done. We are not to ask what the vineyard represents, or who the workers represent, or what the one denarius signifies. These are details to make realistic a story which teaches a lesson about God's grace.

This parable does not tell us anything about how to pay wages, either! Our Lord did not intend by this parable to instruct us how to run a business, or what industrial relations should be like, any more than the parable of the unjust steward (Luke 16:1-9) tells us what to do when our employer dismisses us. This last parable only says that we should prepare for eternity now, as the steward prepared for his future in the best way that he could.

There are exceptions to the rule that all the details do not have meanings of their own. The parables of the sower (Matt. 13:1-9,18-23), the drag net (Matt. 13:47-50), the tenants (Matt. 21:33-41), the wedding banquet (Matt. 22:1-14) and the great banquet (Luke 14:16-24) are more like allegories. At least some of their details stand for something or someone.

There are also exceptions to the rule that parables illustrate only one point. The parable of the two sons, for instance, tells us what true repentance is: how God joyfully forgives those who repent; and also speaks of the sins of jealousy and self-righteousness (Luke 15:11-32).

Jesus started using parables at a certain point in his ministry. His disciples noticed the change and asked why (Matt. 13:10). In Mark's Gospel (4:10-12) Jesus' reply seems to say that he used parables in order to hide his teaching. A little later, however, Jesus gives a parable which teaches that all hidden meanings are meant to be known by those who have ears to hear (4:21-23) and the chapter ends by saying that Jesus spoke in parables to the level that his hearers could understand if they wished (v. 33). What v. 12 means, therefore, is what Matt. 13:13 says more clearly. The people's hearts were hard and they were not willing to understand. Because they did not want to understand, they found that they could not understand what Jesus was saying to them.

Parables, then, were to help those people who wanted to understand Jesus' teaching. Those who are humble believers who want to learn, will understand. Those who reject Christ will not be able to understand him. Understanding Christ and understanding his parables go together.

Parallelism

See Poetry.

Passover

God's great saving act in the Old Testament was the exodus from Egypt. He rescued the Israelites from slavery and made them into his own chosen people. On the night that the Israelites escaped, each household killed a year old male sheep or goat, sprinkled its blood on their door frame and ate the meat with herbs and unleavened bread. That same night, the angel of God killed all the firstborn in Egypt, but when he saw the blood on their door frames, he passed over the Israelites. This passing over gave the night and its meal the name — passover. Pharaoh was so troubled by this that he finally told the Israelites to leave Egypt immediately (Exod. 12:1-36).

God told Israel to keep the passover feast on the fourteenth day of the first month of every year from that time on (Exod. 12:2,6,14). The feast was to last seven days and there was to be no leaven in their houses during that period (vv. 17-20). Moses added that after they reached the land, they were to hold the passover in the place where the tabernacle stood (Deut. 16:2).

We read of the passover being celebrated by Joshua (Josh. 5:10-11), Hezekiah (2 Chr. 30), Josiah (2 Kings 23:21-23; 2 Chr. 35:1-19) and the returned exiles (Ezra 6:19-22). Hezekiah celebrated it in the second month, which was allowed under the law in Num. 9:6-13.

The fact that only four passovers are mentioned does not mean that they were not held at other times. These were special occasions. Joshua's was the first to be held in Canaan; Ezra's was the first after the exile. The other two were held at times of reformation and rededication of the temple, being different from others but not the only passovers to be kept (2 Chr. 30:5; 35:18).

In New Testament times, the sacrifice was killed in the temple and the meal was eaten by family groups in their houses in Jerusalem. Groups of friends sometimes made up a household. The Last Supper just before Christ's death was a passover meal (Matt. 26:17-30). During that passover, Christ himself became the real passover lamb (Matt. 26:2; 1 Cor. 5:7). In God's plan of salvation, the passover was a picture of what Christ was to do on the cross.

The Lord instituted a new feast at this passover (Luke 22:14-20; 1 Cor. 11:23-26). Just as the passover celebrated the great redemption of the Old Testament, the Lord's Supper celebrates the greater redemption of the new covenant. The Lord's Supper, therefore, replaces the passover.

In AD70 the Roman army destroyed the Jewish temple. From that time on, ritual sacrifice was not possible, but the Jews still celebrate the passover as a family festival.

Pastor

The Bible pictures God (Ps. 23:1; Isa. 40:11) and Christ (John 10:1; Heb. 13:20) as shepherds. This shows their tender care for the godly (God's 'sheep'). Pastors care for and lead God's people (Jer. 3:15; Eph. 4:11). These pastors are under Christ, who is the chief shepherd (1 Peter 5:4).

The New Testament also calls pastors 'elders' and 'bishops'. These are not three different groups of people. An elder, for example, is also a pastor (or bishop). In Acts 20 we find that elders (v. 17) act as shepherds (v. 28) and oversee the church (v. 28 - 'bishop' means 'overseer'). This shows that the three names are given to the same people. The name pastor emphasizes that the elders of each church should care for the people, feed them on the Word of God and protect them. In fact, they should serve God's sheep (1 Peter 5:1,2).

See Elder.

Peace

When people talk about peace today, they often mean that no one is fighting. Enemies may glare at each other and there may be injustices, but it is still thought of as peace.

Peace in the Bible is not like that. The Bible's word for peace also means harmony, unity between people, a healthy society where everyone may live secure and fulfilled lives.

There is a false peace (Jer. 8:11). True peace can come only where there is righteousness (Ps. 85:10; Isa. 32:17). God is the source of peace (Heb. 13:20) and in his unfailing love makes and keeps his covenant of peace with his people (Isa. 54:10). The wicked cannot share this (Isa. 48:22).

True peace, then, is a time of healing (Jer. 8:15) when there is rest and quiet (1 Chr. 22:9), security (Ezek. 34:25) and opportunity to live fulfilled lives (1 Kings 4:24). Peace comes with the presence of God (Ezek. 37:26) who blesses his people (Num. 6:24-26). All this shows that before people can be at peace, their sins must be atoned for and they must obey God.

The Old Testament looks forward to the Messianic age of peace (Isa. 2:2-4; Hag. 2:7-9). The Messiah is the Prince of Peace (Isa. 9:5). Jesus Christ fulfilled this when he came into the world (Luke 2:14).

Yet Christ's mission to this world was not to bring universal peace (Matt. 10:34). Instead of peace, he brought division. He divides those who love him from those who will not receive him as Lord (vv. 35-42). His peace is different from the false peace offered by others (John 14:27). Christ brings peace but only to those who love and serve him.

God's peace is not cheap. It cost Christ's death on the cross (Col. 1:20). But this gospel peace (Acts 10:36; Eph. 6:15) not only brings peace between God and sinners, it also brings peace between people who were enemies. The great division between Jew and Gentile was joined by Christ's act of peace (Eph. 2:14). Other barriers are also broken in Christ (Gal. 3:28).

Churches should show this peace to those around them. There may be conflicts in surrounding society, but the churches are to make every effort to live at peace. There should first of all be peace among the members (Eph. 4:3) and also peace with those outside the church as far as this is possible taking into account their opposition to Christians (Rom. 12:18).

Note that Paul talks of making every effort to live at peace. As Christians are not yet completely sinless, living peaceful lives will include a struggle against sin. But the Holy Spirit's fruit in Christians includes peace (Gal. 5:22) and therefore they have his power to live at peace. They can then go one step further and bring peace to others who may be in conflict with each other. Such peacemakers are truly children of the God of peace (Matt. 5:9).

Peace offering

Only the fat around the intestines, the kidneys, the liver and the fat around the sheep's tail were burnt in the peace offering (Lev. 3:3,4,9). The priest and his family ate the breast and right thigh in a ceremonially clean place (Lev. 10:14,15) and the worshipper and his family ate the rest (Lev. 7:15).

Peace offerings were made for several different reasons: to thank God (Lev. 7:11,12) or to fulfil a vow, or as a freewill offering (v. 16), or an expression of grief over sin (Judg. 20:26).

The peace offering showed the blessing of peace with God and was therefore a joyful occasion. In addition, there is the theme of communion with God in the sacrifice, because the meal was shared with the priests.

Pentecost

The feast of weeks is the middle one of the three annual feasts of the Old Testament (Deut. 16:16). The name pentecost comes from the Greek translation of the word 'fifty' in the fifty days in Lev. 23:16.

The day after the sabbath following the passover was the day the first sheaf of barley was gathered (Lev. 23:10). Barley was the earliest of the harvests in Palestine. The feast of weeks (or pentecost) took place seven weeks later (vv. 15,16). Although seven weeks is forty-nine days, the Hebrew way of counting included both the first and the last day. This would make seven weeks fifty days.

The Holy Spirit came to the church on the day of pentecost (Acts 2:1). For Christians, therefore, pentecost means the anniversary of the coming of the Spirit. Originally, however, it marked the end of the barley harvest and expressed thanks to God for that harvest.

Perfection

God is perfect. He is perfect in what he knows (Job 37:16), what he says (Ps. 19:7), what he does (Deut. 32:4), what he gives (James 1:17). Everything about God is perfect. There is no sin in him whatsoever (Hab. 1:13).

God has no defects. He is complete in all that he is and does. He has perfect knowledge.

God is perfect in a way that no creature can be. He needs no other being to add anything to him. Also, he cannot be anything less than perfect.

Christ as the Son of God shares the Father's sinless perfection. But as a human being Christ had to be made perfect (Heb. 2:10; 5:8,9). This does not mean that Christ was ever a sinner for he was completely without sin (Heb. 4:15). It means that Christ was made fit for his work as God's high priest (Heb. 5:5). By his suffering and sharing our weakness (Heb. 5:8; 4:15), he became ready to save those who obey the gospel (Heb. 5:9). When the Bible talks about perfection, it sometimes means moral purity, but at other times it means fulfilling a purpose or achieving a goal. Christ fulfilled his purpose by obeying God and dying on the cross. Through his obedience in this way, we are saved.

To be perfect means to be mature. A mature person is able to achieve goals appropriate to a human being which children cannot achieve. In 1 Cor. 14:20 Paul tells believers to be adult in their thinking. The word for adult is 'perfect'. Paul does not expect believers to be all-knowing or sinless, but he does want them to be grown-up in their thinking. Eph. 4:13 is another example of 'perfect', meaning 'grown-up, mature'.

In some places the Bible does talk of people being perfect. Noah (Gen. 6:9), Job (Job 1:1) and Asa (1 Kings 15:14) were said to be perfect. Abraham (Gen. 17:1) and Christ's disciples (Matt. 5:48) were told to be perfect. Elihu claimed perfect knowledge (Job 36:4). Does this mean that believers can be perfect?

Certainly, believers should aim at perfection (2 Cor. 7:1). But the truth is that they will not be perfect until they see Christ face to face (1 John 3:2). Meanwhile, they fight against sin by the power of the Holy Spirit (Gal. 5:16-26), but are not sinless (Rom. 7:14-25; 1 John 1:8).

Those whom the Bible called perfect, still sinned. Job realized his sin (Job 7:21; 9:2; 10:6). When Job protested that he was innocent (9:21) he meant that he wholeheartedly committed himself to God and to God's demands. Job was an upright man. He kept himself away from the wicked and their ways. In Ps. 7:8 David says that he is righteous. He means that he is not guilty of the crimes of which others accuse him (Ps. 7:3-5). David was far from righteous, or perfect in the full sense of the word, as his life showed.

The basic meaning of the word perfection in the Bible, then, means to be complete, or to achieve an appropriate end, or to enjoy an ideal state. The actual state of perfection may differ from case to case.

Persia, Persians

This Indo-European race came from South Russia to Iran about 1000BC. They were part of the Median Empire (625-550BC) but had their own kings. In 550BC Cyrus II rebelled against and separated from his Median overlord. Cyrus was related to the Median kings and gave Medes as well as Persians high offices of state. He also combined the customs and laws of the two peoples (cf. Dan. 6:8). Cyrus enlarged his empire before defeating Babylon in 539BC. He was a tolerant ruler, unlike the harsh Assyrians and Babylonians. He respected local customs, and his order allowing the Jews to return to their homeland (Ezra 1:1-4) is typical of his general policy.

His son, Cambyses II (530-522BC) conquered Egypt in 525BC. Previously, Jews who wanted to rebel looked to Egypt for support, but now Egypt was under Persian control. Cambyses killed himself after Gaumata ursurped the throne in his absence.

Darius I (522-486BC) claimed the throne and defeated Gaumata. However, more revolts followed in different parts of the empire. Haggai and Zechariah prophesied just before Darius restored the situation late 520BC. Darius was an able ruler with policies similar to Cyrus. His reign was the high point of the Persian Empire, although he failed to conquer Greece.

Xerxes I (486-465BC) had to deal with more revolts. Xerxes is the Greek form of his Persian name, the Hebrew form of which is Ahasuerus (Esth. 1:1).

His younger son Artaxerxes I (465-424BC) removed the rightful heir from the throne. He sent Ezra and Nehemiah to Jerusalem. Early in his reign, Egypt rebelled. This may be why he stopped building work in Jerusalem (Ezra 4:7-24). However, in 445BC, about ten years after the rebellion by Egypt, Nehemiah was allowed to rebuild the wall of Jerusalem.

The empire declined and the Greek king, Alexander the Great, conquered it in 331BC.

Persecution

Jesus told his disciples to expect persecution. In the same way as his enemies persecuted him, so they would persecute those who follow him (John 15:20). Indeed, they should rejoice when they were persecuted. They followed the godly people of the past (Matt. 5:12) and they shared in Christ's sufferings (Phil. 3:10; Heb. 13:12,13).

This biblical thinking is very different from ordinary human thinking. We say the oppressed are miserable. Christ said those who are oppressed because they belong to him are blessed, and to be envied (Matt. 5:10,11). The blessing is for those who are persecuted for righteousness' sake, not for doing wrong (1 Peter 4:15). Only persecution for the name of Christ is blessed (Matt. 5:11; 1 Peter 4:14,16).

Of course, believers should not desire persecution. When Jesus sent his apostles on a preaching journey, he said they should go to another town if they were persecuted (Matt. 10:23). Christians should aim to live at peace with everyone (Rom. 12:18).

Christians should not hit back at their persecutors (Matt. 5:38,39). Christ was silent before his tormentors. Christians should say what they believe (1 Peter 3:15) in the Spirit's power (Matt. 10:19,20), and they should seek the good of their enemies. They should bless them (Romans 12:14), meet their needs (v. 20), love them and pray for them (Matt. 5:44).

The book of Acts shows that Jews were the first persecutors of Christians. They hated the Christians' different attitude to the temple and the law of Moses (Acts 6:13,14; 7:48-53; Rom. 6:14). Jewish Christians accepted Gentile Christians as equals in Christ (Eph. 2:11-14).

The Romans allowed the people they conquered to practise their own religions. Paul was protected by Romans (Acts 18:14,15; 21:32; 23:12-35). Sometimes the rulers listened to the crowd (Acts 16:22,23). People like the Philippian citizens often hated Christians, one reason for which was that they were afraid that the gods would avenge themselves on the town because the Christians refused to worship the pagan gods. This may be the background of 1 Peter 4:12.

In AD64 the emperor Nero blamed the Christians in Rome for a disastrous fire in that city. He knew that the Christians were hated and he wanted to find someone to take the blame for the fire instead of himself. This persecution was cruel but confined to the city of Rome. Peter and Paul may have been killed at that time.

The book of Revelation was written during a time of severe persecution, probably about AD90-95 near the end of the reign of the emperor Domitian. He wanted to make sure that the peoples in the Roman empire remained loyal to him and tried to make people worship him as a god, although he allowed them to continue to worship their own gods also. Pagans, who believed in many gods, could do this without any difficulty. Christians, who believed in the only true God, could not. Christians refused; the Romans saw this as treason, and persecution followed, which lasted for a long time.

Perseverance

Perseverance is to continue with something and not to stop, whatever the difficulties. Christians should persevere in living the Christian life (Heb. 12:1). Perseverance is a virtue that all Christians should seek (2 Peter 1:6). Often it comes with suffering when patiently endured (Rom. 5:3; James 1:4). Those who persevere with following Christ and living the Christian life will receive a place in heaven as their reward (Heb. 10:35,36).

Pharisees

Alexander the Great's conquests (336-323BC) spread Greek culture as far as the borders of India. Greek kings first from Egypt and then from Mesopotamia ruled Judaea in the years that followed. By 200BC the Jewish aristocracy began to accept a Greek way of life. Only a small party of Jews called the Chasidim ('loyal ones') resisted Greek culture. They sought to follow God's law fully.

Antiochus IV (175-163BC) tried to force Greek culture and religion on the Jews. In 167BC the Jews rebelled, led by the priestly family of the Maccabees. The Chasidim supported them, but soon found themselves opposing the Maccabean rulers. The party of the Pharisees began at about this time, as successors to the Chasidim.

Because the Pharisees opposed the Jewish aristocracy in regard to the keeping of God's law, being a Pharisee then brought trouble. However, after Rome took control in 63BC, they began to gain in popularity and started to influence the religious life of the Jews. Their strong influence in synagogue worship helped this.

Pharisee means 'separatist'. They separated themselves from all who did not keep God's law as rigidly as they did — Jews as well as Gentiles. In order that they did not break a law by mistake, they added many traditions to cover every aspect of life. They believed these traditions were as binding as the written law itself.

The Pharisees were divided into two parties. One party followed

Rabbi Shammai who held a strict interpretation of the Law. The other party, led by Rabbi Hillel, taught a far more lax interpretation of the Law. One issue between them was what grounds are acceptable for a divorce (cf. Matt. 19:3).

The Pharisees hated Jesus because he did not keep their traditions, such as the thirty-nine laws preventing work on the sabbath (Mark 2:23-3:6). Jesus said the Pharisees' priorities were wrong. They were too busy looking at the letter of the law to understand its true meaning (Mark 7:1-23). He also spoke against their pride (Luke 18:9-14) and their self-display (Matt. 6:1-18).

Their emphasis on law meant that the Pharisees were far more interested in ethics (how to behave) than theology (what to believe). They taught that there was only one God who chose Israel as his special people. Unlike the Sadducees they believed in angels and demons, and also in the resurrection from the dead, with rewards for the righteous and punishments for the wicked (Acts 23:6-9).

The Pharisees kept away from politics. Although they expected the Messiah to come, they did not believe that politics would bring in the messianic age. Instead, they believed that God would act in a special way. In the meantime, they accepted rule by a Gentile nation, as long as they could follow the law of Moses in peace. Most Pharisees opposed the Jewish revolt against Rome (AD66-70). They hated the Romans, but this was mainly because of the heavy taxation imposed which interfered with Jewish giving of tithes to the temple.

After AD70 the Jewish state no longer existed. Not long after this, the Sadducees and Zealots disappeared. The Jewish religion became completely that of the Pharisees.

Pharaoh

This title for the kings of Egypt means 'Great House'. Originally it meant the palace and court. By Moses' day it was given to the king. Its meaning would be similar to 'Your Majesty'. It was not until about 945BC, when Solomon was on the throne of Israel, that the king's personal name was added to his title of Pharaoh. This is why he is just called Pharaoh in Genesis and Exodus, but later we find Pharaoh Necho (2 Kings 23:29) and Pharaoh Hophra (Jer. 44:30).

Philistines

The table of nations shows that the Philistines were descended from the Casluhim (Gen. 10:14). They came from Caphtor, that is, Crete (Amos 9:7) and with other peoples from around the Aegean Sea invaded Egypt. After terrible battles, the Egyptians made the Philistines mercenary soldiers and vassals. They had settled on the Mediterranean coast of Palestine before the exodus (Exod. 23:31). Philistines were at Gerar a few centuries before this (Gen. 20 and 26) but this was a small group which had emigrated much earlier than the main Philistine invasion.

The Philistines were based in the five cities of Gaza, Ashkelon, Ashdod, Ekron and Gath. A lord ruled each city (Josh. 13:2). They soon adopted the religion and language of Canaan.

The Philistines learnt how to smelt iron. As expert soldiers, they took advantage of this new discovery to establish their power in Palestine (1 Sam. 13:19-22). Before iron was smelted, the softer metal bronze was used, which was no match for iron weapons.

The Philistines put pressure on the Israelites throughout the period of Judges and during the reign of Saul. David broke their power (2 Sam. 5:25) but also used them for his personal bodyguard (2 Sam. 8:18 - the Pelethites were Philistines). The Philistines never regained their power although they caused trouble at times (Isa. 9:12).

The name of the country Palestine comes from the word Philistine.

Phylacteries

Moses told the Israelites to tie God's law on their hands and foreheads (Deut. 6:8). About 200 years before Christ, a small number of pious Jews took this literally. They made small cases - phylacteries - in which they placed certain passages of the law and wore these on their left hands and in the centre of their foreheads. In Christ's day only a minority wore them, including the Pharisees.

Jesus condemned the Pharisees for making their phylacteries wide. He is talking about the strap which holds the cases in place. Other people could see a wide strap more easily and would admire the Pharisees for their piety. Jesus spoke against this way of seeking praise from people (Matt. 23:5).

Orthodox Jews still wear phylacteries, but only during their morning prayers. Their phylacteries contain Exod. 13:1-16; Deut. 6:4-9; 11:13-21. In Jesus' day the passages of Scripture would not be all the same and usually included the ten commandments.

Pledge

In biblical times, a pledge was the first instalment of a gift or payment. It guaranteed that the full amount would follow later. Judah gave Tamar a pledge in Gen. 38:17-20.

Paul uses this business-term as a picture of the Holy Spirit in the life of Christians (2 Cor. 1:22; 5:5; Eph. 1:14). God gives his Spirit to those who hear the gospel and believe. This gift is the first instalment which guarantees that they will receive all the blessings of salvation after this life is over.

Poetry

The Israelites loved music and poetry and were known for their songs (cf. Ps. 137:3). Psalms, most of Job, Proverbs, Ecclesiastes, Song of Songs and most of the prophets are poetry.

Hebrew poetry uses many of the poetic devices found in other languages. But it does not use rhyme. Its rhythm only counts the stressed words, not the unstressed.

One important content of Hebrew poetry is what is called its parallelism. This means that an idea stated in the first line is followed by a second line with a parallel idea. Sometimes a further parallel line is added.

The parallel may be the same idea in different words; for example:

Come, let us sing for joy to the Lord,
Let us shout aloud to the Rock of our salvation.
Ps. 95:1.

Or it can be an idea which adds something to the first line:

I said, Oh that I had the wings of a dove!
I would fly away and be at rest.
Ps. 55:6.

Another parallelism gives the opposite idea in the second line:

A wise son brings joy to his father,
But a foolish son grief to his mother.
Prov. 10:1.

Jesus used poetry in his teaching to help his disciples remember what he said. One example is Matt. 7:7 which is a three line parallelism, each line (Ask ... Seek ... Knock ...) giving the same idea. The next verse then gives a further three lines which emphasize the same point about prayer.

Poor

The Old Testament shows that sometimes God blesses the righteous by giving them wealth (Deut. 28:1-14; Ps. 112:1-3) and that poverty is sometimes God's punishment for disobedience (Deut. 28:15-48). But this is not the whole truth. It must also be remembered that at the time Israel was under a special relationship with God in the old covenant.

Job lost all his wealth and his friends said that poverty was always the result of sin. Job, however, maintained that he was innocent. He began to realize that sometimes the wicked are rich and the righteous are poor (Job 21:7-15; 24:2-12). His trust was in God who would bring justice in the end (Job 27:13-23). We find similar teaching in other parts of the Old Testament (Ps. 73:13-17; Jer. 12:1,14; Hab. 1:3-11). So often did the wealthy wicked oppress the poor that the 'poor' and the 'righteous' were usually the same people (Ps. 14:5,6).

The Bible does not sympathize with those who become poor through laziness (Prov. 6:9-11; 2 Thess. 3:10). On the other hand, the wealthy should help those who are poor through no fault of their own (Deut. 15:7-11). God heard the cry of the righteous who were oppressed by the wicked (Deut. 24:15). Christ and his disciples gave to the poor (cf. John 13:29) and the early church helped its poor members, often at great cost to those who gave (Acts 2:45; Rom. 12:13; 2 Cor. 8:1-15).

Riches can make people's lives spiritually unfruitful (Matt. 13:22) because those who love riches cannot follow Christ (Matt.

6:24; 19:21-24). The poor depend on God more readily than the wealthy. Of course, it is not a sin to have possessions. Those who are rich should thank God for providing everything for their enjoyment, but ensure that their hope is in God and not in wealth which can so easily be lost (1 Tim. 6:17-19). Also, those riches should be used in a way that gives glory to God and not to encourage selfishness.

Power

God holds all power throughout the universe. The power enjoyed by the godly comes from God (Ps. 29:11) and even the power held by the leaders of the nations is under God's control (2 Kings 19:25; Isa. 45:1; Rom. 13:1). Human power is as nothing compared with God's power (2 Chr. 20:6).

We see God's power in what he has made (Jer. 10:12) and in his mighty saving acts such as the exodus (Exod. 9:16) and Christ's resurrection (Rom. 1:4). The ark of the covenant was a symbol of God's power (Num. 10:35; 2 Chr. 6:41). The gospel is God's power at work saving people (Rom. 1:16), although unbelievers do not see anything powerful in it (1 Cor. 1:18).

We link the Holy Spirit especially with power. Christ ministered on earth in the power of the Spirit (Luke 4:14; Acts 10:38). Later the Spirit's power worked through the church as she witnessed for Christ (Acts 1:8; 4:31). Today believers can live for Christ and serve him only in the power of the Spirit (Gal. 5:16-18; 1 Cor. 12:4-11).

Christ showed his power while he was on earth through his miracles (Luke 5:17). Now he is above all other power, whether human or angelic (Eph. 1:21). We praise God when we gladly admit that he has power over all (Ps. 29:1; 96:7).

Praise

Praise is one of the marks of the people of God (1 Peter 2:9). The angels also praise God (Job 38:7; Luke 2:13) but the heathen refuse to do so (Rom. 1:21).

Praise expresses joy and delight in God. It is the highest act that human beings can do (Ps. 84:4) because God's people live to praise him (Ps. 119:175). Believers should therefore praise God through all their lives and thereby find complete satisfaction (Ps. 63:4,5).

Joy and delight come from knowing and understanding God. Believers may praise God for his character (Ps. 92:1-3) or for something he has done (v. 4,5). These acts of God include his works in creation (Ps. 104) and in salvation (Ps. 40:1-3).

We should praise God whatever happens to us (1 Thess. 5:18), even if we suffer pain and sorrow (Job 1:21). Of course, we should not praise God for things that are sinful, but we should praise him because he is still in control and works everything for good, even the painful things of life (Rom. 8:28).

The Bible sometimes shows us an individual person praising God, but more often praise comes from the congregation of God's people. This united praise may be through a song, a shout, or a spoken prayer (Ps. 95:1; 1 Chr. 29:10-13). Old Testament saints also praised God through dancing (Exod. 15:20; 2 Sam. 6:14; Ps. 149:3).

Prayer

Prayer brings Christians to God through Jesus Christ. Prayer is not magic, where the act of praying somehow does us good. Prayer helps us because God hears our prayers and answers them.

God does not listen to every prayer. He will not hear the prayers of sinners (Isa. 1:15) unless they come humbly to God, begging for his mercy (Ps. 51). Old Testament prayers were often offered to God with a sacrifice (Gen. 13:4; Ps. 66:13,14), which shows that sin must be atoned for before human beings can talk to a holy God. These Old Testament sacrifices point to the sacrifice of Christ on the cross, which alone opened the way to God (Heb. 4:14-16).

Christ's pattern prayer summarizes a great deal of biblical teaching on prayer (Matt. 69-13):

Our Father in heaven. Christ taught his disciples that God was their Father who cared for them (Matt. 7:9-11). Christians do not approach an uncaring tyrant, but a loving Father who rewards his faithful children (Matt. 6:1,6). This means that they should come to God confident that he will answer their prayers (Mark 11:24). Prayers are made to God. Therefore it is better to pray in a secret place (Matt. 6:6) and wrong to pray in front of other people (Luke 20:47) as a performance.

Hallowed be your name. True prayer seeks only that God's name might be respected. We find good examples of this in the Old

Testament. Some saints told God that he should do as they asked or the heathen would slander his name (Num. 14:10-16). Those who respect God's name will also honour him in their hearts and not use empty words in prayer (Isa. 29:13).

Your kingdom come, your will be done. Prayer seeks God's rule in everything. The Bible clearly teaches that our prayers can have a real effect on what God does (Amos 7:1-6). On the other hand, prayer never forces God to do anything against his will. He did not grant all the wishes even of Moses (Exod. 32:31-34) or Paul (2 Cor. 12:8,9). Christ gives us an example in Gethsemane where he pleaded for an escape from the cross, but at the same time his first desire was for God's will to be done (Luke 22:39-44). We must bear this in mind when we read promises such as Matt. 18:19,20. Jesus is not saying that we will get whatever we ask for. He is saying that if Christians are united in prayer, their prayers are effective because when they meet together they have the mind of Christ who is with them. They ask for the things that Christ wants. Such prayers must be answered.

Give us today. We should come to God feeling our dependence on him, even for the simplest things in life. This does not mean that we need not do anything ourselves. God often answers our prayers through our efforts when we obey him. Nehemiah prayed but also worked hard on the walls of Jerusalem. He had no doubt that it was God who gave them success, and that without God they would not have finished the work, however much effort they put into it (Neh. 1; 2:20; 4:4,5,20; 6:16). Our prayers, however, should not only ask for things for ourselves. The New Testament tells us that praying for others is the duty of all Christians (Luke 6:28; Heb. 13:18,19; 1 Tim. 2:1,2).

Forgive us ... as we forgive. God listens only to the humble (James 4:6). We must be sorry for our sins (Luke 18:10-14) and forgive all who have wronged us (Matt. 6:14,15; 18:21-35).

Lead us not ... deliver us. Prayer seeks for victory. This victory can be over our sin, or over the schemes of other sinners (Ps. 13).

In the Bible, we find people standing (Luke 18:11,13), kneeling (2 Chr. 6:13) and sitting (1 Chr. 17:16) when they prayed. Often their hands were lifted up (Ps. 28:2). In Old Testament days, people faced the holy place (Ps. 28:2), the holy temple (Ps. 138:2) or Jerusalem (Dan. 6:10) because God's presence was symbolized in the holy place in the temple at Jerusalem.

People prayed both as individuals and in groups. They had fixed times for prayer (Dan. 6:10) but could also pray at any time.

Preaching

In the New Testament, preaching means proclaiming the gospel to the unconverted. Today we also say that explaining the faith to Christians is preaching, but the New Testament words for that are teaching and exhortation.

Christ is the authority for evangelism (Matt. 28:18,19). This puts the preacher under compulsion to spread the gospel message (Acts 4:20; 1 Cor. 9:16). Preachers do not simply give facts, but also seek to persuade sinners to repent (Acts 18:4). The power of preaching is not the preacher's skill, but the Holy Spirit at work (1 Cor. 2:4; 1 Thess. 1:5). This type of preaching makes enemies as well as converts.

There are two Greek words which mean preaching. One means to proclaim as a herald (Kerusso): e.g. in Matt. 3:1; Acts 8:5; Rom. 2:21. There are fifty-one occurrences of this verb. The other is to announce good news (Euanggelizo): e.g. in Matt. 11:5; Acts 5:42; Rom. 1:15. There are fifty-five occurrences of this verb.

This good news in Christ's preaching was that God was bringing in his kingdom (Matt. 4:23). In the letters of the New Testament, we find that it is Christ himself who is the good news: Christ crucified (1 Cor. 1:23), Christ raised from the dead (1 Cor. 15:12), Christ the Son (2 Cor. 1:19) and Christ the Lord (2 Cor. 4:5). There is no difference between 'preaching the kingdom' and 'preaching Christ', for God's kingly rule is centred in Christ.

Predestination

God is in control of everything. Predestination means that God has planned in advance certain events and that certain people would be saved. The word appears six times in the New Testament.

Before the world began, God predestined those who would be his children (Eph. 1:4,5; Rom. 8:29). He works out everything according to his plan (Eph. 1:11), including the conspiracy against Christ which led him to the cross (Acts 4:28). In due time, God calls his elect to repentance and faith, cleansing them from their guilt in order that they may share in God's glory (Rom. 8:29; 1 Cor. 2:7).

Pride

Christians often see pride as the central sin which leads to all other sins. The proud refuse to submit to God, preferring to trust in their own abilities. This leads to their destruction. The fall of Satan is said to be through his pride (Isa. 14:10-14). God is against the proud (Prov. 16:5; Matt. 23:12; Luke 1:51).

The Bible's teaching on pride went against the beliefs of the Greeks during the four centuries before Christ. They saw pride as a virtue and believed a good man would think highly of himself. Educated Gentiles who were influenced by Greek thinking would not, therefore, readily accept the Christian call to humility before God.

Priest

A priest conducts religious ceremonies, especially sacrifices. Melchizedek is the first priest mentioned in the Bible (Gen. 14:18). Pagan priests are also mentioned in the Bible.

The Israelite priesthood was instituted by God at Mount Sinai shortly after the exodus. Although in a sense all Israel were priests, the priesthood and therefore the privilege of offering sacrifices was reserved for Aaron and his male descendants (Num. 3:10) who were without physical blemishes (Lev. 21:16-23).

In addition to representing the people before God through offering sacrifices, priests were to guard the book of the law (Deut. 17:18) and teach it to the people (Lev. 10:10,11); to judge difficult cases (Deut. 17:8,9) and control cases of infectious skin disease and mildew (Lev. 13,14). The priests were assisted in some things by Levites. The New Testament teaches that all believers are priests, able to worship God fully (1 Peter 2:5; Rom. 12:1). No priest can represent Christians before God except Christ (Heb. 4:14).

See High Priest.

See also Levites.

Promise

The Hebrew Old Testament does not have a separate word which means promise. Instead, the Hebrew uses one of two words which mean a 'word' or someone 'spoke'. The Old Testament is full of promises and religious faith is built on the assurance that God always does what he has promised (Josh. 23:14; Heb. 11:13-20). In the New Testament, the word used usually means a promise that God makes to give something freely.

Prophecy, Prophets

We find prophets throughout the whole Bible, from Enoch (Jude 14) and Abraham (Gen. 20:7) to John and his brother prophets (Rev. 22:9). The first prophecy was in the Garden of Eden (Gen. 3:15). Moses was the greatest Old Testament prophet (Deut. 34:10). He was the standard by which all later prophets would be measured (Deut. 18:15-19).

A prophet's main task was to be God's spokesman. God spoke to him and he in turn gave that message to God's people. See Exod. 7:1,2. God said Moses was like God and Aaron would be his prophet. Aaron was like a prophet because he spoke on Moses' behalf, except that here Moses was representing God to Pharaoh. The prophets often said words like 'The word of the Lord came to me' (Ezek. 18:1), or 'This is what the Lord says' (Isa. 43:1).

God's message was usually passed on in the form of words. Sometimes, however, the prophet would act his message (Isa. 20:1-6; Ezek. 4). Agabus in the New Testament did the same (Acts 21:10,11).

Prophets often told people what would happen in the future. This was not like fortune-telling, because God condemned sorcery and divination to find out the future (Deut. 18:10,14). When God speaks about the future, he tells people what he intends to do and why he will do it. The prophecies may be about God's judgment on sinners (Amos 5:18-27) or his encouragement of the weak (Isa. 41:8-16). Some events prophesied may be stopped by repentance or falling into sin (Jer. 18:7-10; Jonah 3:4-10).

Among the future events that the prophets saw was the Israelites' exile to Babylon and their return to Jerusalem. The prophets also looked forward to even greater events, such as the coming of Christ as Saviour, the spread of the gospel to the Gentiles and the coming of peace to creation through Christ.

Prophecy, then, gives God's meaning to history. The Hebrew Bible calls the books of Joshua, Judges, Samuel and Kings 'the former prophets'. These books do not only record history, they show God acting in history. The Bible does not portray history as a story of what happened by chance in the past. God is shown to be acting in history and these Bible history books tell us what history means and what it tells us about God. Bible histories have a prophetic purpose.

So far, we have seen a forward look to prophecy (that is, what God intends to do in the future), and a backward look to prophecy (what God has done in the past). Prophecy was to teach the people to obey God. The prophets, therefore, spoke against sin, whether it was in the form of false worship (Isa. 1:10-15), idol worship (Isa. 2:6-21), oppression and immorality (Isa. 3:11-26; Amos 2:6-8). Rich landowners (Isa. 5:8-30), leaders (Micah 3:1-4), false prophets (vv. 5-7), kings (1 Sam. 13:13; 2 Sam. 12:1-14; 1 Kings 17:1) and priests (Amos 7:10-17) as well as ordinary people were opposed by the prophets. The prophets also spoke against the other nations of their day (Jer. 46-51).

God chose his prophets and called them to be his spokesmen (Isa. 6; Jer. 1). Only false prophets took this work on themselves without a call from God (Jer. 14:14). God spoke to his prophets through visions and dreams (Num. 12:6; Isa. 1:1), through ecstatic trances (1 Sam. 19:23,24; 2 Kings 3:15) and through other ways. People thought the ecstatic prophets were mad, but they still believed what they said (2 Kings 9:11-13). Sometimes they seemed to use methods similar to the methods of the prophets of Baal (1 Kings 18:28,29).

We find false prophets in many parts of Scripture. One way of telling that a prophet was false was if his foretelling were proved to be wrong (Deut. 18:22). Even if it came true, he might still be a false prophet (Deut. 13:1-3). The real test was whether his message agreed with what God had already revealed about himself (Deut. 13:4,5; 1 John 4:1-3) and whether the prophet was a godly man (cf. Jer. 23:9-32).

Some prophets earned their living by prophesying. Kings had their own court prophets (1 Kings 22:23). Micah complained that false prophets prophesied good to those who could pay and evil to those who could not (Micah 3:5). Amos denied that he was one of the prophets who earned his living by prophecy (Amos 7:12-15). We read of two schools for prophets: one was perhaps set up by Elijah and Elisha (2 Kings 2:5) and the other for Isaiah's disciples (Isa. 8:16).

Other names for prophets include 'seer' (1 Sam. 9:9), i.e. one who sees [visions], 'man of God' (Deut. 33:1; 1 Sam. 2:27), 'servant of God' (Josh. 1:1; 2 Kings 17:13) and, after the exile, the 'Lord's messenger' (Hag. 1:13). Before the monarchy was established, there may have been a difference between a seer and a prophet, but later they were the same. There are two Hebrew words for 'seer', but again there appears to be no difference in meaning. The last Old Testament prophet was John the Baptist (Matt. 11:13).

Prophets were an important group in the New Testament church, second only to the apostles (1 Cor. 12:28). They looked into the future (Acts 11:28) but their main task was to encourage and build up believers in their faith (Acts 15:32; 1 Cor. 14:3,4). New Testament prophecy was not the same as speaking in tongues (1 Cor. 14:22) and in fact was not ecstatic at all, because we read that the prophets were in full control of their minds (1 Cor. 14:32). There were ecstatic prophets after the New Testament was written, but they gradually fell into disrepute and the practice died out.

Some men and some women (Acts 21:9) in the New Testament church had a special gift of prophecy. All Christians had a potential to exercise this gift (1 Cor. 14:1-5). God may reveal a message which fits the time and circumstances of a church. He uses godly people and tells them a message which agrees with God's Word. Even then, the message has to be carefully considered by the other believers before it is accepted (1 Cor. 14:29).

Christians today sometimes discuss whether prophecy still exists. The first thing we must say is that God's revelation of himself was completed in Christ. That revelation was written down by men inspired by the Spirit during the apostolic age and has been accepted by the whole church since that time. No other message can be equal to Scripture. However, God may reveal a message to a godly person who is trying to understand what God is doing in his church at the present time, and what they should do in the future. Even this message cannot be accepted just on somebody's word that God told him. The church must consider the message, using Scripture and godly wisdom.

Propitiation

Propitiation is appeasing an angry person by offering a gift. In Greek pagan writings, the gods were not thought of as being kind to mankind. Their goodwill had to be earned by propitiation. Their anger had to be turned aside. The Bible shows the true God to be different from pagan gods. God is love, and planned to ransom his people from sin by sending Jesus Christ as the means of propitiation to remove his holy anger against sin (Rom. 3:25; 1 John 4:10).

Some people think it is unworthy to think of God as angry, and therefore translate the word as 'expiation'. There is no thought of wrath in expiation, only removing guilt by paying something. God is slow to anger, and patient (Exod. 34:6; Rom. 2:4), but the Bible clearly teaches that he is a holy God who hates sin (Hab. 1:13) and is angry against sinners (Ps. 7:11; Lam. 4:11; Rom. 1:18).

In Rom. 3:25 and 1 John 4:10 the meaning of the Greek word is shown by pagan writings to be propitiation and not expiation. The main teaching of the Bible agrees with this. God is angry against sinners but he also sent Christ to rescue sinners by dying for them on the cross. Christ bore God's holy wrath against sin.

Providence

The Bible teaches that God is King, in complete control of his creation. He keeps the universe in existence and provides for the needs of all his creatures (Ps. 104; Matt. 6:26-29). Even the ungodly benefit from God's providence in nature (Matt. 5:45). God is guiding and controlling every event that happens (Eph. 1:11,12) however small (Matt. 10:29) and will bring history to its conclusion at Christ's return. In Christ, he has also provided salvation for all those who believe.

Purity

Moses gave laws which allowed for ceremonial purity. Israelites could become unclean for a number of reasons, such as touching something unclean (Lev. 5:2), bearing a child (Lev. 12) or having an infectious skin disease (Lev. 13). Detailed laws told the people what to do if they became unclean and how they might be purified.

Ceremonial purity concerned what the body touched, or what touched the body. It was not a matter of moral purity. The whole point of these laws, however, was to teach the need for moral purity, and therefore the need to be purified from sin (Lev. 16:30). The prophets saw that the Israelites did not understand this. Many people thought that as long as they sacrificed offerings in order to become ceremonially clean, they could behave as they liked. The prophets had to tell them that obeying God's moral laws was more important than offering sacrifices (Micah 6:6-8).

Christ's teaching was similar to that of the prophets. He told his disciples that uncleanness was a matter of the heart, not what the body touches (Mark 7:14-23). The pure in heart are blessed (Matt. 5:8). A pure heart belongs to a person who is wholly devoted to God. Such people want to obey God in every part of life and do not have two masters (cf. Matt. 6:19-24).

The New Testament letters tell us that Christ purified sinners when he died on the cross (Heb. 1:3; 1 John 1:7). No other sacrifice can purify the conscience. Old Testament sacrifices could only make worshippers clean on the outside, that is, ceremonially clean (Heb. 9:9,10,13,14). Sinners are made pure by Christ through confessing their sins (1 John 1:9) and by submitting to the truth of God's Word (1 Peter 1:22).

See Clean and Unclean.

Purple

Purple dye came from the stomach gland of a shell fish found along the eastern shores of the Mediterranean Sea. Kings and emperors wore purple clothes and sometimes nobles did so also. Purple therefore became a symbol of royal or imperial pomp. Lydia traded in purple (Acts 16:14).

Rabbi

Rabbi means 'my great one', or 'my teacher'. It was a title Jews gave to their teachers of the law to show great honour and respect. John the Baptist (John 3:26) and Christ (Mark 9:5) were called Rabbi.

Jesus told his disciples to refuse the title of Rabbi because they were all equal as brothers and only Christ was their teacher (Matt. 23:7,8).

Rabboni (John 20:16) means the same as Rabbi, but even more respect is intended.

Reconciliation

Reconciliation in the New Testament means a change from being enemies to being friends. The reason for a quarrel has been removed. Perhaps a friend helped the people involved to see how they had misunderstood each other, or the person in the wrong apologized and repaired whatever damage had been done. The New Testament talks about people being reconciled to each other (Matt. 5:24; 1 Cor. 7:11) but even more important is being reconciled to God.

Mankind and God became enemies because of sin. People are hostile to God. They do not want to obey God but prefer their own way (Rom. 8:7; Col. 1:21). God is hostile to mankind because he will only accept holiness and people are sinful. God is angry with sinners (Rom. 1:18).

But God reconciled sinners to himself in Christ (2 Cor. 5:18,19). He removed the reason for hostility to himself by sending Christ to die in his people's place on the cross (Rom. 5:10; Gal. 3:13). God has made his people holy, who were once sinners (Col. 1:21). People's hostility to God is changed because they now want to live for God in God's way. God's hostility to his people is changed because he does not see sin in them, but the righteousness that Christ has given them.

God, therefore, is the one who reconciles. If he did not act, mankind would always be his enemies. On the other hand, each sinner must seek to be reconciled with God (2 Cor. 5:10). Only when they repent from their sin and desire to be holy will they find true peace and reconciliation with God.

Redeemer, redeem

A redeemer is a person who rescues someone or something by paying a price for them. The law of Moses said that if a man had to sell his land to pay for his debts, a close relative should redeem the land for him. The relative did this by buying back the land from the new owner and giving it freely to his poorer relative. If a close relative did not redeem the land, the man who sold it could buy it back later if he had enough money (Lev. 25:25-28). A similar law allowed for Israelite slaves to be redeemed (vv. 47-50).

The firstborn of animals not used for sacrifice could be redeemed, otherwise it had to be killed. All firstborn children had to be redeemed because all firstborn belonged to God and therefore had to be bought back at a price of five shekels (Exod. 34:19,20; Num. 18:15-17). Israelites could also redeem animals, houses or land which they had dedicated to God in a vow by paying money to the full value plus a fifth.

God redeemed individual Israelites (Ps. 119:154) and the whole nation of Israel (Ps. 130:8). Only on very few occasions is it said that God redeemed from sin (Ps. 130:7,8; Isa. 44:21-23). Mostly God is said to redeem from all kinds of different dangers and troubles. These include slavery in Egypt (Exod. 6:6,7), exile in Babylon (Isa. 48:20), the wicked (Jer. 15:21), enemies (Ps. 69:18), oppression and violence (Ps. 72:14), death (Hosea 13:14). The idea of redemption from sin is firmly taught in the sacrificial system but the word redemption is not used.

The Old Testament teaching prepares us for the New Testament teaching. God redeems his people through his Son (Col. 1:13,14). The price paid as the ransom is Christ's blood, shed on the cross (Eph. 1:7). He redeems his people from sin (Col. 1:14) and the curse of breaking God's law (Gal. 3:13). But New Testament redemption goes further than this. Like the Old Testament teaching, New Testament redemption delivers people from all the troubles of life: in other words, from the effects of sin as well as from sin itself. In its fullest sense, believers' redemption is not yet complete because they wait for the day of redemption to come (Eph. 4:30). Then their corrupted bodies will be redeemed (Rom. 8:23) and they will live for ever in God's renewed creation.

So redemption is more than solely delivering someone from an evil. A price has to be paid. Sometimes paying the price is not an important part of redemption, but redemption cannot be properly understood unless the fact is recognized that a price must be paid (1 Cor. 6:20). Some people have tried to work out to whom the price is paid. This is taking the picture of redemption too literally. The important point is that our deliverance from sin was by a costly payment.

Regeneration

The Bible looks forward to the regeneration of all creation. God is to make all things new again (Rev. 21:5) with a new heaven and a new earth (Isa. 66:22; Rev. 21:1). The first creation was very good in the beginning (Gen. 1:31) but creation was harmed when Adam sinned (Gen. 3:17-19). The creation was harmed by mankind's sin; the natural world will be renewed by the complete redemption of God's people at the end of the age (Rom. 8:19,21).

Not every angel and human being will share in the renewed creation. Part of the renewal is to destroy all that is evil, which includes the fallen angels and those people who refuse to obey God (Matt. 25:41; Rev. 20:15). Sinful people share the nature of Adam. New, regenerate people share the nature of the last Adam, who is Christ (1 Cor. 15:45-49; Rom. 5:12-17). The renewed people are those who are 'in Christ' (Eph. 2:15; 2 Cor. 5:17).

In the Old Testament, the nation of Israel were God's people. Some of the prophets looked forward to the regeneration of Israel, when the people will have new hearts (Ezek. 36:26) with God's law written on them (Jer 31:31-34). But although the prophets looked forward to the nation being renewed, they realized that must be through individual persons being renewed. Each Israelite needed a new heart with God's law written on it. King David asked God to create a pure heart in him (Ps. 51:10).

In the New Testament, the church is God's people, the new Israel made up of both Jews and Gentiles who trust in Christ (Gal. 3:7,29; Eph. 2:14-16; 3:6,7). Christ died for the church, to renew it and make it holy (Eph. 5:25-27). This church is not the same as any organisation on earth, but is the whole number of those saved by God throughout all history. (See Church). The church is made up of renewed individuals, born again believers (John 3:6,7). Without this new birth, no one can be part of God's kingdom (John 3: 3,5).

God gives this new life (John 1:13). Sinful people cannot ask for it because they are dead in sin (Eph. 2:1) and cannot understand spiritual things (1 Cor. 2:14). All Christians enjoy this new life because they share in Christ's death and resurrection from the dead (Gal. 6:14; Rom. 6:4). Christ's new life gives believers new life. The Spirit also is active in regeneration, for the Spirit gives birth to spiritual life (John 3:6) and the Christian's new life is life in the Spirit (Rom. 8:1-17).

Being born again is only the start of regeneration. God renews his people every day (2 Cor. 4:16). They start this new life without any effort on their part (it is God's gift) but they must make every effort to use this new life as soon as they possess it. Christians are to keep renewing their minds (Rom. 12:2), to put off their old way of life and put on the new self as they seek to be like God in true righteousness and holiness (Eph. 4:22-24). Those who are born again will do what is right (1 John 2:29), love other Christians with a godly love (1 John 4:7), believe Jesus is the Christ (1 John 5:1) and follow God's commands (1 John 5:3,4).

God uses his Word when giving new life (James 1:18). His Word challenges us, showing us our sin and our need to be saved by Christ. When we are born again, we must obey God's Word in order to live the new life (1 Peter 1:22-25).

The climax of regeneration is the new heavens and the new earth. When the number of God's people is complete, creation itself will be renewed (Rev. 21:1-5).

Repentance

The gospel tells us that God sent Jesus to save sinners. Repentance is essential to salvation. Gospel preaching must include the demand to repent (Luke 24:47; Acts 2:38) because sinners must change. They must be sorry for their sin and live for God in the future.

When people repent, they move from the kingdom of this world to the kingdom of God (Matt. 3:2; 4:17). God only forgives those who repent (Acts 5:31). Also, the faith that saves is accompanied by repentance (Acts 20:21).

The Old Testament usually describes repentance as turning from sin (2 Kings 17:13; Jonah 3:10) and turning to God (Isa. 55:7; Joel 2:12,13). Repentance not only looks back (a believer has sorrow for the past) but also looks to the future (a believer is determined to live for God).

The New Testament words for 'repent' usually mean a change of mind. People who repent change their whole way of thinking. They now regret what they have done in the past and want to live in an entirely new way in the future. The thought of turning is still there because the call is to repent and turn to God (Acts 3:20).

It takes humility for people to admit they are wrong (Job 42:6). But grieving over the past does not always lead to repentance and salvation, as in the cases of Judas (Matt. 27:3-5) and Esau (Heb. 12:17). Godly sorrow, however, turns believers from sin and they then seek to live for God. This gives them the joy of salvation and not continuing regret (2 Cor. 7:10).

Resurrection

Sinful people crucified Jesus the Christ, but God raised Jesus from the dead. The resurrection was the centre of the message of the earliest preachers (Acts 2:32; 3:15; 4:10). The basis of Christianity is that Christ is risen (1 Cor. 15:17-19).

God's power raised Christ's body. On Easter morning, the tomb was empty, the body had gone (Mark 16:6). If the apostles had only seen a vision or a ghost, the Jewish leaders could have made them look very foolish by pointing out the decaying body to the crowds. But they did not know where the body was, for it had gone. They suggested that the disciples took it away and hid it (Matt. 28:12,13). But the disciples had not hidden the body. Jesus was alive again. They saw him. They saw that he had flesh and bones, could eat food (Luke 24:37-43) and could be felt (John 20:27). The disciples could not have faced suffering and death unless they were convinced that Jesus was alive again.

Christ's raised body was different from his pre-resurrected body. His friends did not always recognize his looks or his voice straightaway (John 20:14; Luke 24:16). He could enter locked rooms (John 20:19) and disappear (Luke 24:31).

Some people suggest that Jesus was not truly dead when the soldiers took him down from the cross. But the soldiers often executed people and would not make such a mistake. One of them pushed his spear deep into the side of Christ's body (John 19:34). Even if it were possible that Christ had some life in him when he was put in the tomb, he would have been far too severely injured to get up and walk over fourteen miles only two days later (Luke 24:13-35).

The resurrection is the most remarkable event of all history. It shows that death is not the end. Christ defeated death. Those who are united with Christ by faith will live again after death (John 11:25,26). Christ is the firstfruits of a great harvest of resurrections (1 Cor. 15:20-23).

The Old Testament talks about the life to come (e.g. Ps. 16:10; Dan. 12:2) but its message mainly concerns this life. The New Testament puts great emphasis on eternal life. Just as Christ's body was resurrected, so will the bodies of Christ's people be resurrected. The old bodies return to dust but the new bodies, no longer weak and prone to decay, are spiritual bodies like Christ's (1 Cor. 15:35-49).

This teaching of the resurrection of the body contradicted the Greek teaching of Paul's day. The Greeks taught that the body was a prison for the soul, but at death the soul would at last be free from the limitations of the body. They saw the body and the soul as two opposites living together, and the soul would therefore be better if it were free from the body. But the Bible teaches that God made the body as well as the soul. The body and the soul are not two separate things, but two different ways of looking at what makes a human being. Our souls need our bodies just as much as our bodies need our souls.

This explains why the philosophers at Athens rejected Paul's message (Acts 17:31,32). Only a few of them could accept a resurrection of the body. Another group who rejected the resurrection were the Sadducees, the priestly party of the Jews.

Christ's resurrection gives believers more than hope of defeating death. Through their union with Christ, they have put to death their old sinful nature and now live a new life in Christ (Gal. 2:20; 6:14). This does not mean that believers are now perfect, for they have a continual struggle with their old nature to live a Christlike life.

Christ's resurrection also shows that God accepted Christ's sacrifice on the cross as an atonement for the sins of his chosen people. Christ's resurrection means that God accepts his people as those who are not guilty of sin (Rom. 4:25). Those who do not have faith in Christ and are therefore not united with Christ in his death and resurrection, will be raised - but only for damnation (John 5:29).

Baptism is a picture of believers sharing in Christ's death and resurrection, giving them a new life now and the promise of a bodily resurrection in the future (Rom. 6:1-14).

Revenge

God is the rightful avenger of all wrongs (Deut. 32:35). Individual Israelites were told not to seek revenge but to love their neighbours

(Lev. 19:18). However, the nation of Israel was to carry out God's vengeance on his enemies (Num. 31:2,3). Also, God's vengeance should be carried out by the injured party against those who do violence (Lev. 24:17-21).

When someone committed a murder, the next of kin should execute the murderer (Num. 35:19). "Avenger of blood" means "Redeemer of blood". The loss of life in the murder had to be paid for by the life of the murderer (Gen. 9:6, cf. Deut. 21:8). No other person could legally be executed except the murderer (Deut. 24:16; 2 Kings 14:6). If the killing were accidental, the accused could escape to a city of refuge where he could be safe from the avenger of blood.

Christ taught his disciples not to seek revenge on those who hurt them (Matt. 5:38,39). They should leave all vengeance to God (Rom. 12:19; Rev. 6:10). This does not mean that violent criminals should be left free, for it is the duty of the state authorities to punish evil. By doing so, they are carrying out God's vengeance (Rom. 13:4).

Revelation

Revelation is the uncovering of something which was hidden. God is hidden from mankind unless he reveals himself to them (Isa. 45:15). God is hidden because sin puts a barrier between people and God (Isa. 59:12). But even if people had not sinned, they would still need God to reveal himself to them. Adam in the Garden of Eden needed God's revelation (Gen. 2:16,17). God is too great and wonderful for human beings to understand him unless he shows himself to them in ways they can understand (cf. Job 42:3; Isa. 55:8,9). We know God only as much as he has revealed himself to us (Deut. 29:29).

God wants us to know him. It is part of his character to show himself to us (Amos 4:13; Dan.2:29). In the Old Testament God showed himself in a number of different ways: through nature (Ps. 19:2), dreams and visions (Num. 12:6), the angel of the Lord (Judg. 6:12-23), his Word (Jer. 7:1).

God showed himself by his acts in history and by his messages to his servants which explained those acts (Amos 3:7). When the Israelites were suffering in Egypt, God showed himself as the mighty Deliverer by bringing the plagues and dividing the Red Sea.

He told Moses about these acts so that Moses and the Israelites understood that he was doing them in order to rescue his people from slavery (Exod. 3:1-20).

These acts of God and his messages explaining them are recorded for us in the Bible. But the Bible is not just a record of God's revelation in the past. The Bible is itself God's revelation. The New Testament treats the Old Testament as the Word of God (Acts 4:25,26; Heb. 3:7-11; 4:3).

Central to Old Testament revelation is God's covenant with Abraham (Gen. 12:2,3; 15:17,18). God renewed this covenant with Moses at Mount Sinai. God gave the Israelites his law, which set out their obligations to God under the covenant. Later, the prophets sought to bring the Israelites back to the covenant and warned the people what would happen to them if they continued to break it. The prophets also looked forward to a new covenant written on the hearts of God's people (Jer. 31:31-34).

God's greatest and clearest revelation of himself is in his Son, Jesus Christ (John 1:18; Heb. 1:1,2). Before Christ, much of God's mystery was still hidden (1 Peter 1:10-12) but in Christ God has shown all that he intends to show us (Rom. 16:25; 1 Cor. 2:7-10). In Christ, revelation is complete, apart from the revelation of the man of lawlessness (2 Thess. 2:3-6) and our full salvation (1 Peter 1:5,7) at the Second Coming of Christ (1 Cor. 1:7).

The Old Testament looks forward to this full revelation of Christ. The new covenant, set up by Christ's sacrifice on the cross (Luke 22:20; Heb. 10:11-18), is explained in the New Testament. God reveals himself to his people through his covenants. Covenants require a commitment by both parties, so when God reveals himself to people, he demands a response to trust him and to obey his commands. Other ways of seeking God's revelation, such as sorcery (Lev. 19:26), are forbidden.

God's revelation is not always immediately understood. Nicodemus (John 3:4,9) and the disciples (Luke 8:17-21) did not at first understand Christ's teaching. The psalmist prayed for God to teach him how to understand the law (Ps. 119:27). An unbeliever is blind (1 Cor. 2:14; 2 Cor. 4:4) and cannot understand the truth. The Jews failed to understand the law of Moses because they refused to receive Christ's teaching and to acknowledge him as Messiah (2 Cor. 3:14,15). A humble commitment to Christ and the work of the Holy Spirit is needed before people can properly understand God's revealed Word in the Bible.

Reward

In Old Testament times, God gave blessings in this life to those who were faithful to him (Deut. 28:1-14; Prov. 13:21). Such rewards show that God is just (Ps. 57:11). However, the wicked often seemed to be more prosperous than the righteous (Job 21:7-15; Ps. 73:3-12; Eccl. 8:14). Does this mean that God sometimes fails to reward the righteous and to punish the wicked? No! God is just and his people understand that the time will come for the wicked to be punished (Ps. 73:17). Even in the Old Testament we find that the greatest reward is not one that lasts for this life only, but one which continues into the next (Ps. 17:14,15).

Christ taught that his disciples would receive their reward in heaven (Matt.5:12). This reward is their inheritance (Col. 3:24) and the crown of righteousness (2 Tim. 4:8). In this life, believers are more likely to receive suffering than rewards (Matt. 5:10-12; Mark 10:29,30).

The rewards in heaven are not given as payment for our good works. Salvation is a free gift and cannot be earned (Eph. 2:8,9) but good works are the believers' duty (Luke 17:7-10). Those who refuse to do good works, show that God's Spirit is not at work in their lives (Gal. 5:16-25). The salvation of Christians who serve God for many years is the same as that of sinners who are saved in the closing moments of life (cf. Matt. 20:1-16).

The New Testament also speaks of differences in rewards. The clearest passage is 1 Cor. 3:10-14. Here we are told that those who serve God in a way worthy of Christ will be rewarded, whereas those who do not serve God in a worthy way receive only their salvation. What these rewards are, we are not told.

Rome

Rome began as an independent city. It gradually grew in power, until first it ruled over all Italy, then over the countries stretching from Britain to Arabia. For many years Rome was a republic, but its political system was more suited to a city state than the centre of a vast empire. The republic broke up amid civil wars until Caesar Octavianus took control in 27BC. Octavianus was given the name Augustus. After him, other members of his family ruled until AD69 when civil wars broke out again. Augustus' family died out but his system of government continued, although power increasingly went from the Senate to the emperor.

Augustus' system was to divide the empire between himself and the Senate. The Senate ruled in the more peaceful areas of the empire but the emperor controlled the areas where there were wars and other difficulties. Most of the Roman army was therefore under the emperor's control. This system brought peace to the countries inside the Roman Empire with freedom to travel within its borders and was one of the reasons why the Christian gospel spread so quickly after pentecost.

Special privileges were given to Roman citizens. The populations of countries under Roman rule were not automatically citizens New Testament times, but there were certain Roman colonies in different parts of the empire. All those in such colonies were Roman citizens. Philippi was one such Roman colony.

Romans also rewarded people by giving them Roman citizenship, which was passed on to their children. Paul was a citizen by birth, although he was racially a Jew (Acts 22:28). He made use of his citizenship on occasions (Acts 16:37-39; 22:25; 23:27; 25:10,11).

The Roman Empire later developed more wicked ways. John in Revelation 17 describes Rome, the city of seven hills (v. 9), as the great city which rules over other kings (v. 18). In the eastern parts of the empire when the book of Revelation was written, people were told to worship the emperor as a god in order to prove their loyalty. Jews were exempted from this, but not Christians. Ordinary pagans did not find it difficult to worship their gods and also to worship the emperor, for they believed in many gods. Christians could not worship any other god than the God of the Bible and many died for their faith at this time (v. 6).

Sabbath

Sabbath means 'putting an end' to something. The sabbath was the day which put an end to the week of work - a rest day.

God gave the sabbath to the Israelites soon after they left Egypt (Exod. 16:23,29). The special day reminded them that they were slaves in Egypt, from which situation God had rescued them by his mighty power. Servants were given a rest day on the sabbath as well as their masters (Deut. 5:12-15).

Another reason for the sabbath goes back to the creation (Exod. 20:11). The seventh day of creation was the climax of God's creative acts (Gen. 2:3). Mankind needs time for rest and opportunity to rejoice over God's creation and to think about him. People work to provide themselves a living, but the sabbath day shows that there is something even more important. They need to spend time with God (cf. Deut. 8:3).

The Jewish sabbath was a feast day, a day for the assembly to meet to worship God (Lev. 23:3; Num. 28:9,10). The day was given for the people (Exod. 16:29), for they needed to rest and think about God. It was also a day which belonged to God (Lev. 19:3; 23:3). God has the right to demand people's obedience. Those who broke the sabbath denied God's right to rule over them. So sabbath-breaking was punished by the death penalty (Exod. 35:2; Num. 15:32-36).

As well as the sabbath day, the law of Moses ordered sabbath years (Lev. 25:1-7). This was to give the land rest every seventh year. God promised the Israelites that a large harvest in the sixth year would provide enough food for the seventh year of rest (Lev. 25:20-22). We do not know how often the sabbath year was observed, but it seems to have been ignored for a long period before the exile. Only during the exile could the land enjoy its sabbath rests (2 Chr. 23:21; Lev. 26:34,35).

The Israelites also did not always keep the weekly sabbath (Neh. 13:15-22; Jer. 17:19-27). The death penalty does not seem to have been used at these times. Even when the Israelites did keep the sabbath, they often kept it in a merely ceremonial way, seeing it as a hindrance to business (Amos 8:5) or thinking that as long as the sabbath was kept, justice (Isa. 1:13-17) and faithfulness to God (Hosea 2:11-13) did not matter. The prophets had to remind the people that obeying God was more important than observing mere forms of worship (Amos 5:21-24).

During the years between the Old and New Testaments, the Jews worshipped God in the synagogues on the sabbath day. This worship put much emphasis on the study of the law. Many extra traditions were added to the biblical laws, including those which made sabbath-keeping more rigid.

Jesus went to the synagogue on the sabbath (Luke 4:16) but he spoke against these extra rules on keeping the sabbath. He restored the true meaning of the sabbath as a day for people to use (Mark 2:27) and said that people were allowed to eat on that day even if it meant plucking corn (Matt. 12:1). Jesus said it was right to do good deeds on the sabbath (Matt. 12:9-14). What is even more important, Jesus said he was Lord of the sabbath (Mark 2:28) which is similar to the Old Testament's teaching that God was Lord of the sabbath because the day belonged to God.

In the early days of the church, Christians met for worship on the Lord's Day - that is, Sunday - rather than on Saturday, the Jewish sabbath (see Lord's Day). The Lord's Day was not a new sabbath. The first Christians believed that the sabbath was fulfilled in Christ (Col. 2:16,17). The sabbath was a picture of heaven, which is the final rest to come (Heb. 4:1-11). Christian worship took place on Sunday evenings (Acts 20:7-12) because the Christians would have had to work during the day. It was not until three hundred years later that Sundays became a holiday in the Roman empire.

Although the sabbath has been fulfilled in Christ, it still teaches Christians today. Firstly, there is a need for regular physical rest. Secondly, work is not the whole of life and there is a need to spend time thinking about God in worship, individually, and with others as a church. Thirdly, Christ is the place where spiritual true rest is to be found. He gives believers rest now as they trust him for their salvation and will give them rest in its fulness in the glory to come.

Sackcloth

This coarse cloth was usually made from goat hair, although camel hair was sometimes used (Matt. 3:4). Its dark colour made it a good symbol for blotting out the sun's light (Rev. 6:12; Isa. 50:3). Palestinian shepherds wore sackcloth because it was cheap and did not wear out easily. The same material was used for making sacks (Gen. 42:27).

The Israelites and other peoples wore sackcloth as a sign of sorrow and mourning. This could be for the dead (Gen. 37:34), a national disaster (Lam. 2:10) or sin (Jonah 3:5). It was usually worn as a band or skirt around the waist (Isa. 32:11; Jer. 48:37) next to the skin (Job 16:15; 2 Kings 6:30). People lay on sackcloth (2 Sam. 21:10; Isa. 58:5). Prophets who preached repentance wore sackcloth (2 Kings 1:8; Isa. 20:2; Matt. 3:4; Rev. 11:3).

Sacrifice

Each of the five main Old Testament sacrifices (offerings) — burnt, meal, fellowship, sin and guilt — is described in Lev. chapters 1-5. As well as these offerings by fire, there were other offerings, such as incense (Exod. 30:1-10), wave offerings (Lev. 14:12-13), and drink offerings (Num. 28:7). Sacrificing human victims was condemned strongly (Lev. 20:4).

Each type of sacrifice had its special ritual and meaning. In the burnt offering, the whole animal was burnt. In the peace, sin and guilt offerings, only the fat and kidneys were burnt. In the peace offering, the priest had the breast and thigh and the worshipper took the rest. In the sin and guilt offerings, only the priest had a share, not the worshipper. The burnt offering gave homage to God. The wave offering of the firstfruits (Lev. 23:10,11) gave joyful thanks to God for the entire harvest which he had provided (cf. Deut. 16:9-11).

Each type of sacrifice had its own special meaning. At the centre of the sacrificial system was atonement for sin, through the shedding of blood (Lev. 17:11). Sometimes this atonement made something clean and set it apart to God (Exod. 29:37). At other times it turned God's anger away from the sinner. In the sacrifice, the person's guilt was passed to the animal, which then died instead of the sinner. The animal was a substitute (Exod. 29:10-28).

Sacrifices were costly to offer. The worshipper was giving something which sustained his own life. He should not offer anything which cost nothing (2 Sam. 24:24). And this sacrifice should be one of his best animals, usually a male and always without blemish.

In patriarchal days, the head of the family normally offered the sacrifice (Gen. 8:20; Job 1:5). Moses taught that only priests from his brother Aaron's family could offer sacrifices although the worshipper sometimes killed the animal (Lev. 1:5). All sacrifices were to be made in one place only, the place that God chose (Deut. 12:4-6). Later, the Israelites disobeyed this by offering sacrifices at high places throughout the land (2 Kings 14:4).

The nations around Israel thought that sacrifices were magical. They believed that if sacrifices were offered, the gods would be happy. But in Israel, sacrifices were part of communion with God, where the worshippers sought for forgiveness and their sins were forgiven. Sacrifices, therefore, were without value unless they were made by people with broken spirits and contrite hearts (Ps. 51:16-19). The prophets spoke against the offering of sacrifices without true commitment to God and a desire to obey him. To obey was better than sacrifice (1 Sam. 15:22) and sacrifices without obedience were hateful to God (Isa. 1:11-17; Micah 6:6-8).

Sacrifices were made on many different occasions. Some were offered for the nation as a whole; others for individual worshippers. The various feasts included sacrifices. There were also daily sacrifices.

The New Testament teaches that there is now only one sacrifice which can atone for sin: the sacrifice made by Christ by his death on the cross. His shed blood makes his people clean in God's sight (Heb. 9:13,14). The Old Testament sacrifices pointed towards this one, true sacrifice of Christ (Heb. 9:23-10:14). Christ died as the substitute for sinners. God's anger was on him instead of on his people (Rom. 3:25). Unlike the sacrifices in the Old Testament which had to be offered many times, Christ's sacrifice was made at one place and at one time. No other sacrifice for sin is necessary (Heb. 10:10). Those who see the communion service as a re-enactment of Christ's sacrifice ignore this clear teaching.

The New Testament also describes all Christians as priests who offer sacrifices to God (1 Peter 2:5; Rom. 12:1; Phil. 2:17). These sacrifices do not atone for sin. (Even the Old Testament sacrifices had other purposes as well as atonement). The sacrifices offered by Christians are commitment to God in service, and praise to him. God accepts such sacrifices.

Sadducees

The Sadducees were the rival Jewish party to the Pharisees. Most of the Jewish priests in New Testament days were Sadducees. In fact, it was a party made up almost entirely of priests and certainly only rich Jews belonged to it. Unlike the Pharisees, the Sadducees had no following among the Jewish people as a whole.

Despite their small numbers, the Sadducees were very powerful. In Christ's and the apostles' day they controlled the Jewish council (Sanhedrin). When the temple was destroyed in AD70 the Sadducee party disappeared. Soon after that, the Jewish religion came under the control of the Pharisees.

Sadducees were mainly interested in politics, but they also held views on religion which were greatly different from those of the Pharisees. They held these views strongly and considered it a virtue to argue with their teachers. Being a priestly party, they accepted the laws of Moses but did not accept the additional traditions which the scribes had added to the written law. They denied the resurrection of the body, believing that the soul died with the body. Because they thought that there was no after-life, neither could there be judgment after death. They also denied the existence of fate or predestination controlling people's lives and the existence of angels and demons (Mark 12:18; Acts 23:8).

Salvation, Saviour

People can be saved from many different situations. The word 'salvation' in the Bible refers to a variety of circumstances. A saviour is someone who rescues people from distress and brings them to safety. God sent saviours to Israel to save them from their enemies. These Old Testament saviours were ordinary people but the Bible makes it clear that it was God who saved his people through these human saviours (Judg. 1:18,19; 1 Sam. 14:6).

God is the only true Saviour. There is no salvation for mankind apart from him (Isa. 43:11; Hosea 13:4). The Bible tells us that all three persons of the Trinity are concerned in the work of salvation. The New Testament says that the Father planned to save his people (Eph. 1:3-6), the Son provided that salvation (Eph. 1:7-11), and the Spirit applies that salvation to the elect (Eph. 1:13,14; John 3:6).

In the early years of Israel's history, people were saved mainly from ordinary troubles which all mankind shares, such as an angry brother (Gen. 32:11), death through famine (Gen. 45:5) or war (Josh. 2:13), enemies and oppression (Judg. 6:15; 1 Sam. 4:3). God's great act of salvation in the Old Testament was to rescue his people from slavery in Egypt (Exod. 14:30; Deut. 33:29). Centuries later, when God rescued his people from exile in Babylon, he compared it with that great rescue from Egypt (Isa. 43:11-21).

First, salvation in the Old Testament was sometimes from ordinary, physical distresses which also often had a spiritual aspect. In the exodus from Egypt, God showed his glory over the oppressors (Exod. 14:4). The judges saved Israel from the nations around

(Judg. 2:16). Sin was the cause of the people's trouble (vv. 10-19). In other words, the Israelites were rescued from the results of their sin against God. Also, the psalmists asked God to save them from their enemies as they were in a right relationship with him and sought to obey him, whereas their enemies were evil men (Ps. 7,86,120). Salvation, in fact, is closely connected with God's righteousness (Isa. 45:21; 51:8).

The Old Testament also talks of salvation from sin (Ps. 51:14; Ezek. 37:23). Sacrifices were made to atone for sin and atonement and redemption are part of salvation in the Bible. The Old Testament teaching on salvation leads the way to the New Testament teaching which emphasizes salvation from sin.

Second, salvation in the New Testament is salvation from sin. God sent Jesus into the world to save his people from their sins (Matt. 1:21). The name Jesus means Saviour. He is the only Saviour (Acts 4:12). He saved his people by dying on the cross (1 Cor. 1:18) where he took the wrath of God against sin instead of it falling on the sinner (Rom. 3:23,24; 2 Cor.5:15). As in the Old Testament, so in the New Testament, God shows his righteousness in his saving acts (Rom. 3:21,22).

God gives this salvation as a free gift. However, this salvation is not complete in Christians at their new birth (Rom. 13:11). Throughout their lives here on earth, Christians are being saved from sin (1 Cor. 1:18b; 2 Cor. 2:15). The good deeds Christians do can never earn even the smallest part of their salvation, but these good deeds do show that they are truly saved, and are being saved, by God. True faith always leads to obedience (James 2:14-26).

Salvation will be complete in the new heaven and new earth. The New Testament does not promise Christians salvation now from disease, death, pain and other trouble. Instead, they may expect these as part of their witness to the Christ who suffered here on earth (John 15:20; 1 Peter 4:13). On the other hand, believers are saved from the results of sin as well as from sin itself and this includes salvation from death, disease, oppression, sorrow. They will receive that full salvation, including salvation from all these troubles, not now, but in the world to come (Rev. 21:4).

Samaria, Samaritans

King Omri built the city of Samaria on a hill as the new capital of the northern kingdom of Israel (1 Kings 16:24). His son Ahab built his palace there (1 Kings 22:37,39). Samaria soon became well-known as a place of idolatry (2 Kings 3:1-3; Isa. 10:11; Hosea 8:5).

The Assyrians besieged the city in 725BC and captured it three years later. After the citizens refused to pay a tax, Sargon II of Assyria deported nearly 27,300 captives and replaced them with peoples from other nations (2 Kings 17:6,24-41). Judah remained in contact with the northern Israelites (2 Chr. 30:1-11) but relationships between the Jews and the Samaritans deteriorated soon after the Jews returned from Babylon. By this time, the name Samaritan included those from other towns and villages around the city of Samaria.

When the Jews started to build the temple after their return from exile, the Samaritans wanted to help them. The Jews refused their help, which made the Samaritans try to stop the work on the temple (Ezra 4). The Jews did not accept help from the Samaritans because they were a mixed race of Israelites and other nations, which led to them having an impure religion. Ezra and Nehemiah only sought to ensure that the Jews did not marry people from other nations, for the same religious reasons (Ezra 9; Neh. 13:23-27).

Jesus insisted that salvation was from the Jews (John 4:22) but did not share the Jewish dislike of the Samaritans. He spoke to a Samaritan woman, which led to many other Samaritans believing on him through a two-day stay in Sychar (John 4:1-42). One of his parables had a Samaritan hero, which would have hurt Jewish pride (Luke 10:25-37). When he sent the apostles into the world to preach, Jesus mentioned Judaea and Samaria together after Jerusalem (Acts 1:8). Philip the evangelist preached to the Samaritans, followed by the apostles Peter and John (Acts 8:4-25).

The Samaritans believed in one God and accepted the law of Moses. They thought that God chose Mount Gerizim as the place of sacrifice (cf. Deut. 27:4-7,12,13) and they built a temple there (cf. John 4:19-21). They looked for Moses to return as the restorer in a similar way to the Jews waiting for the Messiah. They also believed in a coming day of judgment.

Sanctification, Sanctify

Sanctification means holiness, and to sanctify means to make something or someone holy. See Holy.

An important use of the word 'sanctification' in the New Testament is the moral and spiritual growth of Christians. When Christians are being sanctified, they become more holy, that is, more like Christ in the way they think and act. Christians are called to be holy (1 Peter 1:16). God sanctifies his people (1 Thess. 5:23). This is part of the work of the Holy Spirit in the lives of believers (Rom. 15:15; 2 Thess. 2:13). God sanctifies them through the truth of his Word (John 17:17) and through their faith in that truth (2 Thess. 2:13) and in Christ (Acts 26:18). Being sanctified through the truth means that believers must struggle against sin and obey God and his Word (Gal. 5:16-26; 1 Peter 1:2,14,15).

There are three kinds of sanctification:

First, sanctification is God's work in Christians, yet it demands effort on their part also (Heb. 12:14) as they seek to obey God increasingly. They should seek greater holiness (1 Thess. 5:23) but will not be fully holy, or completely like Christ, until they reach heaven (1 John 3:2).

Second, sanctification in Heb. 10:10, for example, means that God thinks of believers as holy, and is close in meaning to Paul's use of the word 'justification' (Rom. 5:1).

Third, another use of 'sanctify' is found in 1 Cor. 7:14. This means that the non-Christian partner is pure as far as the marriage relationship is concerned. It does not mean that the partner is morally perfect but that the marriage is not unclean.

Sanhedrin

The Sanhedrin referred to in Matt. 5:22 'council' may be a local court, but elsewhere in the New Testament it means the supreme Jewish council which met at Jerusalem. Although Judaea was a Roman province governed by a Roman procurator, the Jews were allowed to govern the province by its own laws. They had some civil duties and could also administer criminal law as well as judge on religious matters. When the death penalty was passed, the Roman governor had to examine the case and pass judgment.

The high priest presided over the Sanhedrin. Members of the Sanhedrin were appointed, not elected. As well as the high priest, previous high priests, other priests, members of high priestly families, heads of the tribal families, and scribes made up the Sanhedrin. The scribes were experts in Jewish law. The Sadducees were generally in the majority although there were Pharisees in the Sanhedrin as well as Sadducees.

When the Sanhedrin voted on whether an accused person was guilty or not, the members stood, starting with the youngest. Students could speak for the accused to be acquitted, but not for him to be condemned. Members could change from a guilty verdict to a not guilty one, but not the other way round. The accused could be acquitted by a simple majority. Normally the Sanhedrin gave the benefit of the doubt to the accused.

Satan

Satan is the chief devil, sometimes called 'the devil', or Beelzebub (Mark 3:22). The word Satan means adversary. He is a very powerful (1 Peter 5:8) and cunning adversary (2 Cor. 11:14). He can even work through Christ's closest disciples (Matt. 16:23).

Satan deceives people, preventing them from seeing the truth about Christ (2 Cor. 4:4). Everyone who is not a child of God is under Satan's rule but Christ came to destroy Satan's works (1 John 3:8).

All this is part of a great spiritual war which is being waged between God and Satan. God is truth, but Satan is the father of lies (John 8:44). God is life, but Satan rules over death (Heb. 2:14). Christians are those who have crossed sides from Satan to God and will therefore be under attack by Satan, which includes temptation (1 Cor. 7:5) and opposition (1 Thess. 2:18). Christians are called to resist the devil with the knowledge that he will run away (James 4:7), but they can only resist him by using the weapons that God has provided for them (Eph. 6:10-18).

Satan has been defeated by Christ on the cross and the final victory is to come (Rev. 20:10).

Scarlet

Scarlet is a dye which comes from the eggs of cochineal insects which attach themselves to the kermes oak. In Bible times it was highly valued and was connected with luxury (2 Sam. 1:24) and royal pomp (Rev. 17:3,4). The tabernacle included scarlet materials (Exod. 26:1,31; 28:5-8,33) because it was made of the very best materials.

Because scarlet was the colour of blood, it was used in some ceremonies in the Mosaic law to show that something was being purified (Lev. 14:4,49; Num. 19:6). In Isa. 1:18 the Israelites' sins were described as scarlet. Again, this is because it was the colour of blood. They were guilty of shedding innocent blood (v. 15). God can make the deepest dye of sin change to the purest white of righteousness (v. 18, cf. Ps. 51:7).

Sceptre

A sceptre is a staff or rod normally held by kings. It is a symbol of their kingship and authority. (For example of use, see Esth. 4:11; 5:2, etc.)

Ps. 45:6 says 'the sceptre of your kingdom is a right sceptre', meaning that righteousness, justice, characterize God's rule over mankind. Heb. 1:8 quotes this scripture and applies it to the Son's kingdom.

School-Master

This word appears in Gal. 3:24,25 and 1 Cor. 4:15. It refers to a man in ancient Greek and Roman times who looked after a child. The school-master was normally a slave whose tasks included the discipline of the child and taking him to school and back home again. Paul is saying in Galatians that the law looked after the Jewish nation and disciplined them until Christ came, who provided salvation through faith.

The Greek Paidagogos, translated 'school-master', but more accurately 'one who leads a child', gives us our word pedagogy, meaning 'instruction of children'.

Scribes

The scribes were a profession found throughout the ancient world. They were highly regarded, for very few other people could read or write. Scribes wrote letters to dictation, legal contracts, kept records and had other similar activities. Some scribes were important officials of state, with great influence.

After the exile, Jewish scribes became more identified with the priests. Ezra was both priest and scribe (Neh. 8:9). These scribes copied Moses' law, interpreted it, and taught it to the people (Neh. 8:13).

In the New Testament, most of the scribes belonged to the Pharisee party. Like Ezra, they were experts in the law but by this time many extra traditions had been added to the written law of Moses. The scribes were influential in the synagogues and some sat in the Sanhedrin, the supreme Jewish council. Mostly, they opposed Christ and the apostles — for example, see Matt. 23:2.

Scripture

The Greek word simply means 'a writing'. The New Testament often used this Greek word for the written Word of God. In those places, our translations use the word 'Scripture'.

Scripture was written by men. These men's personalities can be discerned in what they wrote. They also wrote what God wanted them to write, because God's Spirit spoke to their minds as they wrote (2 Peter 1:20,21). God breathed his Word through his servants to give us a profitable message (2 Tim. 3:15-17).

Sometimes when the writers could have written 'God said', they wrote 'the Scriptures say' (Rom. 9:17; 10:11). God cannot be separated from the Scriptures. Those who want to obey God must obey the Scriptures. When they obey the Scriptures, they obey God. Of course, Bibles are not God but God meets people when they read the Bible and speaks to them through its words.

Because Scripture is God speaking, it must be obeyed. Because Scripture is God's truth (John 17:17) even the smallest part has its meaning, (as shown in Gal. 3:16 where Paul notes that the word 'seeds' is plural, not singular) and must be fulfilled (Matt. 5:18). The Bible's theme is Christ and shows the way to life (John 5:39).

When the New Testament speaks of Scripture, it usually means the Old Testament. In the earliest days of the Christian church, some of the new Christian writings were seen as Scripture. Paul quotes Deut. 25:4 and a saying found in Luke 10:7 and calls them both

Scripture (1 Tim. 5:18). He may have quoted directly from Luke's Gospel, or both he and Luke may have quoted from another written record which is now lost (cf. Luke 1:1,2). Obviously, Christ's sayings were regarded as Scripture. In 2 Peter 3:16 Paul's letters are set beside Old Testament Scripture. So even before all the New Testament books were written, at least certain parts of our New Testament were regarded as Scripture.

This respect for the New Testament writings continued after New Testament times until in AD367 the eastern churches accepted the same twenty-seven books as we have today as Scripture. The western churches agreed with these thirty years later. Ever since that time, the mainstream of Christian belief has accepted these books as Scripture and we, too, may have full confidence in them.

Seah (Hebrew), or Sata (Greek)

A dry measure for flour and cereals. It held probably about 7.3 litres. Used in Matt. 13:33; Luke 13:21.

Seal, sealing

Seals in biblical days were either stamps or cylinders which made a mark in clay or wax. They were used to show that letters (1 Kings 21:8), royal decrees (Esth. 3:12), land purchase deeds (Jer. 32:10-14), covenants (Neh. 10:1) and similar documents were genuine and had a proper authority. Rulers gave their deputies seals to mark their decrees (Gen. 41:42; Esth. 3:10). We also read of rooms (Dan. 6:17) and tombs (Matt. 27:66) being sealed to make sure that nobody broke into them.

The Bible also uses the word 'seal' as a picture of various things, including something hidden, like a scroll (Isa. 29:11; Rev. 10:4), something that was securely held (Deut. 32:34; Job 14:17), or something that was genuinely owned by someone (Rom. 4:11).

Paul talked of the Holy Spirit as a seal. The Holy Spirit is like a 'deposit' in believers to show that God owns them (cf 2 Cor. 1:22) and that they are genuine children of God. They are 'sealed' with the Holy Spirit when they first believe (Eph. 1:13). This seal guarantees that they will be kept safe at the day of judgment, which for Christians is the day of redemption (Eph. 4:30).

Selah

This word appears seventy-one times in the Psalms and three times
in Habakkuk 3. Nobody today really knows what it means, but it is
probably some kind of instruction for the singers and musicians.

Examples of use : Ps. 3:2; 143:6; Hab. 3:3,9,13.

Seraph, Seraphim (plural)

This name for an angelic creature is only found in Isa. 6:2,6. Isaiah
described them as being human in shape but with six wings. They
used four of these wings to show honour to God and the other two
for flying.

The word 'seraph' comes from the Hebrew word for burning.
Isaiah saw angels bright as fire, which befits God's holiness and the
purity of God's presence. The seraphim were also God's servants
who purified Isaiah's lips with fire.

Shekel

The shekel was a unit of weight used throughout Canaan and
Mesopotamia. Three thousand shekels made up a talent. The exact
weight of a shekel varied according to the time and place.

There were three types of shekel. For ordinary business use, the
common shekel (2 Kings 7:1) was used, which was about 11-12
grams. The sanctuary shekel (Exod. 38:25) was about 10 grams and
the third, the royal (2 Sam. 14:26) or heavy shekel, weighed about
13 grams.

Payment for goods was often made with silver, which was
weighed out according to the appropriate shekel. Coins, which
included shekels, were not used until after the exile of the Jews in
Babylon.

Shekinah

'Shekinah' comes from the Hebrew word which means 'to dwell'.
It is not found in the Bible but the Jews used it to describe the shining

out of God's glory as he lives among his people (Exod. 25:8; 29:45). They were trying to avoid describing in human ways the presence of God that they saw in the Old Testament. The word came into use after Bible times.

The shekinah glory - i.e. the blazing light that signified the presence of God - was to be seen on the mercy-seat in the holy of holies (see Exod. 40:34,35; 1 Kings 8:11; Ezek. 44:4; Lev. 16:13; Rom. 9:4 'the glory'). The concept of God dwelling with his people is found in both Old Testament and New Testament. See John 14:23.

Sheol

This Hebrew word is used in the Old Testament to describe death or the grave. It is pictured as a hungry monster (Isa. 5:14) and a place to which the dead go. Although it is sometimes described as a punishment for sin (Ps. 9:17), good men such as Jacob (Gen. 37:35) as well as bad men like Korah (Num. 16:30) go there.

It is best not to put more meaning to the word 'sheol' than 'the grave'. The Bible teaches that this life is not the end, but everlasting bliss or torment follows. However, going to sheol seems to mean simply dying and going into a grave. A wider reading of both Old and New Testaments will reveal teaching on what happens after death.

The Old Testament links sheol with sin. See Gen. 2:17. Rom. 5:12 agrees that death is the punishment for sin.

Some ancient tombs were dug quite deeply into the ground. The grave was a picture of something going deep into the earth (Job 11:8).

Shiloh

Shiloh was north of Bethel, east of the road from Bethel to Shechem and south of Lebanon (Judg. 21:19). It has been identified with some ruins on a hill nine miles north of Bethel. Earlier this century, some Danes excavated the site and suggested that Shiloh was destroyed about 1050BC.

The tabernacle was set up at Shiloh while Joshua was still alive (Josh. 18:1). The sanctuary remined there at least until the death of

Eli (1 Sam. 4:4,12-18). There is no account in the Bible of the destruction of Shiloh but later biblical writers looked back to it as an example of God's judgment (Ps. 78:59-61; Jer. 7:12-14). Shiloh may have been destroyed by the Philistines shortly after the death of Eli as there is no record of the tabernacle in Shiloh after Eli. In fact, the ark was soon in Kiriath Jearim (1 Sam. 7:1,2) and the priests a few years later were in Nob (1 Sam. 22:11).

Despite its destruction, Shiloh was later inhabited by a few people (1 Kings 11:29; Jer. 41:5).

Shewbread (NIV - bread of the Presence)

This was twelve baked loaves which were put out each sabbath on a table on the north side of the tabernacle. The priests were to make sure that there were always these loaves before God's presence. When new loaves were brought, the twelve put out on the previous sabbath were eaten by the priests in a holy place. The Kohathites from the tribe of Levi were responsible for the shewbread (1 Chr. 9:32).

Sign

A sign is a mark that points to a meaning that needs to be explained. There are many different kinds of signs in the Bible and we should take care to find out what meaning is intended by each sign.

The mark which points to the meaning may be something like a group of stones (Josh. 4:6-8), something that happens, such as a birth (Isa. 7:11) or a death (1 Sam. 2:34).

The Bible usually explains what the signs mean. The stones in Josh. 4:6 were to be a reminder to later Israelites that God had divided the River Jordan for their ancestors to cross over into the promised land. Circumcision was the sign of God's covenant with Abraham which showed that God had made a covenant with his people (Gen. 17:11).

Miracles are a sign that God is at work (Exod. 7:3; John 2:11). They also point out that the miracle worker was sent by God (Exod. 4:8). This can be confirmed by examining the Bible story to see whether the miracle worker was a godly person, doing what was clearly God's will, and whose message agreed with other teaching in the Bible. Miracles can also be a sign that the worker is God's enemy (Deut. 13:1-4; Rev. 13:13) but in those cases, the three points above would not be found in the life of the miracle worker.

See Miracle.

Sin

Sin began with the devil (1 John 3:8) before Adam's fall in the Garden of Eden. People may sin because they are tempted by someone else (vv. 1-5). But they sin because they want to, not because someone forces them to sin (v. 6). Sin starts in the sinner's heart ('pleasing to the eye') and mind ('desirable for gaining wisdom') and leads to doing something sinful ('Eve took some and ate it and gave some to Adam, who also ate').

Sin is opposition to God. In Gen. 3 the attack is on God's truthfulness (vv. 3,4). Sin shows that people prefer to follow the devil and do what they want, rather than obey God (vv. 1-6).

Sin brings shame (v. 7), fear (vv. 8-10), sorrow, pain and death (vv. 16-19). Even creation is spoilt by human sin (v. 17). Human beings are separated from fellowship with God (v. 23). Yet there is still hope, for God is a God of grace. He made something to cover Adam and Eve's shame (v. 21) and hinted at a coming Saviour (v. 15).

Although sin may hurt other people, it is primarily directed towards God (Ps. 51:4; Rom. 8:7). Sinners fail to live up to God's standards. These standards are set by God's holiness (Lev. 11:44; Rom. 3:23) and are given us in his law. Sin is lawlessness (1 John 3:4). But sin is more than negatively failing to meet God's demands. Sinners positively rebel against God's way and set up their own standards in the place of God's.

Adam's sin damaged human nature completely. Because he sinned, all human beings (except Christ) are sinful from the very beginning of their lives (Ps. 51:5). Whether you look at a person's heart (Mark 7:20-23), desires (Gal. 5:17), mind (Rom. 1:28) or in any other way, that person is completely corrupt. This does not mean that people always do the very worst possible. They may think and do things that are right and good, but even then what they do is tainted with sin. Mankind's best acts are not at God's holy standard (Isa. 64:6).

Because people are born sinful, their spiritual selves are dead (Eph. 2:1), they cannot know God or even understand that God's way is right and their way is wrong (1 Cor. 2:14). Their sinful natures lead them to please themselves rather than God. When Adam and Eve first sinned, they had to be tempted by another person because their hearts were pure. Because people's hearts now are sinful, they do not need anyone to suggest sins to them, for now they can lead themselves astray (Mark 7:20-23; Heb. 3:10). They are also tempted to sin (1 Cor. 10:13).

God must react against sin. He is too holy to accept sin in his presence (Hab. 1:13) and his anger must rage against all sin (Rom. 1:18). However, by the salvation that Christ has procured, God has given a way of escape from sin and death.

Sin offering

Sin offerings were made to atone for ceremonial uncleanness and for unintentional sins. The Old Testament did not include atonement for deliberate sins (Num. 15:30).

People who were made ceremonially unclean, such as by touching something unclean (Lev. 5:2,3) or after childbirth (Lev. 12:8) made sin offerings, as well as those who had done something morally wrong (Lev. 5:1,4). The kind of animal offered depended on who did the sin (Lev. 4). Poor people could offer two doves or pigeons (Lev. 5:7) or even flour (Lev. 5:11). The priest burned the fat and kidneys on the altar (Lev. 4:8-10) and with other men in his family ate the meat in a holy place (Lev. 6:24-27). The worshipper did not share in any part of the sacrifice.

Slaves, slavery

Slavery in Bible times was not the same as slavery in more recent times. In the 18th and 19th centuries, slaves were taken against their will from their homes and treated like animals, often with horrible cruelty. Old Testament law did not allow this. Kidnapping people and making them slaves was punishable by death (Exod. 21:16). Slaves had rights and could claim justice (Job 31:13). If their master maimed them, he had to set them free (Exod. 21:26,27) and if he killed them, he was punished, no doubt by the death penalty (Exod. 21:20). If he bought a female slave as a concubine, he had to give her full rights as a daughter-in-law or wife, otherwise he had to release her (Exod. 21:9-11).

Prisoners of war could be made slaves (Deut. 20:11-14). Other slaves were bought from other nations (Lev. 25:44-46), were born in a slave family (Eccl. 2:7), or were slaves because of debt. These latter included thieves who could not pay back what they had stolen (Exod. 22:3), those who were forced into slavery to pay off a debt and those who sold themselves to avoid bankruptcy (Lev. 25:39-43).

Six years' service was enough to repay the debts. After that, a person forced into slavery could go free, although he or she could continue in service if they chose to do so (Exod. 21:2-6). Israelites who sold themselves into slavery were released in the jubilee year (Lev. 25:40) but non-Israelites could be slaves permanently and passed on in a will (Lev. 25:44-46).

Many slaves in Israel worked on the land or in the home. Others worked in mines or on buildings (1 Kings 9:15). Some helped the Levites in the temple (Num. 31:29-31; Josh. 9:23; Ezra 8;20). Some slaves were given positions of trust and authority (Gen. 39:4) and if their master did not have children, could even be heir (Gen. 15:2,3). Women had their own maids and could give the maid to her husband to bear a child for her if she herself could not have children (Gen. 30:3).

God reminded the Israelites that they once were slaves in Egypt. This should lead them to be kind to their slaves. Slaves should share the sabbath rest (Deut. 5:12-15) and foreign slaves could eat the passover after they had been circumcised (Exod. 12:44). In the Old Testament, then, slaves did not enjoy freedom but they did have rights and were treated as people.

Under Roman law, slaves had no rights and their owners could do as they wished with them. They were protected in some states in the empire, such as Egypt. However, even where Roman law prevailed, many masters allowed their slaves a certain amount of freedom, because they realized that slaves would work better if reasonably treated. Some masters were rough, but generally public opinion influenced them to be fair to their slaves. Slaves mostly did labouring work of some kind, but others were doctors or teachers. Some slaves even held high office in the Roman empire.

The churches in the New Testament included many slaves as members. The apostles taught that in the church everyone was equal. Distinctions like being a slave or being free were not important (Gal. 3:28; 1 Cor. 7:21-23). The apostles taught the slaves in the churches to work hard for their masters, doing everything as if it were for their heavenly lord, Jesus Christ (Col. 3:22-25; 1 Peter 2:18-20). The apostles did not tell masters to release their slaves but said the slaves should be treated kindly. Masters should remember that they have a master in heaven (Eph. 6:9).

The Bible does not oppose slavery but does seek to prevent cruelty. Slaves should be treated as human beings and not as animals. In the New Testament, we find that all people are equal before God and this teaching has led to the eventual ending of slavery in many parts of the world...

Some people criticize the apostles for not protesting against slavery. These people forget that this was a different kind of slavery than in more recent days. If masters had freed their slaves in New Testament times, the slaves would have been without work and probably destitute.

Sling

Shepherds used slings to protect their sheep from wild animals (1 Sam. 17:35,40). Slings were also used in Egyptian, Assyrian and Babylonian armies, as well as by the Israelite army. The people of the tribe of Benjamin were famous for their ability with the sling (Judg. 20:15,16; 1 Chr. 12:2).

Slings were leather straps with the middle part broader in order to hold the stone. The slinger held both ends firmly, whirled the sling over his head, and let go of one end of the sling causing the stone to fly out.

The sling in 2 Chr. 26:14,15 was a machine, or a very large catapult.

Sons of God

The Old Testament uses the term 'sons of God' in various ways. Angels (Job 1:6; 38:7), the people of Israel (Exod. 4:23), the Davidic king (2 Sam. 7:14; Ps. 2:6,7) are all described as sons of God. Jewish writings between the Old and New Testaments describe righteous men as sons of God because they obeyed God like good sons. Jesus uses this meaning sometimes (Matt. 5:45; Luke 6:35).

Jesus Christ is the Son of God in a special way. Those who belong to him are made sons of God. (See Adoption, where this is treated more fully.)

Spirit

In both Hebrew and Greek, the word also means 'breath' and 'wind'. As with other words in the Bible, it is used in different ways but it never loses its basic idea of breath and wind.

All living things breathe. Animals (Gen. 7:15; Ps. 104:29) as well as people (Isa. 42:5) have the breath of life in them. The difference between them is that God breathed directly into man (Gen. 2:7) whereas he simply formed the animals (Gen. 2:19). Spirit, then, means life, and the life (or spirit) of human beings is closer to the divine life than is the animals' life. The Bible also calls that part of a person which survives death 'spirit' (Heb. 12:23).

From the wind, we get the idea of a power that is beyond human control (1 Kings 19:11). The Bible says that God is spirit and mankind is flesh. This is not a description of what God and people are made of but teaches that God holds all power and people are weak (Isa. 31:3). Because its behaviour is mysterious, wind is a symbol of spirit (John 3:8).

Spirit also means the mental and personal aspects of a person. A person's spirit may be contrite and humble (Isa. 57:15), jealous (Num. 5:14), defiled (2 Cor. 7:1) and also consecrated to God (1 Cor. 7:34). Caleb's different spirit (Num. 14:24) means that his attitude was different from that of the other ten spies. He trusted God to give them the victory, whereas the others only looked at the difficulties ahead.

The Bible tells us about a spirit world. Angels are spirits who serve God, and evil spirits are those who oppose God (see Angel, Devil). These spirits do not have physical bodies, although they appear in a material form to human beings in order that they may be seen.

God is Spirit (John 4:24). He does not have a physical body. God the Son took a body to become Jesus Christ, and that body was, and is, completely human. The Bible sometimes seems to teach that God has a body, for he walked in Eden (Gen. 3:8) and could smell sacrifices (Gen. 8:20,21). But God is very different from us (Isa. 40:25). God showed himself in human form and talked about himself as if he had a body like ours, in order that we might understand a little about him.

God is Spirit and the spirits of believers respond to God (Rom. 8:16). The Bible uses the word 'spirit' to speak about their relationship to God. In this sense of the word, only Christians are spiritual because only Christians have true contact with God in person. Christians are born a second time, that is, by a spiritual birth (John 3:3-8). The words translated 'born again' are literally 'born from above', i.e. through the power of God.

Sometimes Christians misunderstand the word 'spirit' and think that it means the opposite to 'material'. This is not so. Prayer and reading the Bible are spiritual acts, but so is loving our neighbours by meeting their needs. Spiritual acts are those done out of love for God. God tells us to love and help each other as well as to worship him. The real opposite of 'spiritual' is 'sinful' because sin seeks to ignore and disobey God.

Spiritual gifts

The usual Greek word for spiritual gifts comes from the word for grace, but Paul also used the word which means 'spiritual things'. These words show that the gifts are of God's grace, which the Holy Spirit gives to Christians according to his sovereign will.

Salvation is a gift of God's grace (Rom. 5:15; 6:23). Spiritual gifts usually mean the abilities that the Spirit gives to each Christian. He gives them not to make us feel good but to enable us to use them for the building up of the church (1 Cor. 11:7; 1 Peter 4:10). This includes convincing others of God's power working through us (1 Cor. 14:24,25). These gifts can be very different from each other. We find gifts to help us serve one another in practical ways, as well as gifts of leadership, preaching the gospel and teaching Christians the faith (Rom. 12:6-8; 1 Cor. 12:4-11; Eph. 4:7-12; 1 Peter 4:11). Some gifts are more effective than others (1 Cor. 14:1-5) but no gift gives any believers the right to think they do not need the other members in the church (1 Cor. 12:21-26).

When we read through the lists of gifts in the New Testament, we find that each list is different from the others. This suggests that they are only examples, and not complete lists of gifts. Some clearly do not appear in their fullest sense today (e.g. apostles), and gifts not mentioned in the New Testament may be required today to meet our needs which in some ways are different from the needs in apostolic days.

We read of the Spirit giving people in the Old Testament the ability to serve God (Exod. 31:3-5; Judg. 6:34) by equipping them to do a particular task. The prophet Joel foretold a time when the Spirit would be poured out on all people and not just on the few (Joel 2:28). This was fulfilled at pentecost (Acts 2:16) and from then on all followers of Christ have their own gifts from the Spirit (Eph. 4:7).

Stigmata

See Marks.

Stoics

Stoicism was founded by a Phoenician named Zeno. He taught his philosophy in Athens three hundred years before Paul met Stoics there (Acts 17:18). During this time they placed increasing emphasis on ethics and changed much of Zeno's other teachings.

Stoics believed that reason or the supreme power, sometimes called god or Zeus, controlled everything by natural laws. This supreme power determined everything that happened. Cruelty and injustice may exist, but Stoics believed that suffering these gave them the best opportunities to exercise virtue. Stoics believed that virtue was the only real good. For them, virtue meant wanting whatever agreed with nature.

They thought it was better to co-operate with the supreme power by finding out their place in the natural order. This led them to work in public office, but they did so only to be virtuous, not in order to benefit other people. They also rejected emotions of all kinds. Although their personal behaviour was of a high moral standard, their coldness was in stark contrast to Christianity with its emphasis on joy. Christians do not want things to remain as they are but seek to change things for the benefit of all, while looking forward to the new creation where sin will be absent.

Stoning

The Israelites executed people by throwing stones at them until they died. Legal stoning had to have at least two witnesses of the crime, and these witnesses threw the first stones (Deut. 17:6,7). Afterwards, the body was hung on a tree until sunset (Deut. 21:22). The Egyptians also stoned people (Exod. 8:26).

Stumbling block

This word is used in the Old Testament for something that gets in people's way and makes them fall (Lev. 19:14). It is therefore a clear picture of the harm done by anything that makes someone fall spiritually (Ezek. 3:20; 1 Peter 2:8). A similar word in the Greek New Testament originally meant the trigger that sets off a trap, or a trap itself (1 Cor. 1:23).

Suffering

God made this world perfect (Gen. 1:31). Pain arrived only when sin spoiled God's creation (Gen. 3:16-19). Christ's death conquers sin. It will also deliver creation from suffering (Rom. 8:19-23). In the new heaven and new earth, suffering will disappear for ever (Rev. 21:4).

The book of Job is about suffering. God controls our suffering. Even when Satan wants to harm God's people, he can do nothing unless God allows him (1:11,12; 2:4-6). Job's friends believed that the wicked suffer and the righteous prosper (4:7-9). This was generally true for Israel as long as they kept the terms of the Sinai covenant (Prov. 10:27; Ps. 37:25). It must not be made into an unbreakable rule, as Job's friends made it. They said that because Job suffered greatly, he must have sinned greatly (22:4-11). Job denied this (6:24; 31:1-40) and complained that God was unjust to him (7:17-21; 19:6-20). He saw that wicked people often prospered and righteous people often suffered (21:7-21; 24:1-12). At times Job was very bitter against God, yet his faith can also be seen (19:25-27; 23:10).

At last, God showed his superior knowledge (chapters 38,39) and power (chapters 40,41). He cares for his creation (38:25-27,41, etc.) God does not explain Job's suffering. Instead, he shows himself as a just and powerful God (40:8-14). Nevertheless, Job clearly felt that he had benefited by his experience (42:5,12-17).

God does not always tell us why some people suffer and other people do not. God's ways are hidden from us (Eccl. 3:11). The Bible gives some reasons for suffering. God may be punishing sin (2 Kings 17:1-23), testing faith (James 1:12), strengthening character (James 1:2,3; Rom. 5:3), training by discipline (Heb. 12:7-11). Whatever the reason, we can be sure that God always works for the good of his children (Rom. 8:28).

The godly have always suffered as they served God in a sinful world (Heb. 11:35-38). Jesus taught his disciples to rejoice when they suffer for his sake because such suffering shows that they belong to God and will be rewarded (Matt. 5:11,12). In fact, it is a privilege to share in Christ's sufferings.

When we look at Christ, suffering becomes most precious. Isaiah spoke of the servant of God who would suffer greatly in order to redeem his people (Isa. 50:4-6; 53:3-12). Christ fulfilled this at Calvary where he died as the sacrifice for his people's sin. When Christians see that God in Christ suffered greatly, then they are more willing to suffer for Christ's sake.

Synagogue

When Nebuchadrezzar sacked Jerusalem in 587BC, he destroyed the temple and took many of the Israelites into exile in Babylon. The Jews, therefore, could no longer worship at the temple. Nor could they build another temple in Babylon because it could only be built in the place God chose in the promised land (Deut. 12:5). Instead, the Jews met in synagogues.

Unlike the temple, there were no sacrifices made in the synagogues. They became places where the law and the prophets were read and taught and prayers were made. After the exile, they continued to be a central part of the Jewish religion. There were synagogues in Jerusalem even though the temple was rebuilt.

Synagogues were not only places of worship. Children were educated in them and the local civil life was governed from them. Synagogues were governed by elders. Ten adult men had to be present before a service could be held.

Jesus went to the local synagogue each sabbath (Luke 4:16). The early Christian missionaries preached the gospel to the Jews and Gentile God-fearers in the synagogues (Acts 14:1).

The word 'synagogue' comes from the Greek 'sun ago' — to lead, to gather together.

Syria

In the Old Testament, the Syrians are properly called Aramaeans. 'Syria' is a Greek word and is best used for the Greek and Roman provinces from 312BC onwards.

The Aramaeans were a semi-nomadic people who originated in northern Mesopotamia, near Assyria. Amos tells us they came from Kir, or Assyria (Amos 9:7) and the table of nations closely connects the Aramaeans, Assyrians and Elamites (Gen. 10:22).

The Aramaeans started settling in the area now known as Syria before Abraham's day and kept arriving for a long time afterwards. Abraham's nephew Bethuel and his son Laban are called Aramaeans (Gen. 25:20). This connection with the Aramaeans was remembered by the Israelite who said: 'My father was a wandering Aramaean' (Deut. 26:5).

The most important independent Aramaean state in the Old Testament was Damascus. After the death of Solomon (about 922BC) they became particularly strong and troublesome to the Israelites. Later they declined and Damascus fell to the Assyrians in 732BC.

The Aramaean language was closely related to Hebrew. Aramaic became an international language for trade and diplomacy (2 Kings 18:26) and was the official language of the Persian empire. Parts of Daniel and Ezra were written in Aramaic. In New Testament days, Aramaic was the language spoken by Palestinian Jews and therefore the language that Christ spoke.

Tabernacle

The Hebrew word used of the Old Testament tabernacle means 'a dwelling place'. At Sinai, God gave Moses detailed instructions how to make a dwelling place for him. The Israelites carried the tabernacle with them throughout their desert wanderings. After the conquest it was set up at Shiloh (Josh. 18:1) where it stayed until Samuel's day (1 Sam. 1:9). During Saul's reign it was at Nob (1 Sam. 21:1-6). It later was moved to Gibeon (1 Chr. 16:39). Solomon put it in his temple in Jerusalem (1 Kings 8:4).

The tabernacle was made of ten linen curtains joined together. These were made of blue, purple and scarlet thread, with figures of cherubim woven into them. Wooden frames supported the tabernacle, making it into a tent approximately 13.5 metres long by 4.5 metres wide and 4.5 metres high. A curtain divided it into two rooms. The Holy Place was 9 metres long and the Most Holy Place was a 4.5 metre cube. Goats hair curtains covered the tabernacle and these were covered by rams skin and sea cow hides to keep out the rain (Exod. 26).

The priests went into the Holy Place every morning and evening to attend to the lamps which burned all night, and to burn incense (Exod. 30:7,8). The priests changed the Bread of the Presence every sabbath (Lev. 24:5-9). Only on the Day of Atonement, and then after careful preparation, did the high priest enter the Most Holy Place where God's name dwelt (Lev. 16). The various pieces of tabernacle furniture had special positions in the tent.

A curtain courtyard 46 metres long, 23 metres wide and 2.3 metres high surrounded the tabernacle. The altar of burnt offering (the closest place to the tabernacle to which non-priests came) and wash basin stood between the courtyard entrance and the tabernacle.

The tabernacle and the temples that were built subsequently were central to Old Testament worship. They showed that God lived among his covenant people, but also that he is holy and can only be approached when sin is atoned for. The letter to the Hebrews shows that the tabernacle and its rituals is a picture of the saving work of Christ (Heb. 4:14-5:10; 7:23-10:18).

Tabernacles, feast of

See Booth.

Talent

A talent was a weight of approximately 30 kilograms. It was used to measure metals such as gold, silver, bronze and iron. 3000 shekels made up one talent. For an example of use see 2 Sam.12:30.

Tax (tribute, AV)

Tax was an important part of relationships between nations in the Old Testament world. Weaker nations paid tax in the form of money, goods or slaves. This showed they owed allegiance to the king of the stronger nation. At the same time, the great king made sure that his vassals became even weaker by having to pay the tax, and he thereby became richer. Vassals had to pay tax yearly. If they failed to pay on time, the great king would understand this to be rebellion and would seek to punish the offender.

The Jews paid tax when dependent, and received it when powerful. The tax mentioned in Matt. 17:24,25 was the half shekel paid by every Israelite towards the general expenses of the temple. The tax in Matt. 22:17 was the tax paid to the Romans.

Tax-collectors (publicans, AV)

The government of the Roman empire did not employ their tax-collectors. Instead, they made contracts with businessmen who collected the taxes for them. In the days of the republic, the publicani, — tax-collectors — forced people in the provinces to pay more than the legal amount and by doing this became very rich. Augustus reformed the tax-collection system just before the New Testament era in order to stop many of these abuses. Under his system, each province had a supervisor called a procurator or quaestor. This supervisor collected all the direct taxes but the publicani still collected indirect taxes, occasional taxes and the inheritance tax.

People hated the tax-collectors because they often cheated people and became rich (cf. Luke 19:8). Despite the supervision, tax-collectors still managed to cheat. Strict Jews had an additional reason for hating them. They considered the tax-collectors to be unclean because they worked for and had contact with Gentiles. Jewish rabbis taught their disciples not to eat with tax-collectors.

Jesus, however, did eat with them (Matt. 9:9-11), which made the Pharisees angry. The Pharisees also thought that the idea of God hearing the humble prayer of a sinful tax-collector, but not the proud prayer of a self-righteous Pharisee was outrageous (Luke 18:9-14). God forgives sinners if they repent but not proud and self-righteous people (Matt. 21:28-32).

Temple

King David wanted to build a temple to replace the portable tabernacle but God told him that his son Solomon would build it (2 Sam. 7:1-13). Solomon's temple was about 32 metres long, 9 metres wide and 13.5 metres high. Like the tabernacle, it had a Holy Place and a Most Holy Place. In front of the Holy Place was a porch with two stone pillars. The temple building was made of stone and the inside was lined with cedar wood and then decorated. Store rooms three storeys high were built around the outside of the temple. Some of these rooms were used as the state treasury. An inner court (1 Kings 6:36) surrounded the building and this was surrounded by the great court (1 Kings 7:12). Nebuchadrezzar destroyed this temple when he defeated Jerusalem in 587BC.

During the exile, Ezekiel had a vision of a new temple (Ezek. 40-47). This was an elaborate version of Solomon's. The vision was intended to be a picture of the kingdom of God (see Ezek. 47) in a way that Jews before Christ, and especially a priest like Ezekiel, would understand. The vision is not to be taken as a literal temple.

The returned exiles built the second temple. At the beginning, the builders were forced to stop work but after encouragement from Haggai and Zechariah and a word from the Persian emperor, it was eventually finished. It was 27 metres wide and 27 metres high (Ezra 6:3) and was surrounded by stores and priests' rooms. The ark had disappeared at the time of the exile, so the Most Holy Place was empty. This temple stood for five hundred years.

Herod started building his temple in 19BC. Its main structure was finished in ten years but the whole building was not completed until AD64. Six years later the Romans destroyed it as they quelled the Jewish revolt. The shrine was similar to Solomon's but the porch was much wider and higher. In front of the porch was the priests' court where the altar stood. Jewish men could go into the court of Israel which stood in front of the priests' court. They could also go into the priests' court to the altar during the feast of tabernacles. Jewish women could only go as far as the court of the women. Surrounding all these was the court of the Gentiles where anyone could go. On the inside of the outer wall were porches where scribes held their schools and debates and merchants and money-changers worked.

A great curtain hung between the Holy and the Most Holy Places in Herod's temple. It was a thick, stiff mat of woven silk, made with threads bound into ropes as thick as a man's wrist. It was sixty feet high and thirty feet wide. For such a massive curtain to be torn from top to bottom demonstrated a supernatural force (Matt. 27:51).

Christ respected the temple as the house of God (John 2:13-16). He also said that he was greater than the temple (Matt. 12:6) and when his disciples admired the building, he foretold its destruction (Mark 13:1,2,14).

After pentecost the disciples still worshipped at the temple but led by men like Stephen they began to understand that Christ had replaced its sacrificial system (Acts 6:11-14). In the New Testament letters and the book of Revelation, the church (i.e. the people of God) is seen as the temple of God, the place where God dwells, and not any building (1 Cor. 3:16,17; Eph. 2:20-22; 1 Peter 2:4-8; Rev. 3:12). Because individual Christians are part of God's people, they too can be described as God's dwelling (1 Cor. 6:19).

In the new creation, the people of God (the new Jerusalem) will not need any temple for they will be with God and the Lamb of God (Rev. 21:22).

Temptation

Temptation in the Bible means testing. Both God and Satan test people. Testing can be for good or evil. When God tests people, he does so for good reasons, to prove their faithfulness (Gen. 22:1) or to improve their character (James 1:3). Satan does it to trap people into sin (Gen. 3:13; Rev. 20:10) and show up their weaknesses (Job 1:11). He is called the tempter (Matt. 4:3; 1 Thess. 3:5) but he can only tempt God's people with God's permission (Job 1:12; Luke 22:31,32). Human beings cannot accuse God of tempting them to do evil because he does not seek to trap them. When they are tempted to do evil, their sinful desires are leading them astray (James 1:13-15).

Christ taught his disciples to ask God not to lead them into temptation (Matt. 6:13). By being alert and by praying, they will not fail the tests that come their way (Matt. 26:41). Believers have God's promise that they will not be tested more than they can bear and there is always a way out (1 Cor. 10:13). Also, Christians have the help of Christ who knows from experience what temptation is like (Heb. 2:18; 4:15). The Bible warns us not to put God to the test (Matt. 4:7; Ps. 95:9).

Ten Commandments

God gave the ten commandments to the whole nation of Israel at Sinai (Exod. 20:1-22). He then wrote them on two stone tablets (Exod. 32:16). Other names for them are 'the words of the covenant' (Exod. 34:28) and 'the testimony' (Exod. 25:16).

Treaties in ancient west Asia between great kings and their vassals used to set out what benefits the king had given his servant and what the vassal must do in return. Something similar is found in the ten commandments. Exod. 20:2 shows what God had done for his people and the commandments are obligations that he imposes on his redeemed people. They are the words of the covenant because the covenant gives God lordship over his servants the Israelites. Being also the testimony, the commandments show that the way of life that God outlines in them is imposed by a solemn oath.

The covenant between God and the people he redeemed from Egypt is central to the faith of Israel. As the ten commandments are the words of the covenant solemnly imposed as a testimony, they too are highly important. They, but not the law, were written by God's finger (Exod. 31:18) and placed in the ark (Exod. 25:16). Even the ark (Exod. 25:16; Deut. 10:8) and the tabernacle (Exod. 38:21) were named after these commandments.

The ten commandments were religious and ethical principles from which the laws of Israel were drawn. They are not themselves part of the Mosaic law, but its basis. We find that the New Testament continues to have the highest regard for these commandments (Matt. 19:17-19; Rom. 13:8; Eph. 6:1-3; James 2:8-11).

Tents

Tents were among the earliest homes (Gen. 4:20). They were particularly used by nomadic peoples, which included the patriarchs (Gen. 13:18). Women often had separate tents (Gen. 24:67; Judg. 4:17). Tents were often dark in colour (S. of S. 1:5), made from cloths or skins supported on poles.

During their forty years in the desert, the Israelites lived in tents (Exod. 16:16; Num. 16:26) but when they were in Canaan, they lived in houses. Tents were still used by shepherds (Isa. 38:12), armies (1 Sam. 17:54) and in the summer by people who normally lived in houses. In Jeremiah's day, the Rechabites were still living as nomads in their tents (Jer. 35:7).

In the New Testament, Paul and his friends Priscilla and Aquila were tent makers (Acts 18:3).

Teraphim

Teraphim were idols, often used in divination (Hosea 3:4). These were sometimes seen as household gods (Gen. 31:30). Laban was anxious about these gods because the local law made the husband of the woman who possessed them the person who would inherit the family property.

Testimony

The ten commandments are called the testimony (Exod. 25:16; 31:18). This showed the solemnity of the commandments, which are God's demands in his covenant with Israel (see Ten Commandments). From this, we find the word testimonies used to mean God's law (Ps. 19:7; 119:2). This shows that the Old Testament law was given by God's authority.

Tetrarch

Originally tetrarch meant the ruler of a fourth part of an area. The Romans gave the title to anyone who ruled over part of their eastern provinces.

Thank-offering

The thank-offering was not a separate sacrifice on its own but part of the peace offering (Lev. 7:11-15). It was an expression of praise to God.

See Peace Offering.

Tithing

A tithe is a tenth of what people have, which they dedicate to God. Egyptians, Mesopotamians and other ancient peoples gave a tithe to their gods. Abraham gave a tenth to Melchizedek (Gen. 14:20) and Jacob promised God a tenth of all he had (Gen. 28:22). When Israel became a nation at Sinai, Moses gave laws on tithing.

He told them to tithe their grain, fruit, herd and flock (Lev. 27:30-33). As they were all farmers, this covered most of their income. They were to bring their tithes to the Levites (Num. 18:21) at the tabernacle or at the temple (Deut. 12:17,18) where the giver and the Levites shared a joyful meal together from the tithe. In their turn, the Levites gave a tithe of the tithe to the priests (Num. 18:26-28).

If the farmer lived a long way from the temple, he could bring money instead. However, to avoid cheating, he had to add a fifth to the value of his tithe (Lev. 27:31). Every third year, he gave his tithe in his own home town instead of at the temple and the poor as well as the Levites had a share (Deut. 14:28,29). The farmer still had to go to the temple afterwards (Deut. 26:12-15).

People who failed to tithe robbed God (Mal. 3:8) but this does not mean that it was a painful duty. Rather it was an act of joyful worship (Deut. 12:18). It showed that everything a person had belonged to God. The tenth that was dedicated to God stood for all that the giver possessed. Also, it showed the Israelites their responsibility to support the ministry of the Levites and priests and to help the poor and defenceless.

By New Testament days, the Jews had added extra laws on tithing which made it more of a burden to the Israelites. The Jewish teachers saw tithing as a habit rather than as a joyful act of worship which also showed mercy to the needy (Matt. 23:23).

The New Testament does not command Christians to tithe. Nevertheless, the main principles of Old Testament tithing remain. Churches should support their preachers well (1 Tim. 5:17,18) and help the poor (Acts 4:35; 1 Cor. 16:1,2). Giving should be joyful (2 Cor. 9:7) and an act of worship (2 Cor. 8:5). We should give generously because Christ became poor that we might become eternally rich in him (2 Cor. 8:9). The New Testament considers that what is significant now is what we keep for ourselves, not what we give in tithes.

Tongues, gift of

At pentecost, the disciples all praised God by speaking in other tongues. People around, who had travelled to Jerusalem for the feast of pentecost, heard them and recognized these other languages as from their own home areas. When they heard the languages, some of the crowd were puzzled, while others laughed at the disciples. They could nearly all speak Greek or Aramaic and did not need to be addressed in their local languages. But the use of the local languages was a sign that the Holy Spirit was at work, which fact Peter used in his sermon. As he spoke, many in the crowd were convicted, repented and were converted.

The book of Acts mentions two other occasions when people spoke in tongues, both of which were similar to the day of pentecost. These were at Caesarea, when the first Gentiles were converted (Acts 10:46,47; 11:17,18) and at Ephesus when the Holy Spirit came to disciples of John the Baptist (Acts 19:6). Possibly the new converts in Samaria also spoke in tongues, for we read that others could see that the Holy Spirit had come upon them (Acts 8:17-19).

There are many more accounts of conversions in the book of Acts where there is no hint of converts speaking in tongues. We must remember that the first Christians were Jews, who tended to look down on other races. God prepared Peter very carefully before Peter preached to Cornelius (Acts 10-9-20; 11:4-14). When the same thing happened at the first Gentiles' conversion as happened to the Jews at pentecost, it proved to the Jews that even the Gentiles could be converted (Acts 11:15-18). A similar reason accounts for what happened at Samaria. God showed his love for the Samaritans, whom the Jews disliked. In Acts 19 we find disciples of John who had never heard of the Holy Spirit (v. 2). The repeat of pentecost there showed the reality of the Spirit and their conversion.

Apart from Mark 16:17 we find speaking in tongues mentioned only in 1 Cor. 12-14. There are important differences between the references in Acts and those in 1 Cor. In Acts, everyone in the apostolic group spoke in tongues. They were completely under the control of the Spirit. It happened only at the time of conversion and at least at pentecost some hearers knew the languages spoken. In Corinth, not all spoke in tongues (1 Cor. 12:30); the speakers were in control of themselves (14:27,28); the speakers were not new converts; and no one understood unless someone had a special gift of interpretation.

There were similarities as well. Both in Acts and in 1 Cor., speaking in tongues was an act of worship and the words had true meanings even if they were not always understood. Also, unbelievers were either amazed, or laughed, although Paul says in 1 Cor. 14:21,22 that tongues are a sign of judgment on unbelievers.

Paul did not forbid speaking in tongues (1 Cor. 14:39) and indeed did it himself (14:18). However, he also pointed out that there were other gifts which may not seem as exciting but were more useful, and therefore greater, gifts (14:1-25).

Some Christians are still interested in speaking in tongues today. We cannot be sure, however, that what happens today is the same as what happened in New Testament days. In any case, there were at least two different kinds of speaking in tongues in the New Testament and even the Corinthian type did not seem to be common. If it were more common, we would expect it to be mentioned more often, for instance in Eph. 5:19,20 and Col. 3:16, and certainly in the Pastoral Epistles (Timothy, Titus) and in the list of qualifications for elders and deacons. Since it is not mentioned in these later writings, it would seem that the usage of tongues was disappearing from church life.

Transfiguration

Christ's transfiguration was a revelation of his true majesty (2 Peter 1:16) and glory (Luke 9:32). It took place about a week after Peter confessed that Jesus was the Christ (Mark 8:29) and Jesus foretold his death, resurrection and Second Coming (Mark 8:31-38).

As on some Old Testament occasions (Exod. 19:16; 24:15,16; 40:34; 1 Kings 8:11) God appeared hidden in a cloud (Matt. 17:5). Here God confirmed Jesus' messiahship and revealed his divine sonship to Peter, James and John. The words 'Listen to him' remind us of Deut. 18:15 where Moses told the Israelites to listen to the great prophet when he came.

Moses and Elijah represented the law and the prophets, which Jesus fulfilled. These two men also spoke to Jesus about his coming departure, literally, his 'exodus' (Luke 9:31), which meant his death, resurrection and ascension. However, what is even more important is the connection between the transfiguration and Christ's second coming. All three Gospels describe the transfiguration after Christ's prediction of his coming again, and Peter also links the two events (2 Peter 1:16-19). The transfiguration is a foretaste of Christ's coming again in glory.

Tribes of Israel

Jacob had twelve sons, each of whom founded a tribe. The twelve tribes made up the whole nation of Israel, the Old Testament people of God. The tribe of Joseph was divided into two. His sons, Ephraim and Manasseh, whom Jacob adopted as his own (Gen. 48:16) each became a tribe. This should make a total of thirteen tribes but they are always listed as twelve.

The small tribe of Levi was different from the others. They alone had duties at the tabernacle. They did not fight in the army nor did they receive a territory of their own in Canaan. Some lists of tribes, therefore, omit Levi (Num. 7; 13:4-15). Others include Levi but combine Ephraim and Manasseh as the tribe of Joseph (Gen. 49; Deut. 33).

Although some Jews knew their tribal identity even in New Testament days (Luke 2:36; 3:21-28; Phil. 3:50), distinctions between the tribes became less important after the defeat of Judah in 587BC. We should probably read Rev. 7:5-8 to be a symbol of the entire people of God, rather than a literal list of Jews from distinct tribes. The fact, then, that Levi, Joseph and Manasseh are included in this list, but Ephraim and Dan are missing, is not important. What is important is that the Old Testament people of God was made up of twelve tribes and this is a picture of the entire people of God, Jew and Gentile, who are saved by grace.

Tribulation

The Bible words for tribulation carry the idea of being under pressure, such as being pushed through a passage which is too narrow, or being crushed by a heavy weight. It therefore means being in distress. Christ (John 16:33) and his apostles (1 Thess. 3:4) taught that Christians will face tribulations, especially just before the Second Coming (Matt. 24:21-27). Christians must face any tribulations that come their way with patience (Rom. 12:12) because Christ knows all about the tribulations (Rev. 2:9) and God comforts them during the tribulations (2 Cor. 1:4). By God's power, Christians may defeat any trouble that afflicts them, knowing that nothing can separate them from God's love (Rom. 8:35-39). Christians may rejoice in tribulations because they can strengthen them (Rom. 5:3-5) and in any case will soon disappear for ever while believers enjoy the fullness of God's kingdom (Acts 14:22).

Trinity

This word is not found in the Bible. About three hundred years after Christ, church leaders formed the doctrine of the Trinity to settle a controversy by making clear what the Bible taught about God.

The Father is God (Eph. 1:2), the Son is God (John 1:1; 20:28), the Spirit is God (1 Cor. 2:10-14), yet there is only one God, not three (James 2:19). Each person of the Trinity is distinct from the others. The Father is not the Son (John 3:16) and neither of these is the Holy Spirit (John 14:6). All three persons are equally God and fully God and not a part of the divine nature. Each person is eternal, with no beginning and no end (1 Tim. 1:17; John 1:2; Heb. 9:14).

The Trinity is a difficult concept for human beings to understand. We cannot see how three separate persons can each be the whole of one God. The fact that we do not understand his divine nature does not mean that it cannot be trinitarian. God is an infinite being very different from ourselves.

Trumpets, feast of

This festival took place every year on the first day of the seventh month, Tishri. It marked the fact that this was the seventh month, the number seven signifying holiness. Later that month, two of the most important festivals would take place, the Day of Atonement and the feast of booths. The feast of trumpets, then, reminded the people to prepare for these solemn events. It is described in Lev. 23:24,25 and Num. 29:1-6.

Truth

Truth and faith are closely linked in the Hebrew language. Both words come from the same root, which means 'certainty'. So we learn something about both truth and faith. Our faith is in something that is true, not something that may or may not be true. Also, truth is not simply fact as opposed to fiction, but something reliable, something we can trust in.

A statement is true if it agrees with something that exists, or has happened (1 Kings 10:6; Deut. 17:4; Mark 5:33). But the Hebrew mind was less impressed by facts than by the character of the person who said those facts. People may not be able to know the facts for themselves but if the person who tells them is reliable, then the facts can be believed.

God is the God of truth (Ps. 31:5). We can rely on what he says, not only that he is telling us what is right, but that he will keep his promises. He in turn expects truth in his people (Ps. 51:6; 119:151).

Jesus Christ is the truth (John 14:6). We can rely on him because he is the all-powerful and faithful God. He is also the truth in the sense that he shows us the real meaning of life and is full of righteousness and peace (John 1:9). Without Christ, life has no meaning, is dark with evil, and there is no solid ground as a base for living.

Because Christ is the truth, the gospel about him is also the truth (Eph. 1:13). Christians are those who believe the truth but this does not mean merely agreeing with the facts that the gospel brings us. It means committing ourselves to Christ by obeying him (Gal. 5:7). Refusing the truth does not merely mean that you do not believe the facts about Christ, but that you are living an evil life (Rom. 2:8).

The New Testament also uses the word 'truth' in another way. Truth is something that is real, as opposed to something that only appears to be real. The true tabernacle is a heavenly reality. Moses' tabernacle was only a shadow of that reality (Heb. 8:2-5). The manna was a picture of the real bread from heaven, which is Jesus Christ (John 6:31-35).

Unbelief

Unbelief is more than a refusal to accept Christian teaching. It means to disobey God, or to rebel against him (Heb. 3:12-18). Just as the faith of believers commits them to God as they obey him and rely completely on him, so unbelief is a rejection of God and his ways. This is why unbelief is sometimes described as the central sin and the basis of God's judgment on sinners (John 3:18: 16:9).

Urim and Thummim

The high priest kept the urim and thummim in his breastpiece (Exod. 28:29,30; Lev. 8:8). When a leader wanted a decision from God, he asked questions which demanded an answer of either yes or no. The High Priest would then use the urim and thummim to reveal God's decision (1 Sam. 23:9-12). God was not compelled to give an answer and the urim and thummim might say 'No answer' (1 Sam. 28:6).

After the early years of the monarchy, we do not read any more about the urim and thummim until after the exile. Even then the decision had to wait until a priest arose with this means of making decisions (Ezra 2:63). The urim and thummim probably came into disuse because God began to speak through his prophets instead. Along with other things at the temple, the breastpiece with urim and thummim seems to have disappeared at the time of the exile.

Vanity

Vanity in the Bible means something worthless, without any sense, meaning or purpose. Idols are worthless and people who worship them also become worthless (2 Kings 17:15). Even work done by God's people can seem to come to nothing and fulfil no purpose (Isa. 49:4). In Ecclesiastes, the preacher says that if we try to make sense of life by our own efforts, we will fail. We seem to achieve nothing (2:11) and there seems no point in being wise (2:15,16) or good (8:14). Ecclesiastes says that we do not understand what God is doing (3:11; 8:17) and that is why everything seems so senseless. In actual fact, life is really full of meaning and there will be true justice in the end (12:13,14).

The third commandment tells us not to take God's name in vain (Exod. 20:7) which means using God's name in an empty, or false, way. Swearing falsely and using profane language is included, but so is using God's name in any thoughtless way.

Veil

Women in Bible times did not cover their faces with a veil as they do nowadays in Islamic cultures, although there were exceptions (Gen. 38:15). Normally, however, it is obvious that people in Bible times could see a woman's face (Gen. 12:14; 1 Sam. 1:12). Veils were long shawls which could be pulled up to cover the hair. The way women, and indeed men as well, wore their hair was important (cf. Num. 5:18).

Moses wore a veil to cover his face in order to hide the fact that the reflection of God's glory was fading (Exod. 34:33; 2 Cor. 3:13).

For Veil of Temple see note on Temple (curtain).

Vine, vineyard

Growing grapes was an important part of life in Bible times. Grapes were grown very early in biblical history (Gen. 9:20) and were grown in Canaan before the conquest (Num. 13:23,24).

When digging a new vineyard, the farmer dug a trench around the site in which he built a fence or planted a prickly hedge. The soil was very carefully prepared and stones taken away. The vines were planted in rows about 2 metres apart and when the branches grew, they were lifted above the ground on supports. Each spring, the workers pruned the vines with special hooks. After harvesting, helpers trod the grapes in a winepress hewn out of the rock. As they did this, the workers would shout and sing together. The wine was left to ferment in new goat-skin bags or in large clay jars. Some of the harvest was kept as raisin cakes. The owner built a watchtower nearby to protect the crop from thieves during the vintage period.

The vine and the vineyard were symbols of peace and prosperity (1 Kings 4:25) and also of Israel (Ps. 80:8-16; Isa. 5:1-5, cf. John 15:1-8).

Virgin birth

We do not base our belief in the virgin birth only on the words translated 'virgin' as both the Hebrew word in Isa. 7:14 and the Greek word in Matt. 1:23 can be translated 'young woman'. We base our belief on the whole birth narrative in Matthew and Luke. Luke 1:34,35 is a crucial passage - the Son of God was conceived by the Holy Ghost coming upon Mary. Thus, the Bible clearly teaches that Mary was a virgin when she conceived Jesus and remained so until after he was born (Matt. 1:25). Afterwards, Mary and Joseph had children in the normal way (Mark 6:3).

In ordinary births, God creates a new person at conception (Ps. 139:13-16). Christ, however, existed as a person from eternity. In the incarnation, the eternal Word of God, God the Son, became flesh (John 1:14). He became a human being while remaining God the Son. At the conception, therefore, the eternal Word entered the womb of Mary.

Because Christ's humanity was an entirely new creation and not physically descended from Adam, he did not inherit sin as all other human beings do. He was born sinless and remained sinless throughout his life.

Vow

In the Bible, vows are always promises made to God and not to other human beings. This could be to promise to do something if God gives help (Gen. 28:20-22; Num. 21:2), a commitment to do something for God (Ps. 132:2-5), or a dedication of oneself to God (Num. 6:2). A vow offering was a type of peace offering (Lev. 7:16-18).

The law of Moses did not demand that people make vows. It was therefore not a sin if anyone failed to make a vow (Deut. 23:22). However, once a vow was made, it had to be carried out (Num. 30:2). This meant that people should not make rash promises to God (Prov. 20:25; Judg 11:35). The only exceptions to this were that a father or husband could cancel vows made by their womenfolk, so long as they did this immediately (Num. 30:3-15).

No one could vow to give God something which was already his (Lev. 27:26), nor could they vow to give something that God hates (Deut. 23:18).

Watch

A watch was a period of time at night when a guard was kept. The Israelites had three watches each night, including the middle (Judg 7:19) and the morning watches (Exod. 14:24). The Roman system had four watches to each night (Mark 6:48). As the night was from 6.00pm to 6.00am, the Jews had four hours and the Romans three hours for each watch.

Wealth

The Old Testament shows that God sometimes blesses the faithful by giving them riches (Gen. 13:2; Ps. 112:3). This is not an unbreakable rule. Sometimes the wicked and not the righteous are rich (Ps. 73:12). Also, people can become rich by sinful means (Prov. 11:16; 28:8). In the New Testament, we still find that God provides people with material things, but the New Testament puts far less emphasis on material blessings and sees wealth as a snare (1 Tim. 6:17-19).

God gives people riches (1 Chr. 29:12; Eccl. 5:19) but these riches must be used to honour God (Prov. 3:9). This includes giving generously to those in need (Deut. 15:9,10; 2 Cor. 9:11). Wealth can turn people away from God because they can think that they become rich solely through their own efforts (Deut. 8:17), forgetting that it was God who blessed them with wealth. Also, they can trust in wealth (Hosea 12:8; Rev. 3:17), forgetting that it is worthless and unable to help in times of crisis (Prov. 11:4; Isa. 2:7-22). Christ told his disciples to be concerned with spiritual rather than material wealth (Matt. 6:19-24).

Wealth is neither good nor evil. What is important is how people use wealth. Love of money leads to all kinds of evil (1 Tim. 6:9,10) and can lead people away from Christ (Matt. 13:22; Mark 10:22). Love for Christ can lead those with wealth to use it in God's service, remembering that all they possess belongs to God (Acts 4:36,37). On the other hand, Christians without wealth have Christ's assurance that they possess the greatest riches of all, the kingdom of God (Luke 6:20; Rom. 8:17).

Wickedness

Wickedness is doing what is wrong (Ps. 37:21) but it is more than that. It is a hostile attitude to God (Ps. 10:13; Mal. 3:15) and God's people (Ps. 94:3-7; Hab. 1:4). Some men in the Old Testament struggled with the question, 'Why do the wicked prosper?' (Ps. 73:3; Jer. 12:1). By faith and God's revelation, they understood that in the end the righteous will be rewarded and the wicked punished (Ps. 73:17; Dan. 12:3).

The wicked are not necessarily immoral people, or criminals. Even those who practise religion can live lives hostile to God (Luke 11:29; Acts 2:23). Christ redeems his people from their wickedness (Titus 2:14) and in him Christians are reckoned to be righteous (Rom. 4:5,20-25). Those who continue to be wicked will be punished by God (Matt. 13:49,50).

See Sin.

Widow

Widows were usually poor (Exod. 22:22; Mark 12:42) and vulnerable in Bible times because they did not have a husband to support and protect them. God calls himself the widow's defender (Deut. 10:18; Ps. 68:5) and he expects the godly to help them and to give them justice (Deut. 24:17-21; James 1:27). To ill-treat widows was a sign of great wickedness (Ezek. 22:7; Mark 12:40). Being a childless widow while still young enough to bear children was seen as a disgrace (Isa. 4:1; 54:4).

New Testament churches had lists for widows over sixty years old of good character who needed help. Paul recommended that younger widows remarried rather than be included on the list. Also, families should support their own widows, leaving the church to look after those without any means of support (1 Tim. 5:3-16).

Wife

A good wife is a great blessing from God to a man (Prov. 18:22; 31:10). Marrying the wrong woman, however, can be a torture (Prov. 19:13) and she can encourage her husband's sinfulness (1 Kings 11:4; 16:31). The patriarchs took great care over the wives whom their sons married (Gen. 24; 28:1,2) and when they married unwisely, problems followed (Gen. 26:34,35).

Ezra and Nehemiah spoke against those who married wives from other races (Ezra 9:1-15; Neh. 13:23-31). Normally, the Israelites in the Old Testament married Hebrew women but the law allowed them to marry women from other races who were captured in war (Deut. 20:14; 21:10-14). These women would not affect the religious purity of their Israelite husbands, whereas the foreign wives in Ezra and Nehemiah's day did. The lesson for us today is that Christians should marry believers, not unbelievers (1 Cor. 7:39). The Bible does not forbid marrying a wife from a different race, but does forbid marrying a wife from a different religion.

Old Testament men sometimes had more than one wife. These could be full wives, or concubines and slaves, but the Bible nowhere supports polygamy. (See Marriage).

Husbands were to provide for their wives' needs, including food, clothing and marital rights (Exod. 21:10). Barrenness in a wife was a curse (Gen. 20:17,18) but blessing came through a wife who bore several children (Ps. 128:3). It was important for a Hebrew man to have male children, for it was through his male children that his name carried on after him.

Wilderness

Deserts in the Bible include sandy areas with very little life (Deut. 32:10) but grassy areas suitable for grazing animals are also called deserts (Ps. 65:12). Often these would be burnt up in the hot, dry summer (Jer. 23:10). Some deserts had towns spread out in them.

The Sinai desert where Moses led the Israelites for forty years before they entered Canaan is mainly a hilly, desolate area. However, wells, springs and wadis (river beds) bring vegetation to some areas.

Wine

Wine is the juice of grapes which has been fermented. In the Bible, it was always light wine, that is, wine with no extra alcohol added. This makes it less strong than today's heavier wines but it could still lead to drunkenness.

The Bible sees wine as a gift from God (Ps. 104:15), an example of God's blessings (Gen. 27:28), showing rest and prosperity in a settled, farming community (Deut. 33:28). Wine, therefore, could be offered to God (Exod. 29:40), and was tithed (Deut. 12:17). The Israelites did not drink wine while they wandered in the desert (Deut. 29:5,6). Later, the Rechabites did not drink wine because it was not part of the nomadic way of life (Jer. 35:5-10).

Priests on duty (Lev. 10:9) and people who have dedicated themselves to God (Num. 6:3) were to abstain from wine. This was part of the discipline that they were under. And today church elders must be people who only drink a little wine because they must be men with true self-control (Titus 1:7). Paul told Timothy to drink a little wine to help his health (1 Tim. 5:23).

Jesus refused some wine during his crucifixion (Mark 15:23). This may have been given to help relieve some of the pain but, in any case, Jesus refused to drink it because he wanted to keep control of his mind.

Wine can also be a sign of over-indulgence (Isa. 5:12). The Bible warns against the abuse of wine (Prov. 20:1).

The Bible uses wine as a symbol of the work of wisdom (Prov. 9:2), God's wrath (Jer. 25:15), violence (Prov. 4:17), Christ's teaching (Mark 2:22). Its red colour also makes it a fitting symbol of blood (Deut. 32:14,38; Luke 22:20).

Wisdom

Wisdom in the Bible is practical knowledge, understanding. A wise person knows what to do and how to do it. Such wisdom is more effective than brute force or stirring up people's feeling by loud speeches (Eccl. 9:13-18).

Any skill in the Bible is called wisdom. The same Hebrew word is used to describe people like Bezalel who made the tabernacle (Exod. 31:2), wood carvers (Isa. 40:20), professional mourners (Jer. 9:17), sailors (Ezek. 27:8).

Israelite leaders needed wisdom to do their work (Deut. 34:9; 1 Kings 3:7-12). Kings of other nations had their wise men to give them advice (Gen. 41:8; Dan. 5:7). We read of the wise in Israel (Eccl. 12:11) and during the monarchy the wise were a third group of leading men along with the priests and prophets (Jer. 18:18). Later, when the apostles sought to choose leaders in the church, they looked for men who showed wisdom (Acts 6:3).

Not only leaders need wisdom. Everyone needs to know how to behave. The book of Proverbs in particular teaches wisdom and therefore how people can lead disciplined and prudent lives (Prov. 1:2-4). All Christians, not just church leaders, need wisdom (James 1:5). Some people will have a particular gift of wisdom, such as the wise women in David's day (2 Sam. 14:2,3; 20:21,22) and those in the church with a word of wisdom (1 Cor. 12:8).

True wisdom belongs only to God (Job 12:13). He created the world (Prov. 3:19,20; Jer. 10:12) and saves sinners by his wisdom (Eph. 3:8-11). People must have a true fear of God in order to receive God's wisdom (Job 28:28; Ps. 111:10; Prov. 1:7; 9:10). Note how this true wisdom shows itself in obedience to God and keeping away from evil (see also Ps. 119:97-104; James 3:13-18). True wisdom is to evaluate things with the same values as God. If we lack wisdom, then it is God whom we ask (James 1:5).

There is also a false wisdom outside of God's will which is the wisdom of this world (1 Cor. 1:21,26). Such wisdom cannot understand God's ways because God's wisdom is so much greater than that of any person (v. 26). Pagan wisdom is referred to in Isa. 19:11-15 which incites God's wrath.

Witness

A witness is someone who has seen or heard something and who declares this to others, particularly in a law court. The witness may know about the crime directly, or may have learned about it from another person (Lev. 5:1). Moses' law demanded that at least two witnesses testified before anyone was proved guilty (Deut. 19:15). Christ (Matt. 18:16) and Paul (1 Tim. 5:19) applied this rule to the churches. The law recognized that people might testify to lies and dealt severely with such (Deut. 19:16-21).

Contracts that were made also had witnesses (Jer. 32:10). Sometimes monuments (Gen. 31:48; Josh. 22:26,27) served as a witness because they reminded the parties involved of the agreement they had made. Accepting a gift could also be used in a similar way (Gen. 21:30).

God's people are witnesses as they tell others the facts about God and what he has done (Isa. 43:10-12; Acts 1:8; 3:15). An apostle was one who had seen Christ during his ministry on earth and after his resurrection (Acts 1:21,22).

God sees all that people do, and can be called on to act as a witness (Judg. 11:10; 1 Sam. 12:5; Rom. 1:9). The ten commandments (Exod. 16:34) and law of God (Ps. 119:2) are God's witnesses. Christ is the faithful witness (Rev. 1:5), who speaks about God and his ways (John 3:11-13,31-34). The Father joins Christ in witnessing to himself (John 8:18).

Woe

Woe is the opposite of blessedness. When called upon oneself, it is an expression of despair and misery (Isa. 6:5; Lam. 5:16). Generally it is called upon others, where it is a threat of misery to come.

In the Old Testament, the word is mainly found in the prophets. In the New Testament, it is mainly found in the Gospels (e.g. Luke 11:42,43) and Revelation (e.g. 8:13).

Women

The Bible treats women as people of equal dignity to men, which was a contrast to many societies including the Jewish which existed at the time the Bible was written. Both male and female bear God's image in mankind (Gen. 1:27). In the Old Testament, no woman could become a priest but they could worship God by themselves without going through their husbands (1 Sam. 1:10; 2:1-10). There was one woman political leader in Israel, the judge Deborah (Judg. 4:4) and some women prophets (Exod. 15:20; 2 Kings 22:14; Neh. 6:14).

Men led in the home, although children were to respect both parents, not just their fathers (Exod. 20:12). Property was passed down to male descendants, except when a man left no sons. His daughters then became heirs (Num. 27:1-11). Women could have their own money and property and engage in trade (Prov. 31:16-18) although this may not have happened very often.

Christ treated women with respect and as people with dignity and able to have faith. He healed some (Mark 5:21-43) and taught some (Luke 10:39; John 4:7-26). His apostles were all men but several women accompanied him and some gave him financial support (Luke 8:3). Women were the first to know ,about Christ's resurrection (Mark 16:1-8) and a woman was the first to see him alive again (John 20:1-18). This all stresses the importance that Christ put on women, whereas Jewish teachers sometimes saw them as unteachable and inferior to men.

Paul taught that all people are equal in Christ and distinctions of status disappear (Gal. 3:28). Paul warned that women should not seek to dominate (1 Tim. 2:12). Women were highly active in the early church although elders were chosen from the men (1 Tim. 3:11). Women prayed aloud in church services, prophesied (1 Cor. 11:5), worked as deacons (Rom. 16:1; 1 Tim. 3:11), evangelized (Phil. 4:3) and no doubt did other work as well.

See also Family, Mother, Wife.

Word

The Word of God is at the centre of biblical thinking. By his Word, God created the universe (Gen. 1:3,6, etc; John 1:1-3), commands people and makes covenants with them (Exod. 19:6-8; 34:27,28), speaks through the prophets (Jer. 1:2). Christ is the Word made flesh (John 1:14) and the gospel message is the word of Christ (Rom. 10:17). The Word gives new life and must be obeyed (1 Peter 1:22-25).

God reveals himself to mankind. The greatest tragedy for human beings is when God does not speak (1 Sam. 3:1; Amos 8:11-12).

God speaks in words, but he also speaks in what he does. The Hebrew for 'word' can also mean 'acts'. The New Testament tells us that Christ is the Word of God because he is God's message to mankind. This message is found in the person of Christ as God's Son and in the things he did, as well as in the words he spoke. Christ's death is the word of the cross (1 Cor. 1:18) because in the cross God speaks to sinners about the way to be reconciled to himself (2 Cor. 5:19) and therefore to be saved (Acts 13:26).

God's Word describes his character. It stands firm for ever (Isa. 40:8), has full authority (Deut. 12:32), is living (Heb. 4:12) and effective (God keeps his promises - Isa. 55:11). It is the Word of truth (James 1:18) which judges our thoughts and attitudes (Heb. 4:12).

When someone speaks to us, the first thing we do is to try to understand what they are saying. After we have understood, we can then respond to whatever they said. The fact that God communicates with his people only by his Word, shows that he wants to instruct their minds so that they can understand him. The Spirit explains this Word to them (John 14:25,26; 1 Cor. 2:13). It is not enough, however, to hear God's Word. If Christians truly understand it, they will obey it (Matt. 13:19,23; James 1:22-25).

The Bible is God's Word because it is God's revealed truth in written form. When the Spirit explains the written Word to believers, they realize that God's active Word is speaking to them about themselves and Christ, who is the principal Word of God (Heb. 1:1-3).

Work

God made human beings to work (Gen. 2:15) and by working they provide themselves with all their needs (2 Thess. 3:10). Adam worked before he sinned, but after sin came into the world, his work became much harder (Gen. 3:16-19). Work can become an idol because it can be an end in itself (Eccl. 2:4-11) instead of being used for God's glory (Col. 3:23,24).

In their work, people follow God, who is himself a worker (Gen. 2:2; Deut. 3:24). Christ also worked, not only as a carpenter (Mark 6:3) but also in his ministry (John 5:17). Work, then, is good; idleness is bad (Prov. 10:4; 2 Thess. 3:6).

People cannot earn God's favour by anything that they do. Salvation cannot be earned. God saves his people by a free gift. Good works follow salvation (Eph. 2:8-10).

World

The most obvious meaning of world is the planet Earth on which we live. The Bible tells us that God made it (Gen. 1:1), owns it and everything it contains (Ps. 24:1) loves it (John 3:16) and keeps it going (Col. 1:17). In the New Testament, however, we find at least two other meanings to the word. It often does not mean everybody in the world.

1. It can mean 'human life in the world' and not the planet itself. For example, Luke 2:1; John 16:21. Satan offered Jesus the kingdoms of this world (Matt. 4:8,9).

2. It is sometimes the world of 'human beings who, are in rebellion against God'. This world is controlled by the evil one (1 John 5:19) but Christ's disciples do not belong to it (John 15:19). The principles which govern this rebellious world are themselves against God. Christians must not be enslaved by them (Gal. 4:3). Christians are to be crucified to this world (Gal. 6:14).

Worship

Worship means bowing down in submission to God (Gen. 24:26; Ps. 96:9; Rev. 19:4). Serving God is worship (Exod. 3:12; Deut. 6:13; Josh. 24:14-24; Luke 2:37). Bowing down often accompanied worship. Servants and slaves bow down in submission to their masters. A conquered king would bow down before his conqueror and see himself as his conqueror's servant (1 Kings 20:32). Similarly, worshippers in the Old Testament bowed before God in awe. All worshippers give homage to him.

Worshippers confess God to be their Lord and Master. They can therefore only truly worship one God (Exod. 34:14). God is jealous and demands his people's complete devotion to him (Deut. 6:5,14,15).

People may worship God individually (Ps. 5:7) but the emphasis in the Bible is the worship of congregations of God's people. The Old Testament feasts and the New Testament Lord's Supper must be celebrated with other people. The early Christians met each day for worship (Acts 2:46) and, a little later, on the first day of the week

(Acts 20:7; 1 Cor. 16:2). Some disciples stopped meeting with other Christians for worship, but even in times of persecution, Christians were told that they should continue to meet as congregations in order to encourage one another (Heb. 10:25).

Wrath (anger)

Anger is a strong emotion and although it need not lead to sin (2 Sam. 12:5; Ps. 4:4) it can easily do so (Gen. 4:5-8; Prov. 27:4). Wise people try not to become angry (Prov. 29:8; Eph. 4:31) because it is not part of a righteous life (James 1:20). It is part of the old sinful attitudes which Christians seek to remove from their characters (Col. 3:8).

God's anger is different because his anger is holy anger. In a similar way, Christ's anger at the stubbornness of unbelievers (Mark 3:5) was holy. By contrast, the devil's fury is evil (Rev. 12:12). God is angry against sin because his holy and righteous nature must react against everything that is in any way corrupt (Isa. 5:24,25; Rom. 1:18).

Angry people lose control over themselves. God, however, is slow to anger and shows mercy to the sinner (Exod. 34:6; Jonah 4:2). The Hebrew word for 'anger' is the same as 'nose'. When a person is angry, his nose swells and his nostrils tremble! Being slow to anger is written in the Hebrew as being long in the nose, the idea being that God holds his breath before he shows his anger.

God's anger is fierce (Jer. 25:37) and no one can stand before it (Ps. 76:7). God's anger chastises (Ps. 6:1) and punishes (2 Sam. 6:7). Human anger may cool after a while, but God's anger remains until he expresses that anger, or the cause of his anger is removed (Num. 25:4; Josh. 7:26).

At the end of time, the day of wrath (Zeph 1:14-18; Rev. 6:15-17) will destroy all that is evil (Rom. 9:22). The fact that God is slow to anger should not lead people to think that they need not repent (Rom. 2:4,5). Repentance is essential if they are to be saved by Christ from the wrath to come (Rom. 5:9; 1 Thess. 1:10).

Yoke

A yoke is a wooden bar which joins two animals together for work. In Bible times, the yoked animals were usually oxen. Because animals yoked together are under the farmer's control, the Bible uses the yoke as a picture of a conqueror's control over the people he defeated (Jer. 27:2,8,11,12). When the conqueror in turn was defeated, his yoke was said to be broken (Nah. 1:13).

The picture of a yoke is also used in a good sense in the Bible. It is used for serving God (cf. Jer. 2:20) and Christ (Matt. 11:29,30). Paul calls someone a yokefellow (Phil. 4:3) because they served Christ together like a pair of oxen.

Zealot

One of Jesus' apostles was Simon the Zealot (Luke 6:15). The name zealot may mean that he belonged to the Jewish political party called by that name, or it may mean that he showed plenty of energy and enthusiasm in all that he did. If he belonged to the party of Zealots, he would not have been able to remain a member as an apostle because their views were opposed to Christ's teaching about the kingdom of God.

The party of the Zealots was founded by Judas the Galilean in AD6. He led a revolt against the Romans who had removed Herod Archelaus from the throne and made Judea a province ruled direct from Rome. Judas opposed a census which the Romans held to decide how much tribute (see Tax) the province should pay, because he believed that paying tribute to Rome was treason against the Jews' true King, God.

The Romans crushed Judas' revolt but the Zealots continued. Their views on the law of God were similar to those of the Pharisees but they believed that they should fight to gain Jewish independence and thus bring into being the kingdom of God. Their view of the kingdom of God was, therefore, a political one, whereas Jesus preached a spiritual kingdom of God.

The Zealots engaged in murder in a terrorist-type campaign, until AD66 when the Jewish War broke out. At first they had some success but the Roman army captured Jerusalem in AD70 and massacred the Zealot stronghold at Massada in May, AD73.